BUTTEVANT

Buttevant:

A Medieval Anglo-French Town in Ireland

Edited by Eamonn Cotter

Eamonn Cotter

Published 2013 by:
Eamonn Cotter,
Ballynanelagh, Rathcormac, Co. Cork, Ireland.
In conjunction with Buttevant Heritage Group

© Copyright the authors and the publisher.

All rights reserved. No part of this publication may be reproduced, stored in a retrieval system, or transmitted in any form by any means without the prior permission of the authors and publisher.

ISBN 978-0-9576755-0-6 (Hbk)
       978-0-9576755-1-3 (Pbk)

Printed by:
Carraig Print inc. Litho Press
59 St. Mary's Road, Midleton, Co. Cork, Ireland.
Tel: 021 4883458 / 021 4631401

Contents

Page

CONTRIBUTORS

PREFACE

1	The archaeology of Medieval Buttevant. *Eamonn Cotter*	1
2	The awakening of the urban world in the Middle Ages: New villages and towns in southwest France. *Jean-Loup Abbé.*	19
3	Medieval Buttevant: 1100-1400AD *Paul MacCotter*	29
4	The *bastides* of southwest France: a reinvented urbanism. *Jean-Loup Abbé.*	39
5	Liscarroll Castle: a note on its context, function and chronology *Tadhg O'Keeffe*	51
6	Reconstructing the landscape of the mendicants in east Munster: the Franciscans *Anne-Julie Lafaye*	67
7	The sequence of construction of Buttevant friary church in the thirteenth century *Tadhg O'Keeffe*	83
8	Denny Muschamp and the ploughlands of Grange *James O'Brien*	103
9	The revival of the Middle Ages: Buttevant in the 19th Century *Dagmar Ó Riain-Raedel*	113
10	St Mary's Church, Buttevant 1828-1886: Notes on its building history *James O'Brien*	143

Contributors

Jean-Loup Abbé is professor of medieval history at the University of Toulouse II Le Mirail and deputy manager of the UMR 5136 FRAMESPA (University of Toulouse II-CNRS). He is the author of *À la conquête des étangs. L'aménagement de l'espace dans le Languedoc méditerranéen (XIIe-XVe siècle)* (Presses Universitaires du Mirail, 2006, coll. Tempus). He led a *Histoire de Limoux* (Privat, 2009) and *Une longue histoire. La construction des paysages méridionaux* (Méridiennes, 2012). He has written several papers on the new towns of southern and northern France.

Eamonn Cotter is an independent archaeologist and researcher. He has excavated many sites of all dates around Ireland and has also worked on excavations in Germany, Russia and Egypt. His main area of interest is medieval churches and castles, particularly the tower houses of the later medieval period. He has carried out numerous historic building surveys, including a detailed survey of the historic churches of county Cork for Cork County Council.

Annejulie Lafaye was born in Normandy and completed a degree in history and archaeology at the University of Rouen. Having studied at post-graduate level at the Sorbonne, she engaged in PhD studies at the O'Cleirigh Institute in UCD, researching mendicant settlements in East Munster, and completed her doctoral thesis in August 2012. She has now taken a post-doctoral position with the Centre André Chastel at the Sorbonne in Paris.

Dr. Paul MacCotter began his career as a genealogist and independent scholar with an especial interest in the lineages originating during the Anglo-Norman period. Obtaining his MA in 1994 and his Ph.D in 2006 in UCC, he extended his research interests to include the administrative structures of Anglo-Norman Ireland and of High Medieval Gaelic Ireland. He has published three books and numerous journal papers in local and national journals. Dr. MacCotter worked as principal historical consultant to the Making Christian Landscapes project in the school of Archaeology in UCC, and won a two year IRCHSS fellowship to study the lands of the Irish Church, in 2010. His most recent book, Medieval Ireland: territorial, political and economic divisions, has been described by one reviewer as 'a paradigm shifting work'. MacCotter's research interests include medieval economic and administrative divisions in general. He is a part-time lecturer in the School of History, UCC, and lectures in genealogy with Adult Continuing Education in UCC and the Irish Ancestry Research Centre of UL.

James O'Brien is a priest of the diocese of Cloyne and a graduate in arts and theology of St. Patrick's College, Maynooth.

Prof. Tadhg O'Keeffe, who teaches in the School of Archaeology in UCD, specialises in the study of medieval landscape, settlement and architecture, Irish and European. His published work - nearly 100 items across a diverse range of interests - includes four books on ecclesiastical architecture and many papers on castles. His latest book, *Medieval Irish Buildings*, is due to be published by Four Courts Press in late 2013. He is also co-author with David Kelly of the forthcoming Youghal fascicle in the Royal Irish Academy's Irish Historic Towns series.

Dr Dagmar Ó Riain-Raedel has been a member of the Department of History, UCC, with a special research interest in Medieval History. She has lectured and published widely on the connections between Ireland and Europe during the Middle Ages. She has a special interest in art and architecture and her research in the legacy of the architectural family of Hills, which contributed many noteworthy buildings to Cork, will be published in book form in 2013.

Preface and Acknowledgements

Up until a few years ago my interest in medieval Buttevant, like that of most casual observers was confined to noting its most prominent medieval ruins: the Franciscan friary in the centre of the town, the castle tucked away among trees at the southern end, and the Augustinian priory at Ballybeg, a kilometre outside the town. Then, in the summer of 2010, I was engaged by the Buttevant Heritage Group to carry out an archaeological assessment survey of an area to the east of the friary which it was planned to develop as a public park. It soon became clear to me that there was little point in surveying one small area, and that the entire town would have to be considered as a unit. That survey led me to identify surviving fragments of the town's enclosing walls, and the geometrically regular pattern of its grid plan. Using the evidence of nineteenth-century map and descriptions of the town, allied with measurement of the surviving blocks and detailed visual inspection of the walls, it was possible to propose a reconstruction of the original town layout.

During the course of my research into the town I discovered that Professor Tadhg O'Keeffe had previously compared Buttevant with the bastides of south-west France, probably the first to do so. The comparison is certainly apt, not just because of the similarity of layout, but also because of the decidedly French origins of the name Buttevant. Those origins are discussed more fully in this volume, making is clear that the name derives from a type of medieval fortification, not, as tradition holds, from the war-cry of the Barry family.

The significance of Buttevant as a medieval town was now becoming clear, as was the need to promote its importance to wider audience. Following suggestions by several colleagues, a conference, which proved to be highly successful, was held at Springfort Hall, Mallow in March 2011. This book is principally based on the presentations to the conference, with some subsequent additions. The papers here cover the full span of Buttevant's medieval history from the twelfth to the twentieth century, and consider its origin and development, its decline and its nineteenth-century revival. In addition two papers from France deal with the emergence of urbanism in medieval Europe and the development of bastides in south-western France, thus setting Buttevant in the wider context of the foundation of medieval towns across Europe.

The phenomenon of the New Towns of medieval Europe has been widely researched and discussed by historians and archaeologists across Europe. These new towns are found from Ireland to eastern Europe and are a feature of the great economic expansion experienced across Europe over the twelfth and thirteenth centuries in the main. They are distinguished by the regularity of their grid-plan layout, characterized by long main streets interspersed with cross-streets running at right angles and dividing the towns into blocks or insulae. Given the towns' principal function as trading centres the market place was a central element, usually taking the form of a central large square. The other principal elements were the church and usually, though not always, a castle. The clear parallels between Buttevant and many of these new towns both in Britain and across Europe shows clearly that Buttevant was no idle spectator, but was an active participant in that great economic expansion, one of the greatest movements of medieval European history.

This work is but a beginning in the study of the history and archaeology of Buttevant and the wider North Cork area, and the role of that area in the medieval settlement of Ireland.

I wish to acknowledge firstly the tremendous support of the Buttevant Heritage Group, mainly in the person of Lilian Sheahan, who works tirelessly to preserve and promote Buttevant's heritage. Her tremendous work made the conference, and thereby this book, possible. Both my initial survey, and the subsequent conference, were generously funded by the local Leader organisation, Avondhu Blackwater Partnership Ltd., assisted by Christy Roche, and by the Buttevant Heritage Group. Financial support for the publication was provided by the Buttevant Heritage Group and by DP Energy Ireland Ltd., Buttevant.

Finally, I wish to thank the authors, for the high standard of their contributions to both the conference and to this book, for their time and efforts, and for patiently enduring my nagging.

Eamonn Cotter

CHAPTER 1

THE ARCHAEOLOGY OF MEDIEVAL BUTTEVANT

~ EAMONN COTTER ~

Buttevant is situated approximately 10km north of the Munster Blackwater, in the heart of the great limestone plain that stretches across north County Cork and northwards into Limerick (Fig. 1 and Plate 3). The town itself is situated on the western flank of the Awbeg River valley where it flows from north to south. A short distance to the south of the town the river turns sharply eastwards for another 14km before turning south again and falling into the Blackwater at Castletownroche. It is an area rich in medieval archaeological sites, including numerous moated sites, castles, churches and monasteries. The wider hinterland of the town is also densely populated with ringforts, indicating a substantial pre-Norman population in the area.

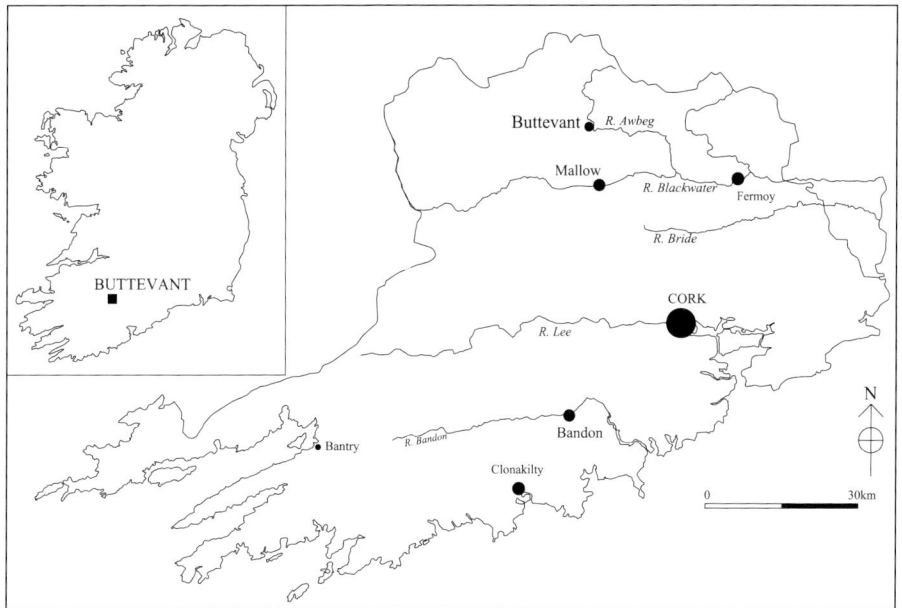

Fig 1: Location of Buttevant

There is little pre-Norman archaeology in the immediate vicinity of the town, but a possible ringfort has been identified approximately 1km south of the town, and a pre-Invasion church dedicated to St. Bridget was located at the southern end of the town. That church became the medieval parish church, retaining its dedication to St. Brigid, and the site is now a graveyard, which surrounds St. John's Protestant church. A large block of collapsed masonry to the rear of the Protestant church, and some architectural fragments used as grave markers, are all that remain of the medieval building. There may well have been a settlement in the vicinity of the church, but no evidence of it survives.

THE MEDIEVAL TOWN

Though the early history of the town is considered in more detail elsewhere (MacCotter, this volume), it will be useful here to give a brief summary of Buttevant's history.

The establishment of the Anglo-Norman settlement of Buttevant appears to have commenced in the early 1200s under William fitzPhilip de Barry.[1] It is likely that the town grew up around the castle and the nearby parish church, and subsequently expanded northwards, perhaps in several phases. It cannot be doubted that it was a walled town, but the dating of the construction of the walls and their full extent must remain somewhat speculative.

The earliest documentary evidence for the development of a town comes from a grant dated 1234 to David de Barry of 'a weekly market on Saturday at his Manor of Botavant, and of a yearly fair there on the vigil and feast of St. Luke the Evangelist and 6 following days [17-24 Oct.]'.[2] A settlement may already have been developing before this grant or, if not, would have emerged shortly thereafter, probably located at the southern end of the modern town, in the vicinity of the castle, parish church and market house. As MacCotter (this volume) has shown, the town was certainly an incorporated borough by 1260, so that the formal layout of the town most likely dates to the period 1234 to 1260.

The walling of the town probably dates to the early fourteenth century following the grant of 1317, by which the sum of £105 owing to the exchequer was released to the town 'to enclose it with walls'. A further grant, in 1375, refers to a 'north gate'.[3] The specific purpose of this grant is uncertain but it may relate to an expansion of the town. The town was said to have been ruined during the rebellion of Murrough O Brien in 1461[4], but the walls are again mentioned in 1479 in the will of one David Lombard of Buttevant.[5]

The town was burned during the Munster rebellion of 1598,[6] and again, apparently, in 1691 during the Williamite wars (Ó Riain-Raedel, this volume). Borlase, in his history of the rebellion of the 1640s refers briefly to Buttevant but does not mention town walls. By contrast he refers to Kilmallock as a town 'environed with a strong wall'.[7] The lack of reference to walls at Buttevant suggests that it was not a place of strength at that time and that the walls were perhaps somewhat decayed by then. However, Charles Smith, writing in 1750, recorded that parts of the walls were still standing at that time, and noted two wall circuits, one outside the other.[8]

Layout of the Town

While Buttevant is in many respects an interesting place from the point of view of medieval history and archaeology, probably the single most intriguing aspect is the layout of the town itself. The medieval origins of the town layout have only recently been identified, through the researches of this author and of Dr. Tadhg O'Keeffe, which have shown that Buttevant belongs to that class of medieval towns referred to by medievalists as *new towns*. These new towns were founded across Europe during the explosion of economic and population growth that was witnessed during the thirteenth century and into the fourteenth. The layout of Buttevant compares particularly well with some of those towns found in North Wales and among the *bastides* of southwestern France. It can hardly be doubted that the Barry founders of Buttevant were familiar with the Welsh towns since south Wales was the base from which they established their holdings in county Cork, and it is likely that they were also familiar with those parts of southwestern France then under the control of the English monarch, particularly in view of the French name they gave to their new Irish town (see both P MacCotter and J-L Abbé this volume for discussions on the Buttevant name).

The town of Buttevant today consists principally of one long street running north-south, parallel to the river which flows to the east of the town, and several cross-streets (Fig. 2). Property boundaries run east and west from the main street. Behind the street-front properties back lanes run from the cross-streets parallel to the main street, giving access to the rear of the houses and separating them from their garden plots. The town's bridge, the medieval element of which still survives, is located at the northern end of the town, and the castle at the southern end. The site of the medieval parish church is located some 150m south of the town and is today the site of a Church of Ireland church and graveyard.

At the northern end of the town New Street runs parallel to, and to the west of, Main Street. New Street is generally believed to have been laid out in conjunction with the military barracks which was established a short distance to the north in the early nineteenth century. However it has been noted by O'Keeffe that the rere-boundary to the Main Street properties (the 'inner wall' in Fig. 3) is approximately equidistant from both New Street and Main Street, leading him to conclude that the modern New Street follows the line of a medieval street which was part of the original town layout.[9] If this was the case then it could explain the odd space between the rere-boundary of the Main Street properties and that of the New Street properties as depicted on the first edition six-inch OS map,

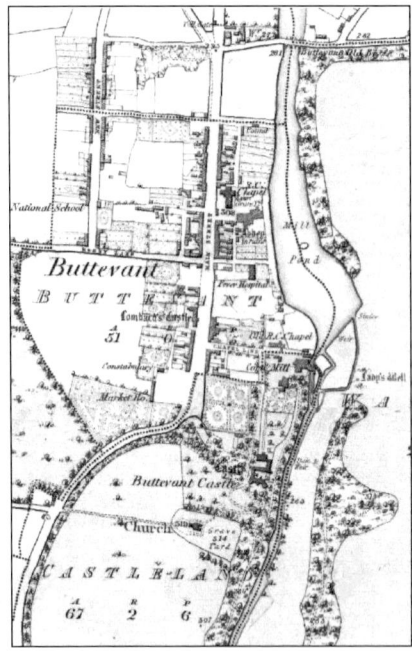

Fig. 2: Buttevant as depicted on the first edition Ordnance Survey six-inch map, c. 1840

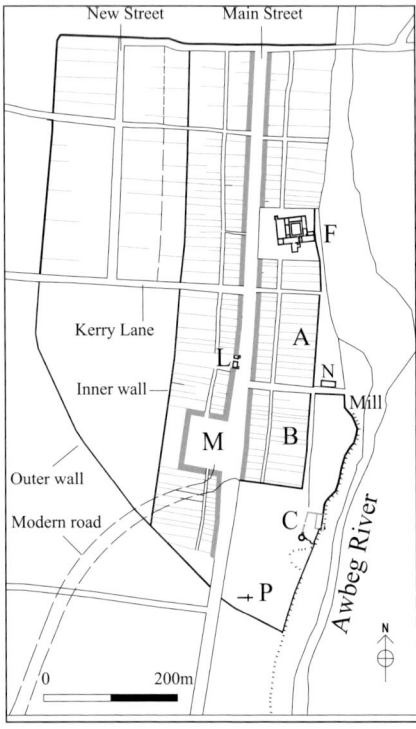

Fig 3: Reconstructed layout of medieval Buttevant based on the 25 inch Ordnance Survey map, surviving physical evidence, and results of geophysical survey.
P = parish church;
C = castle;
M = marketplace;
N = possible nunnery;
F = Friary;
L = Lombard's Castle.
Refer to text for blocks A and B.

which shows a 30-40m wide band of 'no-man's land' between the two (Fig. 2). If the medieval boundaries had become derelict by the nineteenth century, the modern New Street properties may have been laid out without regard to any previous boundaries. Alternatively New Street may have been laid out as part of the medieval town but might not have been developed then but instead remained vacant until the nineteenth century.

At the southern end of the modern town the main street deviates from its straight route and curves to the west (Figs. 2 and 3), something which has led modern observers, including Avril Thomas, to conclude that the starting point of this curve marked the southern limit of the medieval town.[10] As Thomas observed, this left the church well outside the bounds of the town, leading her to suggest that it was not the parish church. However Thomas was unaware that this curve in the road is a modern re-alignment dating to the early nineteenth century. It is clear from documentary and cartographic evidence that this street originally continued in a straight line south, through what is now the entrance to the graveyard and therefore close to the site of the medieval church. Its course can still be traced in the field to the south of the graveyard, and has recently been detected by geophysical survey in the field to the north of the graveyard.[11] The road only assumed its present course at the whim of an early nineteenth-century occupant of the castle, Sir James Anderson, so that it no longer ran through his demesne.[12] This account is borne out by the evidence of Charles Vallancey's map of 1796 (TCD MS2891) and the Grand Jury map of Cork of 1811, both of which agree in showing the road continuing in a straight line south from the town. Both of these maps show the town extending on each side of the main street as far as what is now the access lane to the Church of Ireland graveyard, site of the medieval parish church of St. Brigid. Whether the medieval town extended this far is uncertain, though an entry in the medieval *Pipe Roll of Cloyne* suggests it did. This entry delimits the lands around the castle held of the lord Bishop of Cloyne by David Barry in 1364. These include the castle of Buttevant, its orchard, and the tenements lying between Mill Street 'as far as the roadway and church of St Bridget on the south side'.[13] Comparison with other contemporary towns in Wales would suggest there was an open area to the west of the castle, keeping it separate from the town. That open area might have functioned as a fair green, located as it is under the shadow of the castle and close to the market square. The corresponding area on the west side of the public road, south of the market house, is now occupied by modern houses so that it is impossible to know for certain if there were tenements in that area.

There is one known documentary reference to a town gate at Buttevant. This, as noted above, comes from a 1375 grant to the town. The reference to a 'north gate' suggests there is likely to have also been a south gate. No above-ground evidence survives for either and their exact locations are unknown. The northern boundary of the town in particular is problematical. The nineteenth-century Ordnance Survey six-inch map (Fig. 2) shows that the two blocks at the northern end of the town were vacant at that time, with tenements continuing only as far as the townland boundary, suggesting the townland boundary marks the northern limit of the medieval town. However the line of the rere-boundary to the properties on the west side of Main Street continues north through the vacant block to the cross-street which runs westwards from the bridge and it is likely that the town extended to that road, in which case the town walls would have encompassed the bridge, a more usual situation than leaving the bridge outside the walls. It is likely that the town as originally laid out extended as far north as the bridge but the two northern blocks were either never developed or were developed and subsequently decayed when the town's fortunes declined in the later medieval period.

Locating the south gate must remain equally speculative. It was suggested by Thomas, and is generally assumed, that the south gate was located at Lombard's castle, partly because of its location near the presumed southern end of the town and partly because of its tower projecting onto the street and giving the impression of a narrowing of the street at this point. However, if the south gate was at this point, then the market place would have been outside the gate, a situation which is most unlikely. A more likely position for the south gate would be in the vicinity of the graveyard to the south of the town, probably on the southern boundary of the graveyard, so it would enclose the medieval church site within the town walls.

The layout of Buttevant can be compared with many towns built across Europe around the same time. A striking feature of those towns is the application of precise geometric shapes in the layout of the towns, which are laid out in regular blocks in a grid pattern. This pattern can also be seen in Buttevant. Property boundaries remain relatively intact on the west side of the main street, where the tenements stretch approximately 94m back from the street. Assuming the same tenement length on the east side of the street allows us to reconstruct the town outline with some confidence, and throws up some interesting patterns. The block between School Lane and Mill Street (Block A in Fig. 3) is a rectangle measuring 94m x 133m, giving a length to breadth ratio of 1:1.4142. This was a significant ratio that was widely used in medieval times in the layout of buildings and towns and was almost certainly applied in the layout of Buttevant (See also O'Keeffe Chapter 5, this volume). If we replicate that rectangle to the south of Mill Lane (Block B) we find that it extends precisely to the boundary wall of what are now the school grounds. This wall is clearly of nineteenth or early twentieth century date but the lower courses have a different construction style and may well be medieval. Extending the line of this wall across the street to the south of the market house we find that the area between the market house and Kerry Lane comprises a block which divides precisely into three squares. This is significant for several reasons:

1. It means that the market square would have been a precise square which is the norm in the European New Towns (see Abbé, this volume).

2. The square to the north of the market square extends exactly to, and encloses, Lombard's Castle.

3. Each of these squares encloses an area of approximately two acres. It is recorded that in 1669 a grant was made to one John Gifford of 'Castle Lombard with two acres behind the castle'. Therefore if the extent of the Lombard's Castle property was two acres in 1669 it is reasonable to assume that was also its extent in the thirteenth century and that this was the Medieval layout of this area.

Looking then to the northern part of the town, we find a pattern of regular blocks, here a combination of both squares and rectangles, something which can also be found in European towns. However the Franciscan Friary is out of line with the main street, which might suggest it is earlier than the town. Furthermore it was normal in medieval times for Franciscan friaries to be located outside the towns. It may be that the original town was smaller and the Friary was outside it but the town expanded to incorporate the friary. It is likely that an embryonic settlement grew up close to the castle in the years prior to the 1234 grant of a market and fair. Given that all the principal elements of a medieval town, viz. the castle, parish church, mill, and market house are all clustered close together this area must have been the core of the early town, which subsequently expanded northwards.

The Town Walls – Surviving Evidence
As noted above Charles Smith, writing in 1750, referred to two wall circuits at Buttevant. He wrote 'There are still to be seen the remains of a wall that surrounded the town; and they also shew the traces of an outward wall, which enclosed the other, and took up a considerable circuit of ground'.[14] The reference to 'traces' of an outward wall suggests that a full outer circuit did not survive in Smith's time, and it is unclear if this outer circuit completely enclosed the town originally.

His assertion that the outer wall 'took up a considerable circuit of ground' suggests that it was located quite a distance out from the inner wall. Thomas suggested these two circuits are represented by the parallel property boundaries between Main Street and New Street.[15] However, one of these is, in part at least, a modern boundary. A more likely candidate for Smith's outer wall is a field boundary which extends to the northwest from the main road approximately 100m south of the market house and which forms the boundary between the townlands of Buttevant and Knockbarry (Fig. 3). This boundary is more substantial than other field boundaries in the area, comprising an earthen bank c.1m high and almost 2m thick, with well constructed stone facing on its southwest side. Ground level inside the wall (i.e. on its east side) is c.0.6m higher than it is on the outside. This boundary today extends to the southeast as far as the modern main road to Cork and northwards to Kerry Lane. Recent geophysical survey has detected a continuation of this boundary in the field to the northwest of the graveyard, suggesting that it originally continued southeastwards through the graveyard, to the Awbeg River.[16] At its northern end it may also have extended much further northwards and swung towards the river somewhere north of the bridge, thus enclosing the town. It may be that this was the original boundary enclosing the town as originally laid out, including New Street, and that when it became necessary to strengthen the town's defences in the early fourteenth century a new town wall, built with the 1317 grant, excluded the New Street area which had not been then developed.

Unfortunately, among the myriad walls edging the back lanes and marking the property boundaries behind Buttevant's houses none can be positively identified as medieval, particularly on the western side of the main street. Along the eastern perimeter of the town long stretches of walling survive extending along the cliff-edge from the castle to the corn mill and from north of the mill to the northeast corner of the Roman Catholic graveyard, though with some significant gaps. Similarities in construction style can be observed in three sections, one running northwards from the castle, one on the north side of Mill Lane, and one extending northwards from the Franciscan Friary, indicating the three were contemporary. The section on the north side of Mill Lane retains the outline of a blocked window, obviously part of the building marked *Old R.C. Chapel* on the 1840 map (Fig. 2, and N on Fig. 3). The window still survived in the mid nineteenth century when it was described as a 'small trefoil-headed two light window'.[17] The same author also describes some worked stone on this wall, noting that 'moulded caps are worked on the stone'. These capitals are now incorporated into the grotto erected in the window embrasure on the inner (north) face of the wall. The form of the capitals, coupled with Brash's description, indicates this was a thirteenth century window, therefore it can be assumed that this section of walling was of that date. Given the similarity of construction style of this wall section and the sections to the north of the castle and north of the Friary, it can be proposed with some confidence that these three wall sections are medieval in date. However, only those sections close to the Friary are likely to have been incorporated into the town walls.

Along the southern perimeter of the town, in addition to the possible outer wall already described there is likely also to have been an inner wall, though there is no obvious survival of this. There is however one possible candidate for this element of the circuit, namely the southern boundary of the modern school grounds immediately northwest of the castle. A cursory glance at this wall shows the regular linear coursing typical of more recent walls in the area. However, a closer look reveals that the lowest courses, close to ground level, are of a different construction style, and are likely to belong to an earlier wall. As noted above it fits well with the grid-pattern layout of the town.

BUTTEVANT'S MEDIEVAL ARCHITECTURE

Buttevant Castle

While Buttevant Castle has been very obviously modernised in the nineteenth century, it is possible to suggest how it might have looked in the thirteenth century (see Fig. 4). In its present incarnation it comprises a rectangular enclosure with a circular tower at the southwestern corner and a semi-circular tower at the southeastern corner (see Plates 1 and 2). Between the towers the entrance block contains an ornate ogee-arched doorway (Plate 2) which is a nineteenth-century creation but which closely resembles both the fifteenth-century doorway to the Franciscan friary in Buttevant and the doorway to the Carmelite friary at Castlelyons, another Barry foundation. The interior of the enclosure is now a jumble of overgrown ruined walls, mostly of the nineteenth century. The southwestern tower is original and dates to the thirteenth century. It had two floors under an unusual 'sail' vault and another two floors above. A slender tower projecting 3m to the north, and a thick wall with mural passages and stairs projecting 3.5m to the east are also probably original, though since most of the walls are plastered it is impossible to be certain of this. Parts of the west wall of the enclosure may also be original but rebuilding and repair have been so extensive it is impossible to be certain what is modern and what is medieval. Along the eastern side of the northern half of the enclosure a wall standing on the cliff edge is almost certainly original. Four blocked window opes can be traced with evidence of inserted fifteenth-century lights in three. At the southern end of this wall a fragmentary rectangular tower projects eastwards and below it a semi-circular tower extends down the cliff face to the valley floor below. These are certainly the remains of a medieval hall with a projecting garderobe tower at its southern end, probably the hall mentioned in the medieval *Pipe Roll of Cloyne,* which refers to the 'castle of Buttevant with its orchard and hall'.[18] The hall would have been 20m long internally, but its width is unknown as nothing survives to indicate the location of its west wall.

Reconstruction of the original castle complex must necessarily be speculative. The south-western tower is original, as noted above. Assuming that the wall and tower projecting from it are contemporary would suggest that the tower was a corner tower of an enclosure castle. The entrance to the enclosure is most likely to have been to the north or west, facing the town, and this is supported by the fact that the ground to the south originally sloped away steeply before it was raised in the nineteenth century to create the approach to the new entrance door.

A possible layout is suggested in Figure 4, where it is shown side-by-side with Dinefwr castle in South Wales, a place which must have been familiar to the Barrys, based in nearby Manorbier.[19] The comparisons between the two are clear, particularly the juxtaposition of the hall and circular keep.

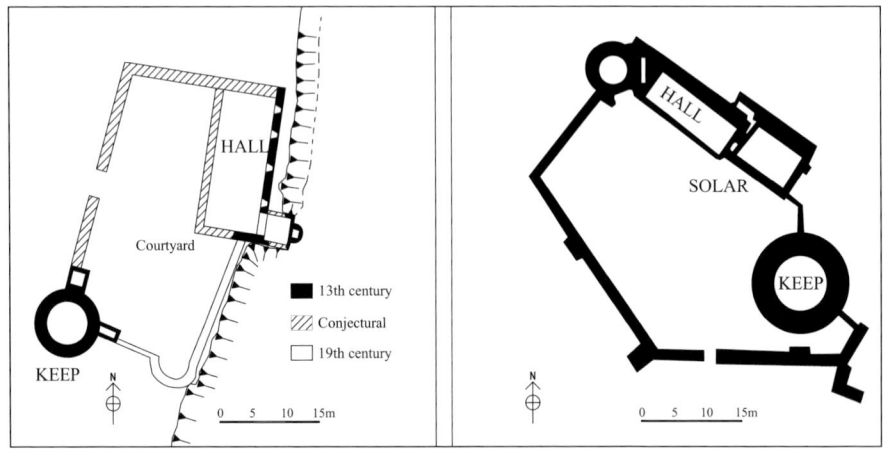

Fig. 4 Plan of Buttevant castle (left) with suggested reconstruction, and (right) plan of Dinefwr Castle in south Wales

The Franciscan Friary
As noted above the Franciscan Friary is likely to have been established outside the boundaries of the original town, which expanded to incorporate it. The foundation date of 1251 ascribed to it by the Annals of the Four Masters seems likely and it was certainly in existence by 1260 (MacCotter, this volume). Only the church survives, comprising a nave, choir and southern transept (see Fig. 5). The crossing tower collapsed in the nineteenth century but some evidence of it still survives. The north wall of the church was extensively rebuilt in the nineteenth century, incorporating architectural fragments salvaged from the ruins. It is not necessary to go into further detail here as the building and its architecture have been fully described elsewhere.[20] A few further points can be made however. Protruding stonework on the north face of the church marks the location of the claustral buildings, and recent vegetation clearance in the graveyard has exposed the full extent of the east range. The northern end of this range lines up well with a slender medieval tower incorporated into the nearby Roman Catholic church. This tower has traditionally been referred to as 'Desmond's Tower' and is believed to have had some connection with the Earl

of Desmond. However, there is no evidence for such a connection, and it seems highly unlikely. A recent suggestion that the old main street ran close by the friary entrance and that the tower was on the opposite side of the street is entirely wrong.[21] The location of the tower in relation to the friary church and the east range shows that it was part of the friary complex and stood at the northwest corner of the cloister. Such corner towers are a common feature of medieval monastic sites, as at Bridgetown, Co. Cork, Kells, Co. Kilkenny and others.

Though the friary has been described in detail in several publications a number of curious features around the west end of the church have largely gone unremarked. Along the external face of the west wall, directly over the entrance doorway, is a row of corbels and beam sockets, and above them a strip of stone flashing such as is normally seen marking the line of a lean-to cloister roof (see Plate 8). These were recorded by Cochrane, who also recorded a feature which no longer survives at the southwest corner of the church.[22] His drawing of the south elevation of the church shows what appear to be traces of a high archway opening to the south. Taken together these features suggest a roofed space in front of the west door with access from the south. It is also worth noting that the corner tower mentioned above does not align well with the west end of the church or with the west claustral range. However a building projecting from the west façade of the church could have aligned with the tower (but see Chap. 7 this volume, for an alternative interpretation).

A number of features along the north wall of the friary church are also worth remarking on (see Fig. 14, Chap. 7). A large central section of that wall is a nineteenth-century rebuild, built to about half its original height and incorporating numerous window and cloister fragments. To the west and east of this rebuild the wall stands to its original height. Along the top of the western section is a continuous row of closely-spaced gutter-stones. The curious feature of these is that the row should have been interrupted by the gabled roof of the west claustral range, so that, though there is evidence for the walls of the west range there is none for the roof. Another curious feature is the row of beam sockets high on the north wall at its western end, immediately west of where the west claustral range would have stood. These sockets seem to be evidence of an intermediate floor in a building which formerly stood here, but again there is no evidence for the roof of such a building and the row of gutter-stones above shows that no roof existed when they were put in place. A likely explanation for these anomalies is that the buildings suffered a period of decay, after which the upper levels of the walls were rebuilt, and the church possibly re-roofed, but the west claustral range demolished. Other evidence of such works can be seen along the wall–top at the angle of the nave and the south transept where worked fragments have been reused. Another later medieval embellishment was the addition of a base-batter and outer 'casing' to the south wall of the transept supporting the unusual arch over the south window. The wall walk above was probably also contemporary. Taken together the evidence suggests extensive later medieval refurbishment, during which several new windows were inserted, part of the claustral ranges demolished and the south transept extensively embellished.

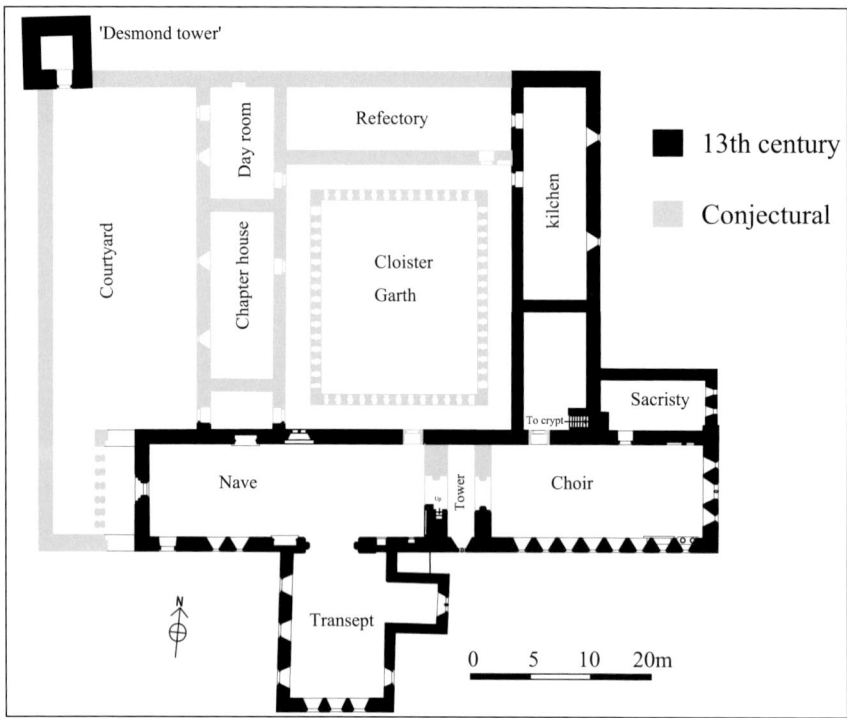

Fig 5: Plan of Buttevant Franciscan Friary with suggested reconstruction

An unusual, if not unique, feature of the friary is the two-level crypt below the choir. The crypt is today accessed via an external stairs on the north side of the choir, but this stairs would originally have been within the east claustral range, of which only the foundations now survive. It is also possible that the stairs was originally accessed from within the choir, but this is uncertain due to extensive repair work on the north wall of the choir. The function of the crypt has recently been discussed by O'Keeffe who proposes the intriguing suggestion that the crypt might originally have been a pre-Norman castle.[23]

Until recent times the upper level of the crypt was piled high with human bones. Local tradition, probably derived from Charles Smith's History of Cork, held that the bones were of those slain at the seventeenth-century Battle of Knocknanuss. However, a more likely explanation was provided by Brash, who was informed that the bones came from nearby Ballybeg Augustinian priory, where they had been disturbed by the farmer to whom the lands of Ballybeg had been granted at the beginning of the eighteenth century.[24] The bones were originally piled on either side of the main entrance to the friary and were moved to the crypt around 1850 by the then parish priest, the Rev. C. Buckley. In recent times they were removed from the crypt and reburied in the adjacent cemetery.

Lombards' Castle

The town is said to have had "several small town 'castles'",[25] though it is not clear at what date they were constructed. The only castle surviving within the town today is Lombards' Castle, a short distance north of the market house. The remains, which are fragmentary and much altered over the years, comprise a façade with traces of an entrance door and blocked windows, a room with fireplace behind the southern end of the façade, and a small tower projecting onto the street from its northern end. The tower is too small to have been residential and is more likely to have been a corner tower, possibly one of a pair, to a walled enclosure. The surviving architectural detail dates to the fifteenth/sixteenth century period. The Lombards, a family of Italian origin, were noted for their close involvement with trade and commerce in medieval Ireland, so that the location of their castle immediately adjacent to the market square is entirely appropriate.

The Nunnery?

Charles Smith in his history of Cork, first published 1750, refers to 'part of another ruin' near the friary. According to Smith this ruin was said to have been a nunnery dedicated to 'St Owen…or…St John the Baptist'.[26] This was in all probability the building named *Old R.C. Chapel* on the 1840 map (Fig. 2, and marked N in Fig. 3), which stood at the south wall of the present convent grounds. As noted above, the southern boundary wall of the present convent grounds retains a section of medieval walling with traces of the medieval window described in the nineteenth century by Brash. Fragments of the window's architectural detailing survived when Brash saw the site, but these have since been removed and some incorporated into the modern grotto dedicated to St. Joseph (See Plate 15). Other than the reference from Smith there is no corroborating evidence for a nunnery dedicated to St. John the Baptist here. The dedication might suggest an association with the Knights Hospitallers who had a preceptory at Mourneabbey some 16km to the south, though this seems unlikely. A more likely explanation is that Smith misinterpreted a fourteenth-century reference to an endowment of lands by John de Barry and others to the nun Agnes de Hereford to support her nunnery dedicated to St. John the Baptist in Cork.[27] Whatever the truth of the matter, there was certainly a church in that location in the early nineteenth century which was used for Catholic worship until the modern St. Mary's was built (see O'Brien this volume). It is most likely that it was originally a medieval church, quite possibly a nunnery, which fell into decay and was renovated in the late eighteenth century and reused for Catholic worship. If it was originally a nunnery there is a fitting symmetry in the fact that it became incorporated into the present convent grounds in the nineteenth century.

Buttevant Bridge
The medieval bridge is located on the northern outskirts of the modern town and, as suggested above, it was probably just within the northern bounds of the medieval walled town. It is described in detail by O'Keeffe and Simmington (1991) in their study of Irish stone bridges. They regard it as being of thirteenth century date and therefore 'a landmark bridge in the national context' (p. 144). The bridge was built in two phases with the southern, downriver side being the earliest and reckoned to date to the thirteenth century. The earlier section is described as having four pointed segmental arches, with roughly cut limestone voussoirs. The depiction of Buttevant in Vallencey's eighteenth century map of the south of Ireland (TCD MS2891) shows a second bridge at the end of Mill Lane just north of the castle. This would have been an ideal location for a bridge, at the centre of the town, close to the castle and at a narrow point in the river just below the mill pond. Construction of the present mill and its associated races and sluices has of course wiped out any trace of such a bridge, if indeed it ever existed.

Buttevant Mill
The modern mill is one of the most prominent buildings along the east side of the town (see Plate 14). It is located on the riverbank between the town and the original castle grounds and is accessed directly from the main street by a laneway which even in medieval times was called 'Mylnstrete' (Mill Street),[28] indicating that the medieval mill stood in the same location. The present mill is a substantial and well-preserved building standing six storeys high, and was built *c.* 1810.[29] The reference in the *Pipe Roll of Cloyne* to 'the mill of Buttevant'[30] shows that the town had just one mill. Its proximity to the castle was surely no accident – there, access was easily controlled and the burgesses of the town were no doubt required to pay a tax to have their corn ground at the lord's mill.

The seventeenth-century Down Survey map shows two mills further to the south, one on the east bank of the river as it flows south, the other on the south bank, where the river bends sharply to the east. Traces of the former can still be seen in an overgrown mound on the riverbank. The mill on the south side of the river must surely have belonged to nearby Ballybeg Priory, and the other may also have been a priory mill.

CONCLUSION

The context for the founding of the town of Buttevant was the enormous economic expansion across Europe in the thirteenth century. Hundreds of new planned towns were founded across Europe, to take advantage of the growth in trade. Located as it was on the main route between the port towns of Cork and Limerick, Buttevant was well-placed to function as a market place where farm produce such as wheat, oats, wool, hides, meat, and live animals was purchased from the farmers of the surrounding areas and transported to those port towns for export. Contemporary records show that huge quantities of these products were being exported to England and France in the thirteenth century. As well as normal trade there are also records of purchasers being appointed in Ireland to purchase wheat and livestock specifically for export from Cork and Youghal to feed the armies of King Edward I during his various wars in Scotland and Wales, and in Gascony in south-western France.[31]

However the Norman colony suffered a serious decline from the early fourteenth century. Edward Bruce's invasion in 1314 in furtherance of his war against Edward II of England sparked off rebellions against the Norman colony. The native Irish lords began to reassert control in parts of the west and southwest, and even some of the Norman lords, including the Earl of Desmond, rebelled against the crown. This resulted in ongoing political unrest and warfare for much of the fourteenth century. This was exacerbated by the Black Death in 1348 which caused widespread devastation, especially in the towns where the concentrations of population meant that plague spread more quickly than it did in the countryside.

As so often happens in times of economic crisis, there was a great increase in the level of emigration, with large numbers of labourers and craftsmen emigrating, thus accelerating the decline of the economy. The problem became so acute that in 1410 parliament declared that "the husbandry and tillage of the land is on the point of being altogether destroyed and wasted" and numerous laws were passed forbidding emigration, but without much success.[32]

All these factors led to a serious decline in economic activity, to the extent that the port towns of Cork, Youghal and Kinsale, which had been major exporters of agricultural produce during the thirteenth century, now became importers. This decline had a serious impact on the larger towns, but must have completely destroyed many of the smaller towns, which were simply abandoned. It was probably around this time that Kilmaclenine, a town only a short distance from Buttevant, was abandoned, and it is likely that Buttevant went into decline also around this time. The turmoil of the fourteenth century abated somewhat during the fifteenth century when the great lords like the Earls of Desmond and Ormond established control over their own territories at least, which probably contributed to some economic recovery. However, in the middle of that century, in 1461, it is recorded that Buttevant was one of several walled towns ruined during a rebellion by Murrough O Brien. Nonetheless the walls are again mentioned in 1479 in the will of David Lombard. The town was said to have been "fearfully devastated" during the Wars of the Roses.

Towards the end of the sixteenth century the brutal suppression of the Desmond rebellion brought with it widespread famine, disease and deprivation, and the town of Buttevant was said to have been burned by the rebels in that rebellion. Following the Battle of Kinsale, the subsequent imposition of central control and the influx of new settlers including farmers, tradesmen etc. from England, a degree of stability was restored. The first half of the seventeenth century appears to have been a period of economic growth, with an increase in economic activity, exports, and the foundation of many new towns and villages around County Cork and the expansion of existing settlements.[33] Buttevant clearly survived the destruction and deprivation of the previous centuries and the census of 1659 suggests it had a population of about 800 people.[34] It also records that a small garrison of 14 English troops was stationed at Buttevant at that time, as well as 47 troops at Ballyclough and 117 at Mallow,[35] so the area was well protected, which would have facilitated trade.

Buttevant appears to have declined again however, in the second half of the seventeenth century, when other neighbouring towns thrived. Mallow expanded, probably due to its location on the Blackwater, while new towns and villages such as Charleville, Doneraile, and Churchtown benefitted from the involvement of local landlords who took an active part in promoting their town. It was of course very much in their own interests to do so as they benefited from increased rents. Buttevant, on the other hand, must have suffered from the decline in the power and influence of the Barrys, whose main base at this stage was in their fine new mansion at Castlelyons, and only experienced a revival when the Barry estates were purchased by Anderson in the early nineteenth century (see Ó Riain-Raedal, this volume).

1. MacCotter, this volume.
2. H. S. Sweetman, (ed.), *Calendar of documents relating to Ireland*, vol 1, (Dublin 1875), 322
3. Thomas, A., *The walled towns of Ireland*, vol 2 (Dublin, 1992), 28
4. F. H. Tuckey, *Cork Remembrancer*, (Cork 1837), 38
5. A. F. Ó Brien, 'Politics, economy and society: the development of Cork and the Irish south-coast region c. 1170 to c. 1583', in P. Ó Flanagan and C. G. Buttimer (eds), *Cork History and Society*, (Dublin, 1993) pp 83-156; 131
6. 'Report by Henry Smith of the State of Munster, 30th October 1598'. Paper presented to the Cork Cuverian and Archaeological Society, *Journal of the Cork Historical and Archaeological Society* 11, (1905) 27-31.
7. Borlase, *The history of the excecrable Irish rebellion*. (London 1680)

8. Charles Smith, *The ancient and present state of the county and city of Cork*, (2nd ed. Cork, 1815), vol. 1, 313.
9. T. O'Keeffe, 'Landscapes, castles and towns of Edward I in Ireland: some comparisons and connections', *Landscapes* 11-1, (2010), 60 -72; 69.
10. Thomas, *Walled towns*, 28
11. The geophysics survey was funded by Cork County Council and carried out by J. M. Leigh Surveys.
12. James Grove-White, *Historical and Topographical Notes, etc. on Buttevant, Castletownroche, Doneraile, Mallow and Places in their Vicinity*, 4 vols (Cork, 1906-15; vol 1, 364.
13. P. MacCotter and K. W. Nicholls, *The pipe roll of Cloyne*. (Cloyne, 1996), 29.
14. Smith, *History of Cork* 1815 vol 1, 313
15. Thomas, *Walled towns*, 28.
16. J. M. Leigh Surveys.
17. Richard R Brash, 'The local antiquities of Buttevant', *Transactions of the Kilkenny Archaeological Society*, 2:1, (1852), 83-96; 96.
18. MacCotter and Nicholls, *Pipe Roll*, 1996, 29. The original text is uncertain but 'hall' is the interpretation favoured by the authors.
19. My thanks to Tadhg O'Keeffe for alerting me to the plan of Dinefwr, from S.E. Rees & C. Caple, *Dinefwr Castle and Dryslwyn Castle*. [Cadw Guidebook] (Cardiff 2007).
20. H. G. Leask, *Irish churches and monastic buildings,* (Dundalk 1960), 110; D. Power, and S. Lane, et al., *Archaeological Inventory of County Cork.* vol 4. (Dublin, 2000), 548.
21. See P. Conlon, 'The Franciscans in Buttevant', *Journal of the Cork Historical and Archaeological Society* 107, (2002) 195-8; 196 for this suggestion. Conlon clearly mistook the back lanes of the town for the original main street.
22. R. Cochrane, 'Notes on the structures in the county of Cork vested in the Board of Works for preservation as Ancient Monuments' *Journal of the Cork Historical and Archaeological Society* 18:94 (1912), 57-76; 68.
23. T O'Keeffe, 'Buttevant friary and its crypt', *Archaeology Ireland* 26/3 (2012), 23-5.
24. Brash, Antiquities, 93-4.
25. K. W. Nicholls, 'The development of lordship in county Cork 1300-1600', in P. Ó Flanagan and C. G. Buttimer (eds), *Cork History and Society, (Dublin, 1993)*, 157-212; 176.
26. Smith, *History of Cork* 1815 vol. 1, 314)
27. A.Gwynn, and R. N. Hadcock, *Medieval religious houses: Ireland,* (Dublin 1988) 316.
28. MacCotter and Nicholls, *Pipe Roll,* 1996, 29.
29. Power et. al. *Archaeological inventory*, 701) See also O'Riain-Raedal this volume.
30. MacCotter and Nicholls, *Pipe Roll*, 1996, 29.
31. Ó Brien, 'Politics, economy and society', *passim*.
32. A. Cosgrove, 'The emergence of the Pale', in A Cosgrove (ed.) *A new history of Ireland*, vol. 2 (Oxford, 1987), 553.
33. P. O'Flanagan, 'Three hundred years of urban life: villages and towns in County Cork c. 1600-1901' in P. Ó Flanagan and C. G. Buttimer (eds), *Cork History and Society*, (Dublin, 1993) 391-468; 392.
34. (ibid., 396)
35. S. Pender, *A census of Ireland 1659*. (Dublin, 2002).

CHAPTER 2

THE AWAKENING OF THE URBAN WORLD IN THE MIDDLE AGES: NEW VILLAGES AND TOWNS IN SOUTHWEST FRANCE

~ JEAN-LOUP ABBÉ ~

During the eleventh, twelfth and thirteenth centuries, a fundamental reorganization of territories occurred across Europe, resulting in the growth of a multitude of towns, villages and hamlets. This agglomeration of population was sometimes the result of proactive policies by local lords. Historians have applied the term "new towns" to these foundations, and have written extensively on this phenomenon, which produced the present urban landscape, like that of Buttevant, that brings us together for this conference[1]. In this paper I will try to offer some insights into the new towns research, in the context of medieval and southern France, concentrating on the following points:

- research on the French new towns, especially the *bastides* : the process of discovery;
- the meaning of the medieval expression *villa nova* (new town): is it really a new foundation? is it really a town?
- the connections between new towns, *bastides* and the feudal world.
- the new towns and Buttevant.

THE FRENCH NEW TOWNS AND BASTIDES: RESEARCH HISTORY

The *bastide* is a medieval new town, or more correctly, a village (rarely a town, in fact), voluntarily founded by one or several lords (in the latter case it is named in French a *paréage*). The word itself refers in the south-west of France to the new villages founded in their hundreds in the thirteenth and fourteenth centuries, between the Atlantic Ocean and the Mediterranean Sea. This mass phenomenon, combined with the regularity of the streets and of the plots, has long attracted researchers, architects, art historians and historians.[2]

It was during the eighteenth century that the *bastide* became identified with an agglomeration. In the early nineteenth century, the *bastides* became part of the rediscovery of the Middle Ages. They were associated with the communal movement, becoming a symbol of the freedom of the people against the lords and a sign of democracy. Curie-Séïmbres, in 1880, synthesized the nineteenth-century research.[3] Later, the art historian Pierre Lavedan, in his *History of Town Planning* (1926), and *Town Planning in the Middle Ages* (1974), proposed a typology of new towns. Plans called checkerboard, with a regular grid, occur in many *bastides*. He was the first in France to study the new towns as a whole.

The model constructed in the late nineteenth century has several flaws. First, it is a "regionalist" history, not compared with other regions and countries (except for Lavedan's work). Furthermore, major elements of the *bastides*, like urban walls, covered market, "cornières" (arches around the market place), presented as if linked with the period of foundation, are almost always much later (late Middle Ages, sixteenth century). Also, the focus is on the village itself, and the surrounding rural land is not taken into account. Finally, the *bastide* is often presented like a town, focusing on its planning, on crafts and trade, on liberties supposed to be urban. The ambiguity is maintained with the term "new town" and their names that sometimes take the name of big towns (Barcelona, Bruges, Cologne, Valencia, Granada, etc.). In reality the vast majority were villages in the Middle Ages, as they are now.

A significant advance was achieved in the work of two historians, Charles Higounet and Maurice Beresford. Since the end of the forties, Higounet (professor of medieval history, University of Bordeaux) worked on the new towns of southwestern France, but also the Paris Basin, eastern Germany and Italy (Piedmont, Tuscany).[4] He offers a more flexible, more nuanced vision, breaking with the rigidity of the earlier pattern and highlighting several phases of foundations:

- *sauvetés* (from the word *sauf* = safe); the first phase village foundations, founded by the Church before the mid-twelfth century;
- *castelnaux* (new castles), the second phase (twelfth-thirteenth centuries);
- finally, *bastides*, the third phase (second half of the thirteenth and early fourteenth century).

The successors of Charles Higounet at the University of Toulouse, Benoît Cursente and Maurice Berthe,[5] have deepened and expanded his work from the eighties until today.

In 1967, Maurice Beresford, professor of economic history at the University of Leeds, and author of *The Lost Villages of England* (1954), shed important new light on the foundations in Gascony, Wales and England.[6] Beresford sought to understand the new towns on a European scale, specifically across the territories of the kings of England, and focused on the role of political authorities (kings, seneschals) as authors of true foundation policies (e.g. Edward I). He considered the bastides in the context of trade, especially the wine trade, and integrated the grid plan with a central market place into a broad chronology, a

European geographical area and a typology of market towns.

These scientific contributions are essential and remain valid, even if research has evolved in the meantime. In the 1980s, the phenomenon of *bastides* became popular in France (heritage, tourism), leading to the creation, in 1983, of the Centre d'Etudes des Bastides, an association dedicated to the study of *bastides*. 'New Towns' research took on new directions in the years 1990-2000. The three-phase model of *sauveté-castelnau-bastide* has expanded, with the addition by F. Hautefeuille of a new category of new towns of the twelfth century, the *bourgs mercadiers,* similar to the market towns.[7] Another direction is the analysis of landscape around the new towns. Indeed, it is notable that the regular morphology of new towns is sometimes accompanied by a reorganization of the land, especially with the later *bastides* in the late thirteenth and early fourteenth century, of which there are about twenty.[8] The 'new town' is not solely about building a town; it can also be a redevelopment of agricultural land. Finally, in England and in the Anglo-Saxon world, researchers study and debate the geometry of the *bastides*, particularly in the journal *Urban Morphology*. The studies of scholars such as K. Lilley, T. Slater, W. Boerefijn and A. Randolph focus both on survey techniques, measurement and meaning of geometric shapes. Boerefijn's thesis is the first academic thesis on the new towns (2010).[9]

THE MEDIEVAL EXPRESSION *VILLA NOVA*

While much has been said about the new towns, there was less interest in the medieval vocabulary, such as the expression *villa nova*. In particular, is it possible to make the link between this term and a regular urbanism? Since the nineteenth century, the expression "new town" was adopted by all researchers. Generally, two questions are neglected. Is the *villa* really a town and what exactly did the medieval word *nova* mean?

A survey was conducted on the use and meaning of the term *villa nova* in the south of France.[10] Its conclusions can be summarized as follows. The medieval sources show that during the Early Middle Ages the term *villa nova* signified a rural area. The term expressed the development of rural areas, particularly in the ninth-tenth centuries. The area designed is a landscape, not a townscape. Later, in the process of concentration of settlement, the term refers to the form of new areas around a village or a town, or a creation/foundation of agglomerations. *Villa nova* turns out to be the expression of the control of space by those who organize it. In the first decades of the twelfth century, the *villa nova* accompanies urban expansion and becomes an essential element. These are new neighbourhoods that are mushrooming in the suburbs of existing towns like Montpellier or Toulouse. They are most commonly described in the sources as little rural suburbs with gardens, few houses, and without regularity. However, several *villae novae* do show traces of regular plots, rectangular or grid-like. In Barcelona (Catalonia), Philip Banks has identified not one but nine medieval *villae novae*! He highlights their morphological regularity and their management according to orthogonal frames. They seem at first to be "garden cities" prior to being, mostly, completely built up.[11]

Thus, the *villa nova* can be defined as a planned operation to extend beyond an urban centre, often beyond the town walls. This deliberate action distinguished it from other, more spontaneous suburbs. It involves organizing the suburban land use, responding to the growth of the town or of the village. But, we must see the regularities of the streets and of the plots as a possible, but not necessary, consequence of the organization of the *villa nova*.

The same is also true for foundations like the *bastides* of the thirteenth and fourteenth centuries. They do not necessarily become an agglomeration with a geometric design. Higounet and Beresford had already noted this. The regularity is a sign of recognition, but an optional sign. It is not always possible to precisely equate terms with standard forms, as designed. This means that the vocabulary does not imply a specific form. On the other hand, the *villa* is usually a village rather than a town. And the novelty (*nova*), must be understood as a new space (designed, exploited) and as an extension (first, of land, later, of agglomeration).

NEW TOWNS, *BASTIDES* AND FEUDALISM

In south-western France, the new towns, especially the *bastides*, have been identified since the nineteenth century, either because they are generically named "*bastide*", or because they have a sufficiently geometric layout to be included among those localities with a plan referred to as "regular". But we know now that the *bastides* do not have a monopoly on regularity. Other types of settlements may also have regular elements of their space. Such is the case with ecclesiastical villages or towns, like *sauvetés*, villages or towns founded and protected by the Church, under the asylum and the institution of the Peace of God, with a church as the main focal point. It is also the case with castle villages or towns (*castelnaux*), with a castle or a tower.

We must not oversimplify. A volunteer foundation is not necessarily designed with a regular plan. The planned layout may be influenced by other elements such as monumental focus, topographic or hydraulic management, etc. Therefore, we must avoid identifying the "new town" with a geometric plane. In addition, subsequent decay may mask the early stages of urbanization. On the other hand, the layout of plots may have included an imperfect geometry, for various reasons such as topography, existing urban area, etc.

From recent research in France on new towns and *bastides* in the south-west, some results may be presented.[12] First, a general mapping of identified regular new towns, *bastides* or not, was conducted by the Centre d'Etudes des Bastides. A total of 633 localities with regular plan were identified, representing 11 per cent of all agglomerations in the south-west (Fig. 1). They are present throughout the area surveyed, with the exception of Landes, which was wetland in the Middle Ages. The density increases around Toulouse, especially in the valley of the Garonne. A typology was developed identifying two major families of plans, those with linear plans and those with grid plans. Finally, the chronology was refined, with the period of development of the regular plans identified as spreading over two centuries, from the mid-eleventh to the mid-thirteenth.

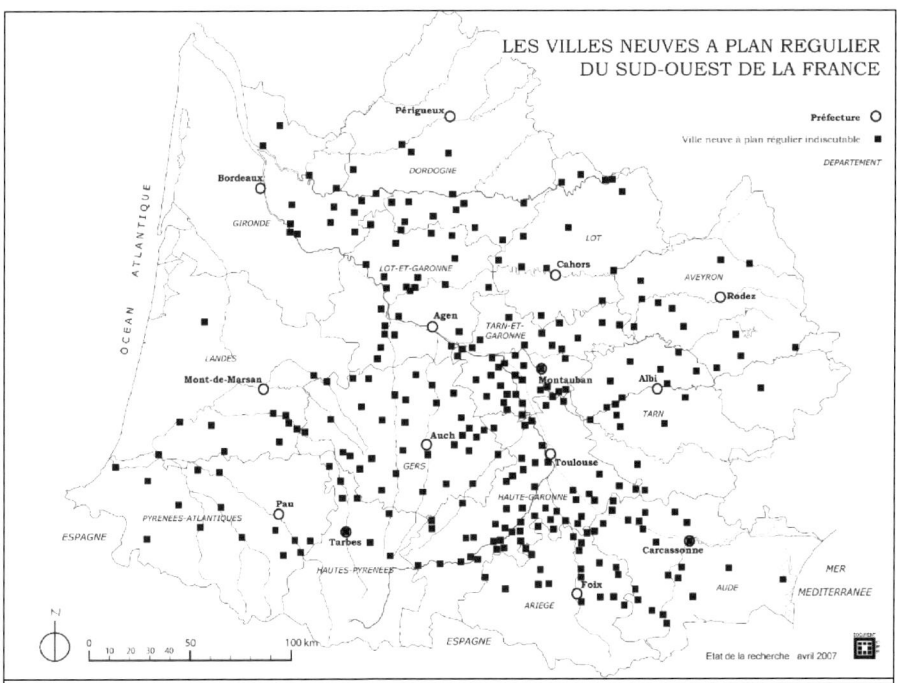

Fig. 1: *Medieval new towns with regular plans in the South West of France.*
(Centre d'Études des Bastides, 2007).

How do we explain this urban dynamic that lasted more than two centuries? And how do we explain the changes in the forms and organization of new towns, *sauveté*, *castelnau* and *bastide*? Historians, architects, urban planners, archaeologists, geographers have offered different explanations. Interest has been mostly concentrated on *bastides*, given their geometry, their large numbers, and the survival of numerous written sources, such as foundation charters and franchise charters. In fact, this thinking is somewhat simplistic.

The formation of villages and towns in the Middle Ages is a European phenomenon. It is first and foremost connected to the economic and commercial development of the rural world and to population growth. But there are wide regional variations in this phenomenon. Why are the new towns and *bastides* so numerous in south-western France? And why are they so scarce in other parts, like Languedoc and Provence? At the beginning of the eleventh century south-western France (Gascony, Languedoc, Pyrénées) was actually a region where the dominant settlement pattern was one of scattered farms (*casal*). Towns and villages were few. Individual lords sought to centralize authority so as to consolidate their power.

The introduction of feudalism played an important role.[13] Aristocratic families gained more and more power from the late ninth century, and replaced royal authority. This consolidation of power is reflected in the proliferation of castles and towers, around which many villages developed. In some cases, however, the local lord took the initiative to found a town to consolidate his authority. This is the case with the Béarn Viscounts, who were responsible for founding several towns. More modestly, these lords were also the initiators of new neighbourhoods to revitalize existing urban areas. The Church was also active. First, by the Peace of God, she tried to protect people from the violence of lords. Thus, spaces around the churches were declared sacred. Bishops, chapters and abbots participated in the creation of towns and villages. The *sauvetés* were protected towns. Their territory was bounded by crosses and could not, in principle, be subjected to violence. The village was built around the church. At the beginning of the twelfth century secular lords, in turn, built *sauvetés* to attract people.

Moreover, the twelfth century was the century when the power of the lords was at its peak. This was the era of counts, viscounts and squires. The south-west was under the control of some very great lords: the Duke of Aquitaine, and, later, the King of England, at Bordeaux; the Count of Toulouse, the Viscount Trencavel, at Carcassonne and, finally, the Count of Barcelona, then the King of Aragon. The new towns of the twelfth century bear their mark. *Castelnaux* were fortified villages around a tower or a castle located on the heights. They provided control of a valley or a territory and demonstrated the power of the lord. They formed a dense network across all of southern France, far from royal power.

Lords were also entrepreneurs who sought to reap the fruits of economic growth and trade. At the very least they could simply benefit from fees and taxes. But the boldest and most powerful founded towns from which they hope for a greater profit. Thus the market towns appear. The Counts of Toulouse, Alphonse Jordain and Raymond V, were the founders of Montauban and Castelsarrasin. The latter was named after the Count's representative, Raymond *Sarraceni*, a wealthy citizen of Toulouse, who directed the foundation.

Fig. 2: The bastide of Cologne (Gers), founded in 1284, on a plan centred on a great marketplace (mercadal).
© *Service de la Connaissance du Patrimoine de la Région Midi-Pyrénées.*

In the thirteenth century, geography and hierarchy of power is significantly altered. Following the crusade against the Albigenses in 1209, the King of France seized the estates of the Count of Toulouse and the Viscount Trencavel. The King of Aragon lost his influence. Only the King of England retained his power in Gascony. The French and English kings were lords of the south-west in the late thirteenth century. That is why the resumption of the foundation of new towns from 1230 to the end of the crusade was usually under their authority. The King of France, who had no estates in the south of France, often collaborated with a local territorial lord, usually a monastery, in the foundation of towns. The thirteenth century was the era of the *bastides*, but also the *castelnaux*, which continued to multiply. Though more numerous, the latter were also smaller. The situation remained the same in the early fourteenth century until the cessation of foundations with the plague and the Hundred Years War, from the years 1330-1340.

C. Higounet and M. Beresford have led the way in comparative research at the European level. These studies should be pursued more vigourously, since studies on a national level alone can not explain everything. The study of medieval new towns across south-west Europe shows up interesting contrasts and comparisons.[14] Thus, in the Iberian Peninsula, the new towns were very often walled, because they were built during the *Reconquista*. In France, where the context was different the *bastides* are built without ramparts. Another interesting comparison is the importance of the marketplace. In the Iberian Peninsula, the marketplace shrank in importance and in size over time, and was often a later addition, while in France, from the mid-twelfth century, it occupies an essential place, with an increasing area (Fig. 2).

CONCLUSION: BUTTEVANT, FROM FRANCE TO IRELAND

What is the place of Buttevant in European urban planning? First it is necessary to examine the name. Buttevant is a particular place name in Ireland. It creates difficulties in interpretation which Westropp had tried to resolve early in the twentieth century.[15] Eamonn Cotter, in his report on the archaeological heritage of Buttevant,[16] expands on Westropp's conclusions. The examples they offer show that the name was used in relation to fortifications, especially strong towers, including a fortification built by King Richard next to Chateau-Gaillard in Normandy, a tower at Corfe Castle, in Dorset, and a tower on Dublin's walls. These three examples all date to the thirteenth century.

The toponymist Ernest Nègre confirms this hypothesis. In his *Toponymie générale de la France* he mentions two other places. The first is *Boutavent*, a village in Picardy (department of Oise), which is mentioned in 1201; the second is *Bouttavant* castle, in Burgundy (Saône-et-Loire, *commune* of Cortambert).[17] The latter is located on a hill and has two round towers. Built in the eleventh century and mentioned in the fifteenth, it belonged to the lords of Brancion, then to the abbots of Cluny.

According to Nègre, *bote avant* (mentioned in this form at Chateau-Gaillard in 1198) is a large tower in front of a ditch. In the 1920s the historian Auguste Longnon had noted occurrences of *Boutavant* in the same context, and its connections with a similar toponym, *Passavant*. Of the fortification near Château-Gaillard, he wrote: 'We read in William the Breton's *Gesta Philippi* in 1198 that Richard the Lion Heart erected in the vicinity of the Andelys's Château-Gaillard a fortress which he called *Boutavant* ... '.[18]

An interesting case is *Boutavent* castle, in Brittany (department of Ille-et-Vilaine, *commune* of Iffendic). It is located on a rocky outcrop in the mythical forest Brocéliande. It is mentioned as early as the late twelfth century. During the thirteenth and fourteenth centuries, it belonged to the lords of Montfort. It consisted of a ditch, rampart, 4 buildings and a round tower (donjon) of 27 meters in diameter, with walls 2 meters thick. It is ruinous since at least the sixteenth century, and since 2005 has undergone conservation, and has become a popular tourist attraction.[19]

Finally, a recent article provides further, decisive confirmation of the meaning of Boutavant. In a study based on the siege fortifications of Normandy, Jacques Le Maho discusses several cases of what he calls *contre-châteaux* (counter-castles).[20] He defines their function as: '*abriter une petite garnison chargée d'empêcher toute sortie des assiégés, d'interdire leur ravitaillement et d'intercepter tout secours venu de l'extérieur ...*'.[21] One of these structures is located in the lower valley of the Seine, at Vatteville (department of Seine-Maritime). The castle of the Count of Meulan, Galeran, was besieged in 1124 by Henry I Beauclerc, King of England and Duke of Normandy. The latter built a *contre-château* which is now identified with a circular motte located about a mile away and still extant. A text of the thirteenth century refers to it as *Boutavant*.

In conclusion, it is possible to say that *Buttevant* is a French term (*langue d'oil*) signifying a fortification, tower, motte or castle. It is used from at least the late twelfth century as a place name and is very active in the thirteenth century. The town of Buttevant probably took the name of the Barry's castle. This small survey has modestly strengthened previous researches and has further integrated this town into a particular family, that of the fortified Buttevant of Northwest Europe.

---

1. I thank Eamonn Cotter and the Buttevant Heritage Group for inviting me to speak on the new towns and the medieval bastides.
2. Florence Pujol, 'L'élaboration de l'image symbolique de la bastide', *Annales du Midi*, 103:195 (1991), pp. 345-67.
3. Alcide Curie-Seïmbres, *Essai sur les villes fondées dans le Sud-Ouest de la France aux XIIIe et XIVe siècles sous le nom générique de bastides*, (Toulouse, 1880).
4. Charles Higounet, *Paysages et villages neufs du Moyen Âge*, (Bordeaux, 1975); *Les Allemands en Europe centrale et orientale au Moyen Âge*, (Paris, 1989); *Défrichements et villeneuves du Bassin parisien (XIe-XIVe siècles)*, (Paris, 1990); *Villes, Sociétés et économies médiévales*, (Bordeaux, 1992).
5. Benoît Cursente, *Les Castelnaux de la Gascogne médiévale : Gascogne gersoise*, (Bordeaux 1980); *Des maisons et des hommes : la Gascogne médiévale, XIe-XVe siècle*, (Toulouse, 1998); Maurice Berthe, 'Les territoires des bastides: terroirs d'occupation ancienne ou terroirs de colonisation nouvelle?', *Annales du Midi*, 102 (1990), pp. 97-108.
6. Maurice Beresford, *New towns of the Middle Ages. Town plantations in England, Wales and Gascony* (London, 1967).
7. Florent Hautefeuille, 'La fondation de villes neuves dans le Sud-Ouest de la France au XIIe siècle du bourg castral au bourg "mercadier"', *Revue de l'Agenais*, 1 (2004), pp. 69-87.
8. Cédric Lavigne, *Essai sur la planification agraire au Moyen Âge. Les paysages neufs de la Gascogne médiévale (XIIIe-XIVe siècles)*, Scripta Varia 5 (Bordeaux, 2002).
9. Wim Boerefijn, 'The foundation, planning and building of New Towns in the 13th and 14th centuries in Europe. An architectural-historical research into urban form and its creation' (PhD, Universiteit van Amsterdam, 2010).
10. Abbé (Jean-Loup), 'De l'espace rural à l'aire urbaine: enquête sur la villa nova en Languedoc méditerranéen pendant le Moyen Âge' in B. Cursente (ed.), *Habitats et territoires*

du Sud, 126e congrès national des sociétés historiques et scientifiques (Paris, 2004), pp. 47-63.
11. Philip Banks, 'Burgus, suburbium and villanova: the extramural growth of Barcelona before A. D. 1200', in A.M. Adroer i Tasis. *Historia urbana del Pla de Barcelona*, vol. 2 (Barcelona, 1990), pp 107-133; 'L'estructura urbana de Barcelona' in J. Sobrequés i Callicó (ed.), *La formacio de la Barcelona medieval, Historia de Barcelona* vol. 2, (Barcelona, 1991), pp. 25-71.
12. J.-L.Abbé, D. Baudreu and M. Berthe, 'Les villes neuves médiévales du sud-ouest de la France (XIe-XIIIe siècles)' in P. Martinez Sopena and M. Mercedes Urteaga (eds), *Las villas nuevas del Suroeste europeo. De la fundación medieval al siglo XXI*, Boletín Arkeolan 14, (San Sebastian, 2009), pp. 3-33.
13. Hélène Débax, *La féodalité languedocienne XIe-XIIe siècles* (Toulouse, 2003).
14. P. Martinez Sopena and M. Mercedes Urteaga (eds), *Las villas nuevas del Suroeste europeo*, Boletín Arkeolan 14, (San Sebastian, 2009).
15. T.J. Westropp, 'The name Buttevant', *Journal of the Royal Society of Antiquaries*, 31 (1901), p. 87.
16. Eamonn Cotter, *Archaeological and Environmental Heritage at Buttevant, County Cork*, Unpublished report for the Buttevant Heritage Group (August 2010), p. iii.
17. Ernest Nègre, *Toponymie générale de la France*, vol. 3 (Geneva 1998), p. 1460.
18. 'Aedificavit aliam munitionem super ripam Sequanae, quam vocavit Botavant, quod sonat " pulsus in anteriora", quasi diceret : "Ad recuperandam terram meam in anteriora me extendo "'. Auguste Longnon, *Les noms de lieu de la France*, 3 vols (Paris, 1920-1929), p. 549. Longnon also mentions another Boutavant in the department of Jura.
19. See the website of the ecomuseum of Pays de Montfort: http://ecomuseepaysmontfort.free.fr/.
20. Jacques Le Maho, 'Fortifications de siège et contre-châteaux en Normandie (XIe-XIIe s.)', *Château Gaillard*, 19 (Caen, 2000), pp. 181-9. I thank Jimmy Mouchard for alerting me to this paper.
21. Le Maho, p. 184. (Editor's note: this can be translated as: "to shelter a small garrison charged with preventing any sortie by the besieged, to prevent their re-supply and to intercept any aid from outside"

Chapter 3

Medieval Buttevant: 1100-1400AD

~ PAUL MacCOTTER ~

THE BUTTEVANT AREA BEFORE THE NORMANS

As Buttevant was an Anglo-Norman foundation the above sub-title is something of an oxymoron. Yet the Irish name for Buttevant demonstrates that there was, at the very least, a church on the site of the present Church of Ireland parish church of Buttevant before the Anglo-Norman invasion. This is indicated by the colloquial name for the town in Irish which occurs in records of the sixteenth century. The 1541 extent of the Franciscan friary of Buttevant gives the friary the alias of Killenenagh or Killnemagh, a name rendered Kilnemullah by the poet Edmund Spenser of Kilcolman near Buttevant, writing his 'Faerie Queene' in the 1590s. A native source, a praise poem on the local O Callaghan chieftain composed around the middle of the sixteenth century, gives the form as Cill na Mallach. This name also occurs in the contemporary fiants, as an alias for the rectory of Buttevant, when rendered Killnemallaghe (in 1578). The Four Masters render the Irish form as Cill na Mullach when referring to the alleged foundation of the friary of Buttevant by one of the Barry family in 1251.[1] All this tells us, of course, is that Cill na Mullach was their effort at a written form of the name as they heard it in the contemporary spoken Irish of the early seventeenth century. Thus we have two possible original forms for this placename, Cill na Mallach or Cill na Mullach. It has been suggested that the former version may derive from *mallaigh*, curse, in the sense perhaps of a saints' curse.[2] If the latter form is chosen it gives the sense of a church built on high ground (*mullach*), and indeed the church lies on the top of the steep enscarpment of the Awbeg river here.

The prefix *cill* here: church, is in itself a useful dating tool as I believe that this onomastic element ceased to be productive perhaps as early as the 'reform' period of the Irish Church from 1100 onwards, or at the very least from the period of the Anglo-Norman invasion. The dedication of Buttevant parish further confirms this chronology. As early as 1364 we have record of this church as *ecclesia beata Brigida*.[3] In general the Anglo-Normans dedicated their churches after saints of their own tradition, that is, saints of the Roman Calendar rather then the Irish Calendar of the Church. Therefore it would appear that the dedication to Saint Brigid here must also predate the Invasion.

This dedication gives us another useful clue to pre-Norman Buttevant.

While it might be thought at first glance that this dedication refers to the great Brigid of Kildare the early hagiography records the existence of another Brigid, a sister to Saint Colmán Mac Leinín, the patron of the diocese of Cloyne, and thus local.[4] Colmán is also patron of the once important church centre of Kilmaclenine, a few kilometers south-west of Buttevant. Although direct evidence is lacking, this seems to have been an important church in the immediate pre-Invasion period, as it certainly was in the post-Invasion period, when the caput of the large episcopal manor of Kilmaclenine which included all of the church-lands of the large cantred of Muscridonegan.[5]

The record of these church-lands contains an intriguing detail. The immediate demesne of Kilmaclenine itself contained just the townlands of Kilmaclenine and Knockaunavaudreen, giving an area of just over one-thousand acres. One would have expected the termon-lands of such an important church to have been larger then this. The remainder of the lands of this manor consisted of medium and large parcels of land ranging in size from several hundred to several thousand acres, as is the normal pattern with church-lands. The one exception to this pattern is the area of Buttevant Castle and Buttevant Church. The 1364 rental of Kilmaclenine describes these lands as:-

> the castle of Buttevant with its orchard and hall, and all the tenements which lie between the middle of the mill of Buttevant [the old cornmill] and the lane called Mylnstrete [Chapel Lane] on the north side of the said orchard, and extends to the public highway of Buttevant on the west side [Main Street], as far as the roadway and church of St. Bridget on the south side and the riverbank.[6]

This precise area is preserved to this day in the northern half of the 67 acre townland of Castlelands, which contains the southern half of the town of Buttevant.

Such an isolated small holding is extremely rare in episcopal rentals, and needs an explanation. A possible explanation arises from a study of the landholding pattern between Buttevant and Kilmaclenine. Both parcels of church-land here, Kilmaclenine and the castle-lands of Buttevant, are linked by the lands of the Augustinian priory of St. Thomas the Martyr alias Ballybeg. The foundation date of this priory is unknown. Lodge gives the foundation date as 1229 and the founder as Philip de Barry, but Philip had been dead for a couple of decades by this time. Sir James Ware is probably nearer the truth with his statement that William fitz Philip de Barry was the founder and that the priory was further endowed by his son, David de Barry, in 1237.[7] Usurpation of church property by the great magnates was common and we know William de Barry to have been in dispute with the bishop of Cloyne for lands in Barrymore a little earlier.[8] It is perfectly feasible for William to have obtained the lands of Ballybeg in a dispute with the diocese, and it is probable that he did indeed endow Ballybeg with these lands.

If this is the case it would suggest that the church of Cill na Mallach/Mullach was an outlying foundation of the powerful church of Kilmaclenine in the pre-Invasion period, and would explain the dedication of Buttevant to Brigid, sister of Colmán.

BUTTEVANT: NAME AND FOUNDATION

The cantred of Muscridonegan was among those cantreds granted to Philip de Barry by Robert fitz Stephen during the early years of the invasion.[9] Philip is unlikely to have made any settlements here, and it seems certain that the arrival of the Barrys was in the time of his son, William, who had certainly come of age by 1208.[10] The location of Buttevant Castle has significance. It lies just inside the cantred of Muscridonegan on a highly defensible site on a cliff above the river Awbeg.

The name derives from the French term *botavant*, and not, as has traditionally been thought, from the French phrase *Boutez en Avant* (which may perhaps be translated as 'push forward' or 'be in front'), the family motto of the de Barry lords. Indeed, it seems clear that the reverse is the case, with the motto being erroneously derived from the name of the town. A *botavant* describes a kind of military fortification, an advanced or projecting mural-tower along a defensive wall (see also Chap. 2 for further discussion). The placename element occurs as Boutevent when applied to several places in northern France, and as Botenan in Langedoc, and as Botevant in Yorkshire. In Ireland there was, in addition to the Co. Cork example, the Buttevant tower, one of the former mural towers of Dublin Castle, and 'Betavaunt', the name of a parish in Co. Laois found in early fourteenth century documents.[11]

The order of development in Buttevant is likely to be as follows. Firstly a (timber?) fortification on the site of the later castle to hold the terrain as a foothold. We know nothing of the actual details of conquest here, but some resistance by the local Uí Donnacáin (O'Donegan) kings is not unlikely. Secondly the foundation of Ballybeg priory, and thirdly the development of the town to the north of the castle and church. The town is likely to have originated as a small village near the castle, later to have been formally laid out in burgage plots radiating on a west to east axis from the central main street.[12] The dating of these developments can only be estimated approximately. While the existence of some kind of urban 'village' settlement north of the castle may well predate the grant of a license to hold a market in 'Bothon' to David de Barry in 1234,[13] the formal layout of the town between the castle and friary probably postdates this.

Something of the timescale here may be reflected in that of the development of the nearby and smaller town of Kilmaclenine, whose first charter of incorporation was granted in 1237 but which was still being settled and presumably in process of development as late as 1251.[14]

The date of the founding of the Franciscan friary presents some problems of integration within this suggested timescale. This is because it appears that the friary was in-situ before the town developed around it.[15] The traditional dates for the founding of this friary both originate in their present form in the seventeenth century.[16] Ware gives a *terminus a quo* as late as 1272, while the *Four Masters* give a date of 1251. This latter date seems the more likely, and would certainly agree with the archaeology if we allow the possibility that the development of the planned town began in the 1230s but was still in process in the 1250s.

BUTTEVANT: AN INCORPORATED BOROUGH

The earliest surviving court records for Co. Cork are those of the eyre of justices itinerant held in Cork city in the summer of 1260. This record contains three references to Buttevant. Firstly, one Adam fitz William Chater unsuccessfully impleaded John and William de Clentham for a burgage in 'Botavant'. Secondly, the court had view of the death of Elias Tanner who was slain by John and Philip Malgarve *infra portam prioratus de Butheawant* ('inside [or below] the gate of the priory of Buttevant'). Thirdly, the unnamed prior of 'Botavaunt' impleaded Philip fitz Cadogan for three ploughlands in Balidergill and Dyrliemade (perhaps Ballybeg).[17] The first record, with its mention of a burgage plot, indicates that by then Buttevant was an incorporated borough. The third reference certainly pertains to Ballybeg Priory, as the Franciscans did not acquire landed estates. The second reference is less clear. In medieval Latin the word *prioratus* can stand for the English 'priory' or 'friary' without distinction, and so this reference may refer to either Ballybeg Priory or Buttevant Friary. The occasional use of the fuller title: *the priory of St. Thomas the Martyr next to Buttevant* for Ballybeg might suggest that the second reference above may refer to the friary, but in general the priory is simply styled 'Buttevant' or the Latin form 'Bothon' and so we cannot be sure whether priory or friary was the site of Tanner's murder.

An incorporated borough possessed a fixed number of burgesses who held burgage plots in the burgagery for a fixed annual rent of one shilling. These burgesses enjoyed the 'liberty' of being judged by their peers in matters civil and commercial in the borough hundred court, under a set of laws originating in the Norman town of Breteuil, as was the normal practise in Ireland.[18] One of their number was elected by his peers as the town provost. Such boroughs were organized on a bi-partite system, with an inner burgagery and an outer burgagery. The inner burgagery was basically the area of the town itself, with each burgess inhabiting a property or messuage situated along the street front with a large garden to rear, while the outer burgagery consisted of plots of land several acres in extent distributed throughout the area of the outer burgagery. We know both the burgagery area and number of burgesses for several boroughs in Anglo-Norman Ireland.[19] These give acreage sizes per burgage plot of between five to twelve medieval acres. I have reconstructed the area of the outer burgagery of Buttevant (see below) which seems to have consisted approximately of nine modern townlands, five to west of the Awbeg, four to east. If we take it that the burgage plots in Buttevant were an average of those quoted above, this gives eight acres per plot. Using the accepted rule of thumb for conversion between medieval and statute acres, 1:3, we get an average statute acreage of 24 per burgage plot, which further suggests that there were around eighty or more burgesses in Anglo-Norman Buttevant, as the area of the burgagery amounts to at least 2,000 acres (834 hectares). To these burgesses should be added their families and servants, to give a total town population of perhaps as much as 1,000 or so. This was a significant number, and the town's importance is further indicated by its walling during the early years of the fourteenth century, at a time of increasing lawlessness and disturbance.[20] Further indicators of the town's importance are shown by the presence there of at least one large mill, two monasteries and a lazar-house or leper hospital (whose lands and location give the townland name Spital).

THE OUTER BURGAGERY OF BUTTEVANT

This can be reconstructed from a number of sources, in particular its representation on the Down Survey barony map of Orrery and Kilmore of the 1650s and its distinction as one of two sections of Buttevant parish in the Book of Survey and Distribution. By this time the burgagery had greatly decayed, with many of the burgess plots having 'fallen in' to the overlord, and so only isolated plots are shown on the map. The leading burgess at this time, according to the Book of Survey and Distribution, was John Lombard, who possessed twelve plots. These included the three parcels of Castlelombard which, strangely, do not seem to have included Lombard's Castle (whose ruin survives on the Main Street): presumably these plots were considered to 'belong' to the castle in some way. The three plots lay in Creggane while the four plots of Ardlombard lay in Waterhouse. Lombard's other plots were Knockard (in Knockanare) and the four plots of Lagg and Castle Pierse, which all seem to have lain in Knockbarry. John of 1641 was the son of Gregory Lombard of Buttevant, who died in 1619 when John was aged 14.[21] Gregory died seized of one and one half ploughlands at Buttevant called Lumbardsland, which included two castles, clearly the lands later held by John. Just one of Gregory's burgage plots is mentioned, apparently because the Crown had a claim to it. This was the parcel called St. John's House alias Teone (*Tigh Eóin*), which had belonged to the Hospitallers preceptory of Mourneabbey alias St. Johns. The second surviving burgess was John Barry, who owned the six plots of Maghery (in Lackaroe and Creggane), the plot of Boultane (unidentified), that of Farranwasten (in Knockbarry) and the plot of Scruby (Bohernascrub East). The third burgess was Hugolin Spencer of Renny, who owned the seven plots of 'Abbeylands', which seem to have been plots belonging to the Franciscan friary at its suppression. These had no doubt been acquired by the friary over several centuries, perhaps as bequests. Two of these can be identified on the barony map as lying in Creggane. Spencer had inherited these lands from his grandfather, the famous English poet Edmund Spencer of Kilcolman Castle, who had obtained a grant of these lands in the 1580s.[22] The total acreage of these seven burgage plots is given as half a ploughland, or approximately 150 statute acres, agreeing with the average size of Buttevant's burgage plots as suggested above. Other plots were known earlier, but had disappeared by 1641. This is indicated by record of the two gardens and three tenements in Buttevant held by Nicholas Barry of Annagh in 1590.[23]

The rather vague line of the northern boundary of the outer burgagery can be confirmed by the location of Spital townland which, with its lazar-house, must have lain outside of the burgagery, as did the townland of Rathclare. We know this because of several references to this townland as a rural fee. In 1260 Robert Cottrell, John Laghles and Walter de Kery were acquitted of disseising Donenald O Kym of one quarter of a ploughland in Rathclare.[24] This Irishman was one Domhnall Ó Caoimh or O Keeffe. These were the recently dispossessed kings of Fir Maighe or Fermoy, and Domhnall may have been one of the senior line of this family, which retained some minor lands in the area into the fourteenth century.[25] The Anglo-Normans who disseised him were probably locals or even towns-people of Buttevant. The toponymical surname de Kery was that of the family who give their name to nearby Curraghakerry.[26] This may well be the origin of the name Kerry Lane in the town. Rathclare again occurs in 1358, when Robert Tanner had possession of the minor heir of Elias fitz Mathew in 103 acres there. (The heir was Rose.)[27] The barony map and these other sources lead to the conclusion that the outer burgagery of Buttevant probably consisted of the townlands of Waterhouse, Knockanare, Lackaroe, and Lackfrancis to east of the Awbeg and Knockbarry, Creggane, Clashabuttry, Bohernascuab and Pepperhill to west. At the same time the inner burgagery would have contained more or less the present townlands of Castlelands and Buttevant.

Given the prominence of the Lombard family in Buttevant a few words may be written about the origins of this surname here. The ancestor of the family was Cambino Donati del Papa, an Italian banker who had come to Cork under Edward I as part of the fiscal element of the royal administration. He acquired much land in the vicinity of Cork city. The mainline of the family appear to descend from a brother of his, and used the surname Donati for much of the fourteenth century, until adopting the name by which they must have been known to their peers, Lombard, that is, the Italian. John Lombard alias Donati obtained a grant of much land in the Lee Valley around Blarney and Cloghroe in 1353, and the family may have built the original castle in Blarney. Their eventual arrival in Buttevant must owe something to the close if not always cordial relationship the family had with the Barry lords, perhaps being granted lands in Buttevant in exchange for the manor of Rahanisky, which the Barrys had seized from the family.[28]

THE EARLY INHABITANTS OF BUTTEVANT

A number of early references occur to these in addition to what has been adduced above. John de Midia (Mead) of Buttevant was the serjeant of the cantred of Muscridonegan in 1295 and first occurs in 1290. The Meads were a local family whom Ballymee and Cahermee are called after.[29] Around 1301 one Richard fitz Adam was a prominent townsman. Jordan le Taillor failed to recover a messuage in Buttevant against him, as did James le Blount a ploughland at Lyskythe (Liskelly?). Richard also loaned money to local gentry, such as Philip de Barry of Kilbrin. In 1297 Thomas Seys of Buttevant was sued by a wine merchant for payment and, in 1313, a local merchant, Henry Cadwelly, was robbed of his horse and ten marks of silver and slain. In 1295 William de Barry of Caherduggan lost control of his horse and accidentally killed William the Goldsmith 'in the street near the priory of Buttevant'. Other surnames associated with the town at this period are Osborn, Alyng and Cadel.[30]

In 1295 the entire town was found guilty of depletion of food in advance of the arrival of the justiciar and his train en route to Mallow to hold court.[30] Specific mention of the town market is made in this context, and there must have been a physical market square in existence, no doubt that which has today been converted into a childrens' playground. Depletion was a serious charge: an offence where the merchants deliberately hid or failed to make available food and fodder for the arrival of the judicial party as they were unwilling to endure the long delay in payment typical of the administration's way of doing business. In other words, when the justiciar and his large retinue of court clerks, servants and soldiers arrived in Buttevant they could not obtain food and fodder as this had been deliberately withdrawn from sale by the merchants. In 1317 the entire 'community' of Buttevant was pardoned its role in supporting its Barry lord in his war against the Cogan lord of the Lee Valley.[32]

THE MANOR OF BUTTEVANT

The Irish manorial system was complex and multi-layered. We should conceive of the manor of Buttevant as having had two dimensions, that of the senior or capital manor of the cantred of Muscridonegan on the one hand, and that of the demesne manor of the Barry lords on the other. That is, the manor of Buttevant had several other manors appendant while at the same time having its own manorial demesne-land and directly held fees. Therefore one can view the entire colony in Muscridonegan as simply consisting of the manor of Buttevant or one can view the colony here as consisting of four principle manors, Buttevant and its three appendant manors. These manors fitted into two groups (see map Plate 3). Firstly we have the great manor of Ballyhay, consisting of the northern half of the cantred. This had been granted to Philip de Prendergast by the Barrys and would later descend to the Cogans and Rochfords.[33] The half of Muscridonegan which the de Barrys retained was divided into the demesne manor of Buttevant itself and two subsidiary manors, Liscarroll and Ardnecrowan or Adnagrothen.[34] This latter place lay near Newmarket, and is probably to be identified with the later Castlemacauliffe. It appears to have been a manor created out of the unsettled parts of the cantred which remained in the hands of the Irish. Originally they would have been subject to firm colonial lordship and paid stiff annual rents, but the Gaelic Resurgence, which seems to have begun here as early as the late thirteenth century, would have essentially won independence for these Irish under their new MacCarthy overlords, the ancestral lords of Duhallow, who were already attacking colonial Muscridonegan by the 1330s.[35]

The destruction of the Barrymore muniments by fire in the eighteenth century has robbed us of a magnificent local archive which must have contained much material on the manor of Buttevant. We are forced to rely on the few surviving fragmentary references in our effort to gain some idea of the area of Buttevant's demesne manor. An indirect reference to the demesne manor seems to occur in 1298 as part of ongoing litigation between John de Barry and his brother David for possession of the de Barry lordship, where 'half of the half-cantred of Muscry' occurs, in which lay the four carucates of the fee of Cloghynynykyk, held by suit at the court of Buttevant from quinzaine to quinzaine by Robert, minor heir of Robert de Barry. This is apparently the fee of Ballyclogh (probably from Baile Cloiche: the townland of the stone castle).[36] The first-name Robert ran in this branch. A second reference, from the 1620s, confirms that Ballyclogh was held of the manor of Buttevant.[37] Then we have a reference of 1333 to Ardenoyd as being part of the manor of Buttevant. This is the present Mount North in Ballyclogh parish.[38] Two later references, from the early 1620s, show that the lands of Ballygrady (Kilbrin parish) and apparently the entire parish of Knocktemple were also held of the manor of Buttevant.[39]

The lands of the Magners of Castlemagner formed a detached portion of the half-barony of Orrery in the seventeenth century, when owing a chief rent and suit to the manor of Buttevant, as did the Magner lands at Templeconnell and elsewhere in Kilbroney parish. Originally these lands lay entirely within the cantred and the Magners (earlier Manganels) were original Barry tenants here from the time of the settlement.[40] Indeed, the boundaries of the manor on both south and west must correspond to those of the cantred of Muscridonegan here, suggesting that the southern boundary of the manor was the Blackwater and the western boundary the Allua. Many of the fees of the large manor of Ballyhay are known, and the pattern of settlement of junior Barry branches seems to have been confined to Buttevant manor, thus aiding our reconstruction here. Liscarroll was clearly another demesne manor of the Barry lords, but seems to have held no large fees beyond its own demesne whose area is probably represented by that of Liscarroll parish. Therefore the northern border of the manor of Buttevant is represented by the northern borders of the parishes of Knocktemple, Liscarroll, Churchtown (Bruhenny),

---

1. N.B. White (ed.), *Extents of Irish Monastic Possessions* (Dublin, 1943), 153; É. de hÓir (ed.), 'Caithréim Donnchadh Mhic Thaidh Rua Uí Chellacháin' in E. Rynne (ed.), *North Munster Studies* (Limerick, 1967), 519; Fiant Eliz., nos. 3278, 4262; AFM, 1251.3.
2. This is the form accepted by the Irish Place-names Commission (www.logainm.ie).
3. P. MacCotter and K. Nicholls (eds.), *The Pipe Roll of Cloyne* (Cloyne, 1996), 28.
4. P. MacCotter, *Colmán of Cloyne: a study* (Dublin, 2004), 64-5, 83, 125-6.
5. Ibid., 81, 86, 123; MacCotter and Nicholls, *Pipe Roll of Cloyne*, 28-57.
6. *Pipe Roll of Cloyne*, 28.
7. A. Gwynn & R. Hadcock, *Medieval Religious Houses Ireland* (London, 1970),159.
8. *Pipe Roll of Cloyne*, 76-8.
9. P. MacCotter, 'The sub-infeudation and descent of the Carew/Fitzstephen moiety of Desmond', *JCHAS* 101, (1996), 64–80, vol. 102 (1997), 89–106: 76, 101.
10. G. Duckett, 'Evidences of the Barri Family of Manorbeer and Olethan, with other early owners of the former, in Pembrokeshire', *Archaeologica Cambrensis* 46 (1891), 277-328: 280.
11. H. Sweetman (ed.), *Cal. of Documents relating to Ireland* (5 vols, London, 1875-86: henceforth CDI), v, 250; *Calendar of the justiciary rolls or proceedings in the court of the justiciar of Ireland,preserved in the Public Record Office of Ireland* (3 vols, Dublin, 1905–1955), (hence forth CJRI), i, 180. I cannot identify this parish and town.
12. For the early plan of Buttevant see E. Cotter, *Archaeological and Environmental Heritage at Buttevant*, Co. Cork (Unpublished report for The Heritage Council and Buttevant Heritage Committee, 2010), 26-8. Also Cotter, this volume
13. *CDI*, i, 322-4.
14. *Pipe Roll of Cloyne*, 36-8.
15. T. O'Keeffe, 'Landscapes, castles and towns of Edward I in Ireland: some comparisons and

connections', *Landscapes* 11-1 , (2010), 60-72; 69
16. *Medieval Religious Houses Ireland*, 243.
17. NAI RC 7/1, 268, 288, 303-4.
18. *Pipe Roll of Cloyne*, 214 n181.
19. A. Empey, 'Conquest and settlement: patterns of Anglo-Norman settlement in north Munster and south Leinster', *Irish Economic and Social History*, 13 (1986), 5-31: 21-3.
20. H. Tresham (ed.), *Rotulorum patentium et clausorum Cancellariae Hiberniae calendarium* [London, 1828] (henceforth CCH), 25.
21. RIA *Co. Cork inquisitions*, vol. 3 p. 8; vol. 4, 32-5.
22. *JRSAI* 3 (1994), 89-100; 14 (1908), 39-43.
23. RIA *Cork inquisitions*, 4, p. 51.
24. NAI RC 7/1, 238.
25. L. Ó Buachalla, 'An Early Fourteenth-Century Placename List for Anglo-Norman Cork', *Dinnseanchas* (1966–7), 1–12, 39–50, 61–7: 39.
26. *Pipe Roll of Cloyne*, 214 n178.
27. CCH, 73.
28. K.W. Nicholls, '*Anglo-French Ireland and after*', Peritia 1 (1982), 396-7.
29. NAI RC 7/3, 175; CJRI, i, 35.
30. NAI RC 7/8, 325, 331; CJRI i, 70, 95, 162; CJRI ii, 402; CJRI iii, 294.
31. CJRI i, 38.
32. NAI ms K/B Pipe Roll 9-11 Ed. III, p. 53.
33. MacCotter, 'sub-infeudation and descent', 76.
34. BL Add. ms 4790, f. 165v; NAI RC 7/4, 199; 7/6, 30.
35. P. MacCotter, *Medieval Ireland: territorial, political and economic divisions* (Dublin, 2008), 156-7; K. Nicholls, 'The development of lordship in County Cork, 1300–1600', in O'Flanagan and Buttimer (eds), (Cork, 1993), 157–211: 165, 168, 176.
36. NAI RC 7/6, 88; Pipe Roll of Cloyne, 217.
37. RIA Cork Inquisitions, vol. 3, 72.
38. NAI RC 8/17, 89; Pipe Roll of Cloyne, 215-6.
39. RIA Cork Inquisitions, vol. 2, 111; vol. 3, 189-90.
40. *Pipe Roll of Cloyne*, 210-12.

CHAPTER 4

THE *BASTIDES* OF SOUTHWEST FRANCE: A REINVENTED URBANISM.

~ JEAN-LOUP ABBÉ ~

This paper aims to trace the evolution in south-western France of urban planning employing a regular plan, and to place the *bastides* in the context of this development.[1] The question will be asked: is the bastide really a model, admired for its perfect geometry? It should rather be considered as marking the completion of a process of urban development spanning two centuries, from the mid-eleventh to mid-thirteenth. The paper is organized into three parts that follow the three key periods in the development of *bastides*.

PHASE 1:
VILLAGES AND TOWNS WITH
SINGLE AXIS AND LONG PLOTS (1050-1130)

The origin of the development of regular town plans lies in the second half of the eleventh century and early decades of the twelfth. It corresponds to the appearance of single-axis planes formed around one or more longitudinal streets. In a recent book on medieval Gascony, Benoît Cursente studied *sauvetés*, monastic and lay agglomerations of the late eleventh century and the beginning of the twelfth.[2] The *sauvetés* often abandoned the traditional urban form of scattered settlements and took the form of small towns surrounded by walls. The presence of a wall, synonymous with tight construction, was decisive in the initiation of a process that developed in the twelfth century and reached its maximum extent in the thirteenth century with *bastides*. The main locus of these early origins seems to be situated at the foot of the Pyrénées (Pays Basque, Béarn, Bigorre) where several examples of new towns are attested in the documentary sources. But the phenomenon is also apparent in other parts of south-western France.

The most notable lay foundations were in the county of Béarn. Installed around 1070 at Morlaàs (Fig. 1), Viscount Centulle V presided over the foundation of three towns, each surrounded by a moat. The three, Morlaàs Vielle, Bourg Mayour and Bourg Nau, were arranged in line with each other along a single street 1.2km long. A fourth village, Saint-Nicolas (the Marcadet), was

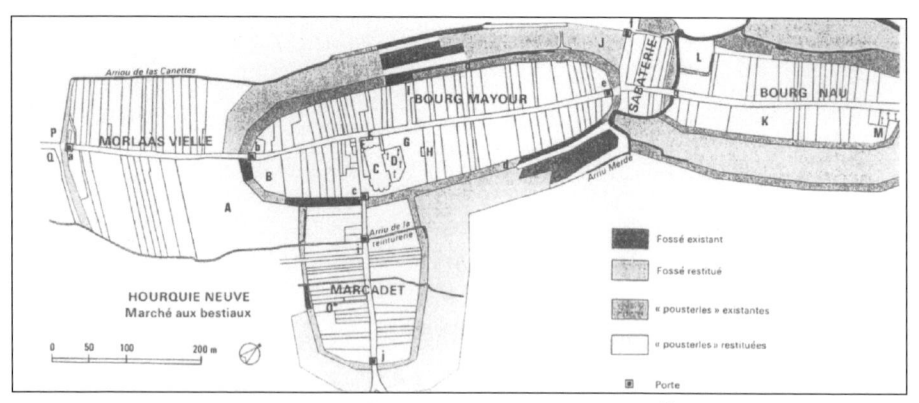

Fig. 1: Morlaàs (Pyrénées-Atlantiques) [3]

added before 1123 and was offset to one side. The towns developed within the space of only half a century and their topography was determined from the first quarter of the twelfth century. Inside the town, the elongated house plots are still clearly visible on the cadastral map of the nineteenth century. Morlaàs offers an excellent example of a plan with single axis and plot strips.[4] The founder, Centulle V, was also involved in the foundation of the towns of Oloron and of Tarbes.

In the same region several contemporary ecclesiastical foundations, the *sauvetés*, display similar regular plans with single axis. The earliest is Nogaro (Gers), founded between 1050 and 1060 by the archbishop of Auch. On both sides of the central axis, the plots extend in long narrow strips reminiscent of Morlaàs and Tarbes. The same is true the case of Bayonne and of the monastic town of Saint-Sever (Landes).

While *sauvetés* and other new towns were being founded in Pyrenean Gascony, a similar movement was emerging in Aragon and Navarra. Jaca, Pamplona, Sangüesa, Puente la Reina and Estella, formed a network of new towns with regular plan. Until the twelfth century, Pyrenean Gascony was within the sphere of influence of the Iberian kingdoms of Navarra, Aragon and Catalonia, which probably explains the synchronicity of the two urban movements on either side of the Pyrénées.

There are numerous indicators of other new towns with regular plans founded in the same period. Further research would probably extend the initial list of linear towns founded between 1050 and 1130, and would confirm the organization of the majority of plans reviewed. The foundations of the late eleventh century and the early twelfth present a plan aligned along a single axis, a type of "village street". The best way to cram a large number of building lots into a small space was to use rectangular plots of equal size, forming long strips aligned on either side of a straight street. This system also facilitated the confinement of the settlement within a rectangular walled space. The regularity can be seen in the street layout and in the regular grid of plots.

PHASE 2:
THE EMERGENCE OF MARKET-TOWNS (1130-1180)

A new boundary was crossed between 1130 and 1180, with the appearance of the first prototypes of the great square and regular plans with two axes. The epicenter of innovation this time was mainly in the estates of the counts of Toulouse, especially in the Toulousain and the Quercy. Such is the case of Montauban (Fig. 2). This town has long been considered a "*protobastide*", almost a century before the first true *bastide*. The novelty was the introduction of a vast central square, 65 to 70 m on each side, determining the layout of streets and that of the wall. Access was provided at the corners. The square commanded the division of the towns into neighbourhoods, each side used like a facade for one of these neighbourhoods.

The foundation of Montauban is now considered the centerpiece of a set of achievements that explain the success of new urban forms. In recent years, several historians have focused on morphological changes from 1130. The first, Benoît Cursente, emphasised the founding of *castral* settlements by princes who were seeking to develop autonomous power centers under the protection of powerful castles. This is the case with two cities, Casteljaloux and Mont-de-Marsan.

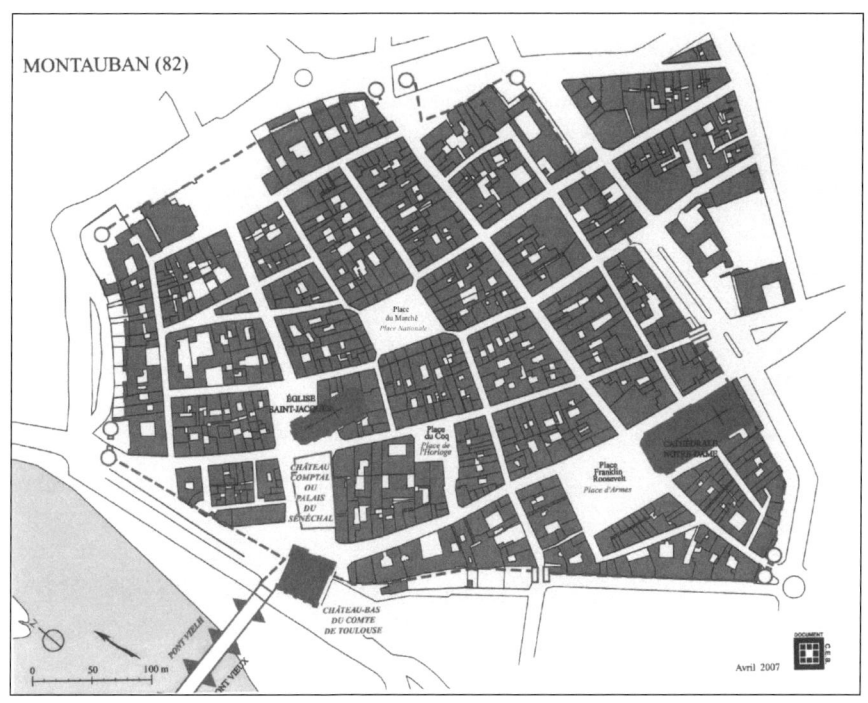

Fig. 2 Montauban (Tarn-et-Garonne)[5]

The second, Florent Hautefeuille, demonstrated the existence in the twelfth century of a wave of foundations of commercial towns, the market towns.[6] They are almost all located in lowland areas, often near a stream. The initiators of this movement are the great territorial princes. Their political power usually results in the presence of a castle on the outskirts of the urban agglomeration. This is the case with the Count of Toulouse Raymond V, regarding the foundation of Castelsarrasin and Montech, but especially of Montauban. Its foundation was an outstanding success, thanks to the development of the commercial activities. From the beginning, the Count had expected that the town would be primarily a market, and for this reason a large central square to accommodate the market was planned from the outset. Other foundations that met the same criteria were Villemur and Lauzerte, L'Isle-Jourdain and Marmande, Mont-de-Marsan, and even the contemporaneous *sauveté* of Saint-Nicolas-de-la-Grave (Fig. 5). All these towns are designed as strongholds, villages and market places. In Montauban, in particular, one can see the juxtaposition of the political function (Count's palace), the military function (Count's castle and fortifications) and the commercial function (market square and port).

The plans of the new towns / market-towns of the twelfth century display a greater regularity relative to their predecessors in their network of streets, blocks and plots. Montauban undoubtedly offers a twin-axis plan forming a grid that foreshadows the orthogonality of the thirteenth century. But the irregularity of the street network has resulted in irregular plot sizes. The towns of this period share a number of other common characteristics:

- the vastness of their associated territories: 17,000 hectares at Montauban, almost 8,000 hectares at Castelsarrasin;
- the area of towns themselves: 25 hectares at Montauban, 14 hectares at Castelsarrasin;
- the regularity of house plots, whose foundation charters give the dimensions and areas. Compared to the eleventh century, the plots are about the same width, but are now much shorter. The ratio is 1 to 2, a proportion often found later in the *bastides*;
- the parish church is usually remote from the square.

The foundation of towns ceased around 1180 throughout the southwest, and did not resume again until about 1220, probably due to a slowdown in economic activity after the long period of commercial expansion in the southern regions between 1130 and 1180.

PHASE 3:
THE *BASTIDES*, RATIONALITY OF FORMS AND COMMERCIALIZATION
(1230-1335)

It was during the second half of the thirteenth century, with the flowering of the *bastides*, that the most successful regular forms appeared and spread.

The medieval term *bastida* had several meanings. The first refers to an isolated fortified residence, often aristocratic, and appears in southern sources from the twelfth century. This meaning persists and in Provence today still means a secluded large farm. The second meaning refers to an urban plan so often orthogonal (or grid pattern), ordered around a central square dedicated to trade. It is generally founded by *paréage* (association) between an ecclesiastical lord (monastery, bishop) and an official of the authority of the counts, dukes or kings. A *bastide* is defined by both its functioning as a market town and its forms - function and form are inseparable. The *bastide* differs from the new towns of the twelfth century in the absence of castle, fortified wall and knights.

There is no fortification in the *bastides* before the fourteenth century and the Hundred Years War. After his defeat by the King of France during the crusade against the Albigenses, Count Raymond VII signed the Treaty of Paris in 1229. One of the provisions of the treaty was that the count should destroy the walls of several towns, including Toulouse. And he was forbidden to build fortified villages.

The *bastides* were founded in large numbers (traditionally the number advanced was 350, but this is probably exaggerated), but with uneven success. They were founded mainly between 1250 and 1320, the outer limits of their foundations being 1230 and 1373. If one focuses attention on their development, it is important to distinguish two main phases:

- the first is their invention and maturation, even in the years 1275-1280,
- the second is then their wide spread throughout the south-west France, after 1280.

It is the time of creation and maturation that interests us most here. Following the work of Charles Higounet, it is generally accepted that the first *bastides* were founded between Toulouse and Albi, by the Count Raymond VII of Toulouse and his officers. It must include two major foundations of the kings of France in the Languedoc, Aigues-Mortes in 1240 and the new town of Carcassonne in 1247.

Foundations prior to 1250 have not been thoroughly investigated. M. Berthe has observed that before 1250 the word *bastida* in the texts never refers to an urban foundation, but to a fortified site.[7] This has caused a lot of misidentification: many places called "*bastide*" (including so called) are not, in fact, new towns. Furthermore, a number of *castra*, not identified in the texts other than by the word *castrum*, have often been incorrectly labelled as *bastides*, on the basis that they had received a charter and had forms of regularity similar to those of *bastides*. Such is the case of Cordes, Castelnau-de-Lévis and Saint-Félix-Lauragais, for example.

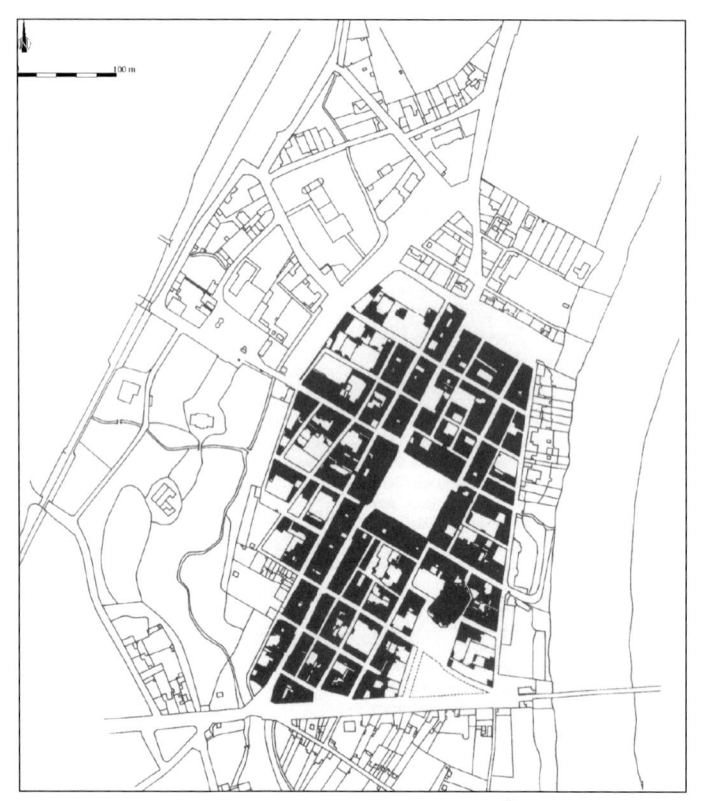

Fig. 3: L'Isle-sur-Tarn (Tarn)[5]

Undeniable *bastides* during the decades 1230-1250 are ultimately very few, Lisle-sur-Tarn (Fig. 3), around 1230, being the first one.[8] It is clear that until the mid-thirteenth century *bastides* are not numerous as compared with fortified villages (named *castra* and *castelnaux*). However, these few new towns, Lisle-sur-Tarn, Montesquieu-Volvestre, and Carcassonne, established a prototype from which the streamlined orthogonality of the southern *bastide* developed.

Shortly after 1250, the movement of creation and maturation of forms accelerates and expands. It is the first foundations of Count Alphonse de Poitiers that mark the real start of the specific phenomenon of *bastides*, whose success was overwhelming. Alphonse, brother of King Louis IX of France, became heir to the Count of Toulouse Raymond VII through his marriage with Raymond's daughter and heiress. Alphonse's officials were responsible for the design of most types of *bastide* plans.

Thus, in the south of France, the first checkerboard plan is that of Carcassonne, in 1247, and the first plan combining square blocks and rectangular blocks seems to be that of Sainte-Foy-La-Grande in 1255. These models were quickly disseminated throughout the lands of the Count of Toulouse and beyond, in almost all sectors of Aquitaine. Of 340 new towns of all types founded in Aquitaine between the 1220s and 1370s, 115 were founded in the decades 1250-

1280. But their widespread dissemination occurs principally between 1280 and 1333, under the direction of the kings of France and England, and all the princes and lords of the southwest, with 182 foundations in that period.

CONCLUSION: THE MULTIPLICITY OF FORMS OF FOUNDATIONS IN THE MEDIEVAL SOUTHWEST... AND BUTTEVANT

The coincidence of fortified villages (*castelnaux*, *castra*, like Cordes) and *bastides* in the thirteenth and early fourteenth century raises the question of specific or general character of regular forms. The two categories of foundation, *bastides* and fortified villages, shared the same principles of orthogonality, grid layout and square. It is not possible to detect a hermetic seal between the two categories. However, the forms are not similar. Those towns with the more refined and more perfect orthogonal plans are certainly, overwhelmingly, the *bastides*. They display the most streamlined and most prescriptive orthogonality of squares, street networks and plots.

Research on the *bastides* needs to progress further. Current catalogues are far from reliable, as they include towns which properly belong to other categories. A long and patient process of sorting is required. Then, the fortified villages of the thirteenth and early fourteenth century, when better characterized, would become a subject-specific study, enabling a more refined investigation of urban morphology in south-western France.

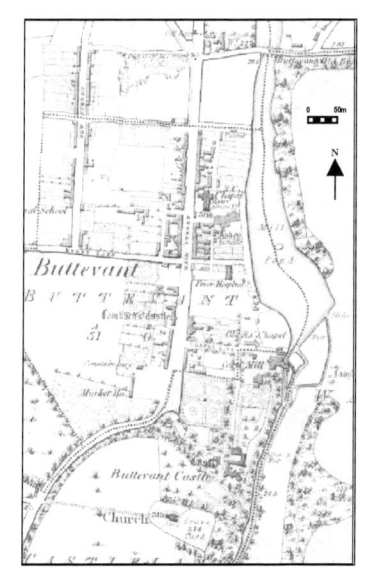

Fig. 4: (left), nineteenth-century OS map of Buttevant. Fig. 5 (right), nineteenth-century cadastral map of Saint-Nicolas-de-la-Grave (Tarn-et-Garonne)[9]. Scale bars in both are 50m

Finally, I will turn to Buttevant (Fig. 4). Comparing it with the new towns of south-west of France and Navarre presents similarities and differences. Take the example of Puente la Reina and Saint-Nicolas-de-la-Grave (Fig. 5). The resemblance is visible in the general structure: very long blocks parallel to a central main street. The plots are thin and elongated. This general structure is actually present throughout medieval Europe. It characterizes the foundations whose major axis is a road or street, existing previously or created. The differences are visible in the localization of the major focal points of the town:

- the market square is a simple extension of the street in Buttevant. Is it an indication of a limited development? In other examples, particularly in the *bastides*, a marketplace occupies a block, rectangular or square. It is central to the layout of the town.
- Buttevant Castle exists, but the plan of the town is not organized around it. The castle is outside, as is the parish church, both to the south of the town. At Puente la Reina and Saint-Nicolas, the church is central. In *bastides*, the castle was completely absent. This raises the question: do the church and castle at Buttevant predate the foundation and did they determine its location?
- collective fortifications, the walls of the village, are attested in the early fourteenth century at Buttevant. Are they contemporary with the foundation or later? If they are later, this trend is common to many new towns, from the *sauvetés* to the *bastides*.

Therefore, it is difficult to assimilate the new town of Buttevant with the foundations of the southwest of France. The relationship with the church and castle, and the shape of the market place are very different, I think. Moreover, the structure and dating of Buttevant are still not fully understood. As suggested by Dr. Tadhg O'Keeffe, one must certainly look to the Edwardian foundations studied by K. Lilley and W. Boerefijn for a better comparison.[10] If Buttevant is French by name, its development seems more characteristic of the British Isles than of south-western France.

A SELECT BIBLIOGRAPY ON THE FRENCH NEW TOWNS AND *BASTIDES*

Before 1990
Bastides méridionales, Archives vivantes, (Toulouse, 1986).
Beresford, Maurice, *New towns of the Middle Ages. Town plantations in England, Wales and Gascony* (London, 1967).
Bernard, Gilles, 'Les bastides du sud-ouest de la France : morphologie et fonctions. Étude de géographie historique', (Thèse de Doctorat de Géographie, Paris, 1983).
Curie-Seïmbres, Alcide, *Essai sur les villes fondées dans le Sud-Ouest de la France*

aux XIIIe et XIVe siècles sous le nom générique de bastides (Toulouse, 1880).

Cursente, Benoît, *Les castelnaux de la Gascogne médiévale - Gascogne gersoise* (Bordeaux, 1980).

Divorne, Françoise, Bernard Gendre, Bruno Lavergne, & Philippe Panerai, *Essai sur la régularité. Les bastides d'Aquitaine, du Bas-Languedoc et du Béarn* (Bruxelles, 1985).

Higounet, Charles, 'Les bastides du Sud-Ouest', *L'Information historique*, (1946), pp.8-35.

— *Paysages et villages neufs du Moyen Âge* (Bordeaux, 1975).

Jantzen, Michel, *Permanence et actualité des bastides*, Cahiers de la section française de l'ICOMOS 9, (Paris, 1988).

Lauret, Alain, Raymond Malebranche & Gilles Séraphin, *Bastides, villes nouvelles de Moyen Âge* (Toulouse, 1988).

Lavedan, Pierre, *Histoire de l'urbanisme. Antiquité, Moyen Âge* (Paris, 1926).

Lavedan, Pierre, & Jeanne Hugueney, *L'urbanisme au Moyen Âge*, Bibliothèque de la Société Française d'Archéologie 5, (Paris, 1974).

de Saint-Blanquat, Odon, *La fondation des bastides royales dans la sénéchaussée de Toulouse aux XIIIe et XIVe siècles* (Toulouse, 1985).

—, 'Comment se sont créées les bastides du Sud-Ouest de la France', *Annales AESC*, 4 (1949), pp. 278-289.

After 1990

Abbé, Jean-Loup, 'Le parcellaire rural des bastides du sud-ouest de la France: l'apport des sources écrites et planimetriques' in G. de Boe & F. Verhaege (eds), *Rural settlements in medieval Europe*, (Zellik 1997), pp. 309-19.

— 'De l'espace rural à l'aire urbaine : enquête sur la *villa nova* en Languedoc méditerranéen pendant le Moyen Âge' in B. Cursente (ed.), *Habitats et territoires du Sud*, 126e congrès national des sociétés historiques et scientifiques (Paris, 2004), pp. 47-63.

— Dominique Baudreu, & Maurice Berthe, 'Les villes neuves médiévales du sud-ouest de la France (XIe-XIIIe siècles)' in P. Martinez Sopena & M. Mercedes Urteaga (eds), *Las villas nuevas del Suroeste europeo. De la fundación medieval al siglo XXI. Análisis histórico y lectura contemporánea. Actas de la Jornadas Interregionales de Hondarribia (16-18 noviembre 2006)*, Boletín Arkeolan 14, (San Sebastian, 2009), pp. 3-33.

Berthe, Maurice, 'Les territoires des bastides : terroirs d'occupation ancienne ou terroirs de colonisation nouvelle?', *Annales du Midi*, 102 (1990), pp. 97-108.

Boerefijn (Wim), 'The foundation, planning and building of New Towns in the 13th and 14th centuries in Europe. An architectural-historical research into urban form and its creation' (PhD, Universiteit van Amsterdam, 2010).

Calmettes, C. (ed.), *New Medieval Towns of the South West with Regular Layout: a Collection of Documents*, (Coimbra, 2007) (CD_ROM; programme INTERREG IIIB-SUDOE).

Coste, Michel, *Afin de planter des vignes ... Essai sur la floraison des bastides et* *autres petites villes médiévales du bassin aquitain, XIIIe – XIVe siècles* (Toulouse, 2006).

—, & Antoine de Roux, *Bastides, villes neuves médiévales* (Paris, 2007).

Cursente, Benoît, 'Les villes de fondation du royaume de France XIe-XIIIe siècles' in R. Comba and A. Settia (eds), *I borghi nuovi secoli XII-XIV* (Cuneo, 1993), pp. 39-54.

— 'Les fondations de bastides dans la France du Sud-Ouest : anciens regards et perspectives nouvelles', *Territori i societat a l'Edat Mitjana*, 2, (1998), pp. 19-31.

— 'Le *bastides* della Francia del Sud-Ovest tra rurale e urbano (1250-1350)', in D. Friedman and P. Pirillo (eds), *Le Terre Nuove* (Florence, 2004), pp. 59-83.

Dubourg, Jacques, *Histoire des bastides. Les villes neuves du Moyen Âge* (Bordeaux, 2002).

Hautefeuille Florent, 'La bastide : une juridiction avant le village. L'exemple du bas-Quercy' in H. Débax (ed.), *Les sociétés méridionales à l'âge féodal (Espagne, Italie et sud de la France Xe-XIIIe s.). Hommage à Pierre Bonnassie* (Toulouse, 1999), pp. 141-8.

— 'La fondation de villes neuves dans le Sud-Ouest de la France au XIIe siècle : du bourg castral au bourg "mercadier"', *Revue de l'Agenais*, 1 (2004), pp. 69-87.

Higounet, Charles, *Défrichements et villeneuves du Bassin parisien (XIe-XIVe siècles)* (Paris, 1990).

— *Villes, Sociétés et économies médiévales* (Bordeaux, 1992).

Ito, Takeshi (ed.), *Bastides, villes nouvelles de la France du Moyen Âge* (Tokyo, 2009).

Les cahiers du C.E.B., 1 - 7, 1992-2004 (Centre d'Études des Bastides).

Lavigne, Cédric, *Essai sur la planification agraire au Moyen Âge. Les paysages neufs de la Gascogne médiévale (XIIIe-XIVe siècles),* Scripta Varia 5 (Bordeaux, 2002).

Pujol, Florence, 'L'élaboration de l'image symbolique de la bastide', *Annales du Midi*, 103:195 (1991), pp. 345-67.

Randolph, Adriian, 'The Bastides of Southwest France', *The Art Bulletin*

---

1. This paper owes much to research conducted with my colleagues Maurice Berthe (historian, University of Toulouse) and Dominique Baudreu (archaeologist, Carcassonne) in the context of a European program Interreg (Spain, Portugal, France) on medieval new towns. The text written by Dr. Berthe was a major source of ours. See J.-L.Abbé, D. Baudreu and M. Berthe, 'Les villes neuves médiévales du sud-ouest de la France (XIe-XIIIe siècles)' in P. Martinez Sopena and M. Mercedes Urteaga (eds), *Las villas nuevas del Suroeste europeo. De la fundación medieval al siglo XXI*, Boletín Arkeolan 14, (San Sebastian, 2009), pp. 3-33.

2. B. Cursente, *Des maisons et des hommes : la Gascogne médiévale, XIe-XVe siècle*, (Toulouse, 1998).

3. After Jean-Claude Lasserre, *Vic-Bilh, Morlaàs et Montanérès - Pyrénées-Atlantiques*, (Paris, 1989), pp. 488-490.

4. B. Cursente, 'Les bourgs castraux dans la Gascogne médiévale', in A. Chédeville and D. Pichot (eds), *Des villes à l'ombre des châteaux. Naissance et essor des agglomérations castrales en France au Moyen Âge*, Actes du colloque de Vitré (16-17 octobre 2008), (Rennes, 2010), pp. 215-26.
5. After Maurice Berthe, 'Montauban' in C. Calmettes (ed.), *New Medieval Towns of the South West with Regular Layout: a collection of documents*, IERU, (Coïmbra, 2007), p. 76.
6. Florent Hautefeuille, 'La fondation de villes neuves dans le Sud-Ouest de la France au XIIe siècle: du bourg castral au bourg "mer*cadier*"', *Revue de l'Agenais*, 1 (2004), pp. 69-87.
7. Abbé et al., 'Les villes neuves'. See also Judicaël Petrowiste, 'Naissance et essor d'un espace d'échanges au Moyen Âge: le réseau des bourgs marchands du Midi Toulousain (XIe-milieu du XIVe siècle)' (Thèse de Doctorat, Université de Toulouse-Le Mirail, 2007), pp. 275-84.
8. Maurice Berthe, 'Quelle a été la première des bastides ?' in J.C. Bouvier et al.,(éde.), Sempre los camps auràn segadas resurgantas, *Mélanges offerts à Xavier Ravier* (Toulouse, 2003), pp. 599-608 and *Les Cahiers du CEB*, 7 (2004), pp. 5-16.
9. Hautefeuille, 'La fondation de villes neuves', p. 74
10. Tadhg O'Keeffe, 'Landscapes, castles and towns of Edward I in Wales and Ireland: some comparisons and connections' *Landscapes*, 2:1 (2010), 60-72. K. Lilley, C. Lloyd, and S. Trick, 'Designs and designers of medieval "new towns" in Wales' *Antiquity,* 81 (2007), 279-93. Wim Boerefijn, 'The foundation, planning and building of New Towns in the 13th and 14th centuries in Europe. An architectural-historical research into urban form and its creation' (PhD, Universiteit van Amsterdam, 2010).

CHAPTER 5

LISCARROLL CASTLE: A NOTE ON ITS CONTEXT, FUNCTION, AND DATE

~ TADHG O'KEEFFE ~

In 1937 Harold Leask published what is likely to remain the definitive description of the architecture of Liscarroll, a de Barry castle of the later 1200s.[1] That work, coupled with its conservation as a National Monument in State Care, placed the castle comfortably in the canon of important Irish castles, a placement acknowledged by Leask's book-writing successors in the field of castle-studies, Tom McNeill and David Sweetman. Yet there has been no real analysis of its architecture. McNeill described it alongside the smaller towered-enclosure castle at Kilbolane near Milford,[2] but really only on grounds of geography, since he did not suggest any particular connection between them; oddly, he reported their measurements almost side-by-side but failed to observe a metrological relationship suggestive of a direct link: averaged, the castles are the same width (±1.5m) and Liscarroll is twice the length (±1.5m) of Kilbolane. Sweetman gave Liscarroll greater consideration – he devoted two-and-a-half pages to it[3] – but his description is accompanied by a plan which is seriously incorrect in its dimensions, in its representation of the orientation of both the west curtain and of the west end of the south curtain, in its phasing of the north wall of the gate-building, and in its representation of how the corner towers are connected to the straight walls. Moreover, his understanding of its general architectural-historical context is, even by the standards of 1999 when his book was published, out-of-date. Contrary to his assertion, for example, that "the later [medieval] castles", in which category he includes late thirteenth-century castles such as Liscarroll, "abandoned the great tower in favour of strengthening its [sic] outer defences and the development of the gatehouse"[4], the history of the 'great tower' (or *donjon*) after 1200 in north-western Europe (including Ireland) is far more closely tied into the history of domestic suites than it is into the history of outer defences. References to great towers are therefore really quite unnecessary when one discusses castles of Liscarroll's general design and vintage. Other questionable generalisations about later thirteenth-century Irish castles – for example, Ballymote Castle, Co. Sligo, Ballintober Castle, Co. Roscommon, Greencastle, Co. Donegal, and Roscommon Castle, were not "all built much to the same plan"[5] – undermine confidence in Sweetman's observations and opinions.

The publication of this book on Buttevant provides an opportunity to look afresh at the architecture of Liscarroll. This short chapter can be no more than an *apéritif* to a proper study, involving archaeological investigations of the castle's interior and of the embanked enclosure adjacent to it on the north side, and ideally comparable investigations at Kilbolane.

THE LAYOUT OF THE CASTLE

Leask's study of Liscarroll is so accessible that there is no great merit in a new description of its architecture, even brief. Instead, we can cut to the chase and highlight the four aspects of the castle which together make it so remarkable.

First, the enclosure is abnormally large (Fig. 1), rivalling in size the contemporary royal castle of Roscommon and exceeded in size only by the royal castles of Dublin (post-1204) and Limerick (1211-12), and by Richard de Burgh's Ballintober Castle of *c*.1300; Trim, Co. Meath, is bigger, of course, but is an entirely different species of enclosure-castle.

Second, it is an *empty* enclosure (Fig. 2), the only obvious accommodation being the fifteenth-century upper part of the gate-building. Spaces for accommodation tended to be quite small relative to overall castle-size in the thirteenth century, so we should not expect to find a large domestic suite in a castle like Liscarroll, but we should expect to find firm evidence of accommodation – a hall and a chamber, at least – contemporary with and physically connected to its curtain wall.

Fig. 1 Liscarroll castle from the east

Third, the gate-building, which looks to be an original late-thirteenth-century feature albeit with significant upper-level modifications (Figs. 3, 4), is somewhat anachronistic in being rectangular in shape[6], and is, along with the west gate-building of Edward I's Roscommon Castle, unique among the pre-1300 rectangular examples in Ireland in having its long axis so markedly perpendicular to the line of the curtain wall. A surprisingly close parallel – and it is merely a parallel rather than a direct relative – is the twin-towered gate-building of Carrickfergus, Co. Antrim, in its completed form of *c*.1300: it and Liscarroll's gate-building were sealed by gates at both ends, and both had portcullises at the interior 'ends' of their passages (Carrickfergus also had one at the 'front' end of its passage), as well as 'murder holes'.

Fig. 2: The interior north end of the castle; putlog holes and horizontal stone courses on this and the other walls show how the curtain wall was built up in layers.

Fig. 3: The gate-building from the south-west; note the difference between the thirteenth-century fabric and, from about halfway up, the later medieval fabric.

*Fig. 4: View along the thirteenth-century gate-passage;
the back wall is a later medieval insertion.*

Fig. 5: The north curtain wall, exterior view.

Finally, Liscarroll's curtain wall is pretty featureless, lacking even fenestration for bowmen. The long stretches of straight wall between the pairs of round towers at its northern and southern ends raise questions about its defensibility: if called upon, those towers could only have provided a minimum of flanking defence, and even that task was rendered more difficult by the orientation of some of the loops away from the curtain wall rather than properly along it (Figs 5, 6).

Fig. 6: The west curtain wall, exterior view; note here the horizontal construction layers.

It is tempting, based on that latter observation in particular, to describe Liscarroll as a poorly-designed castle, and to wonder about the sobriety, even sanity, of a mason/architect who would conceive of such a castle at such a date (the late 1200s) and in such a place (the central Munster 'frontier'). Here, though, is one of those points in historical-archaeological interpretation where we need to suspend our own preconceptions and trust instead that the medieval authors of the archaeological record, such as Liscarroll's mason/architect and his de Barry patron, were knowledgeable agents, capable of evaluating needs and designing accordingly. Liscarroll may have presented a threateningly dour visage to the Gaelic-Irish, its long and high walls hinting at a larger garrison than it actually had, but it was also built to one of the practical/conceptual building blocks of medieval European architectural form and aesthetic, the $1:\sqrt{2}$ ratio (Fig. 7) which was derived from the writings of Vitruvius[7]. Its enclosure inscribed on the

Plate 1 Buttevant castle from the southwest.

Plate 2 Buttevant Castle, Anderson's nineteenth-century entrance façade.

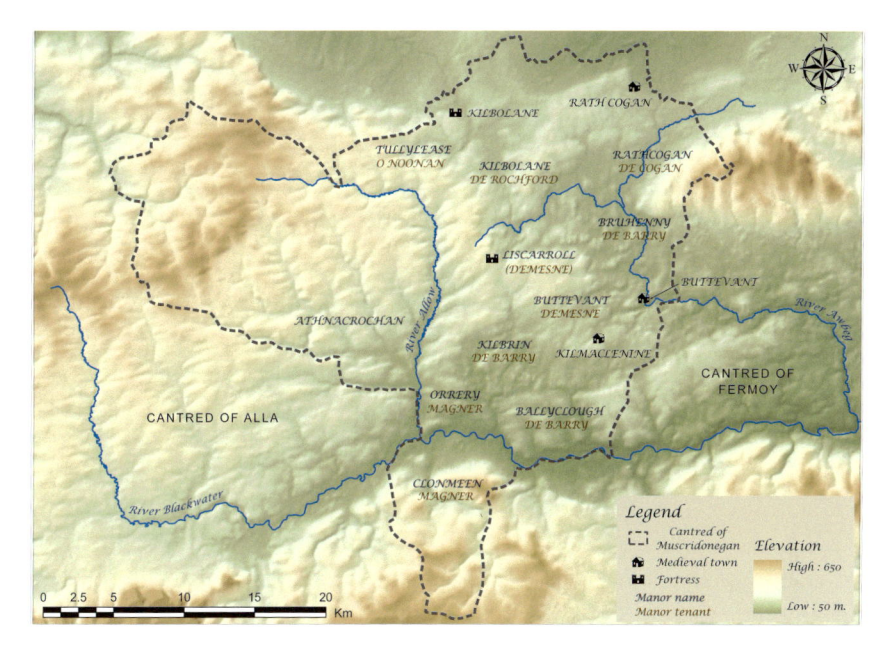

Plate 3 Map of the Cantred of Muscridonegan alias the Manor of Buttevant.

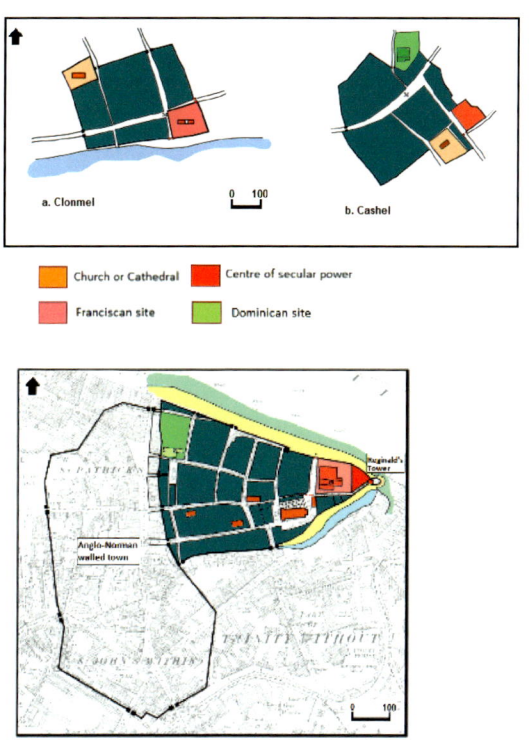

Plate 4 The medieval towns of Clonmel, Cashel and Waterford showing main secular and religious centres. Walled areas in blue.

landscape a rectangle which, based on the diagonal length of its informing square, embodied in the medieval mind both logic and beauty. That it had this proportion was not obvious on the ground, but that was not the point. The great Romanesque and Gothic cathedrals were built with the 1:√2 ratio in their plans and even in their elevations, and while nobody 'saw' that was the case, God, the patrons and the intelligentsia knew of its presence, knew that it infused the architecture with a rigorous logic, and knew that it placed the architecture in a lineage descending from Classical antiquity. The ambitions of Liscarroll's builder were presumably much less lofty, but he still built it that way because that was the proper way to build a rectangular space; it was the proper shape of a rectangle, even a very big one.

This proportional system could be effected on the ground in smaller building operations by simply marking out squares, tying ropes to pegs at two of their corners and then rotating them to determine the lengths of the rectangles. The scale at which Liscarroll was conceived was probably too big for that technique, so we might posit instead that the mathematics were calculated in advance – medieval builders knew to multiply the width of a square by √2 (1.4142) to find the length of a rectangle according to the Vitruvian principle – and that the walls were then built to measure. Proof of a sort comes from the enclosure's slight irregularity: where such boxes were laid out on the ground with pegs and ropes, the sides of the rectangles tended to be metrically parallel, but the scope for a lack of parallelism was greater when the 'Vitruvian rectangles' were too large for the right angles to be measured out carefully on the ground, and especially when the building material was rubble-based (as at Liscarroll) rather than ashlar. It is worth noting that the inaccuracy is apparent at the south end of Liscarroll's enclosure, in the wall which contained the entrance. This suggests strongly that the building of the enclosure began at the north end, where the corner angles are closer to 90°, and that the 'error' of less than 1° in the angle in the north-west corner simply increased as building progressed to the

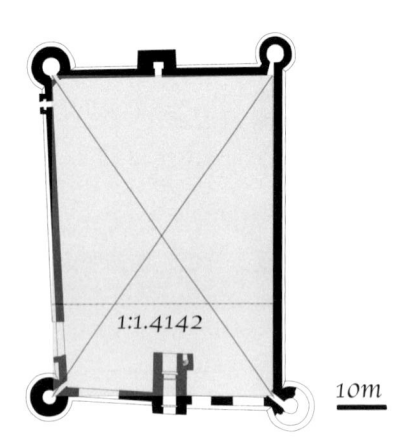

Liscarroll Castle, Co. Cork: metrology

Fig. 7:Liscarroll Castle plan (after Leask, 1937), showing the proportional system (1: √2, or 1:1.4142) which was used in its lay-out. North is approximately at top.

south. Such an interpretation runs counter to our intuitive sense that the building of Liscarroll must have started at the south end, where the gate-building faced the parish church, but the proportions do suggest a north-end starting point.

Liscarroll's builders would certainly have had no option but to calculate the measurements of a 'Vitruvian rectangle' if the curtain wall of the castle was being built around existing structures. I suggest that the enclosure is off-kilter precisely because sight-lines and potential diagonal measurements across the courtyard were so obstructed.

WHAT WAS INSIDE LISCARROLL CASTLE?

This is the question most often asked by visitors to Liscarroll. It will only be answered with archaeological investigations: geophysical survey could establish whether or not the courtyard hosted a light or heavy burden of buildings, while excavation would be needed for more specific information. Interesting as its contents will be, once we know them, just as interesting will be the chronological relationship between those contents and the curtain wall. Given the absence of a suite of stone-built rooms against the inside of the curtain, there is a strong likelihood that this curtain *post*-dates whatever was inside it. In other words, the curtain wall may have been built to contain and protect a complex of buildings *already* on the site. Its adherence to a known proportional system might suggest that whatever it contained was in fact similarly proportioned[8].

Recently-published geophysical work at Ballintober Castle[ix], another large and 'empty' enclosure castle of the later 1200s, confirms the validity (as distinct from the proof) of this hypothesis. That work revealed a complex of large domestic buildings arranged around a small courtyard in the centre of the vast curtain-walled enclosure (Fig. 8), the corners towers of which were designed to contain some additional accommodation. These are presumably the buildings mentioned in the inquisition which followed the earl of Ulster's death in 1333: "an old castle surrounded by a stone wall, which would be very useful for keeping the peace of those parts… In the castle are ruinous buildings, a hall, a chamber, a kitchen, and other houses, worth nothing beyond cost of repairs, because they need great repairs"[10]. One of the buildings identified in the geophysical prospection was externally about 12m by 8m and had external buttresses, a feature which Niall Brady interprets as evidence that it was a chapel[11]. No chapel is mentioned in the inquisition, and that surely rules out that interpretation; chapels are frequently mentioned in descriptions of building-clusters in manorial extents and *inquisitions post mortem* of the later 1200s and 1300s, so if Ballintober Castle had as prominent a chapel, even very ruined, it would have been mentioned. The building in question is better interpreted as the chamber (the main residence, basically), with the hall (the place of

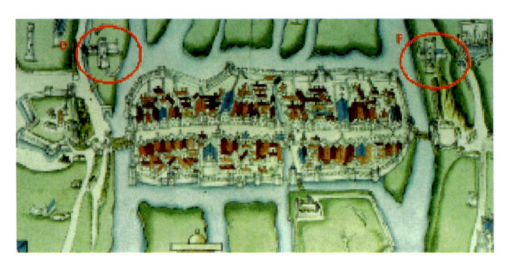

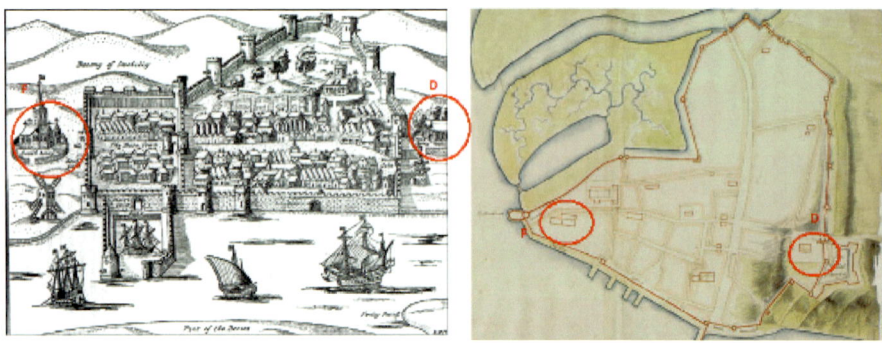

Plate 5 Clockwise from top: 'A description of the Cittie of Cork, with the places adjacent thereto' 1602, (Source: TCD, MS 1209, No. 45); 'The City of Waterford', Phillips, T. 1685, (Source: NLI, MS 3137/13); depiction of medieval Youghal in 1633, (Pacata Hibernia). F and D mark the positions of the Franciscan and Dominican friaries respectively.

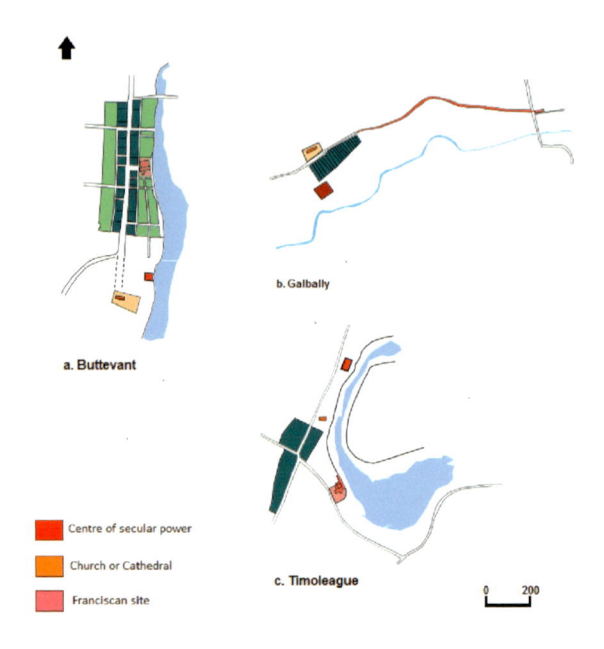

Plate 6 Location of friaries at Buttevant, Galbally and Timoleague.

Plate 7   The Franciscan friary from the southeast. St. Mary's in background.

Plate 8   West façade of the friary. Note flashing line, corbel and sockets below the windows.

administration and feasting) likely to be the building opposite; if the identification of the former is speculative, the identification of the latter is supported by the observation (which nobody seems to have made before, at least in Ireland) that halls are most frequently on the left-hand side as one enters a castle or manorial complex through its main gate.

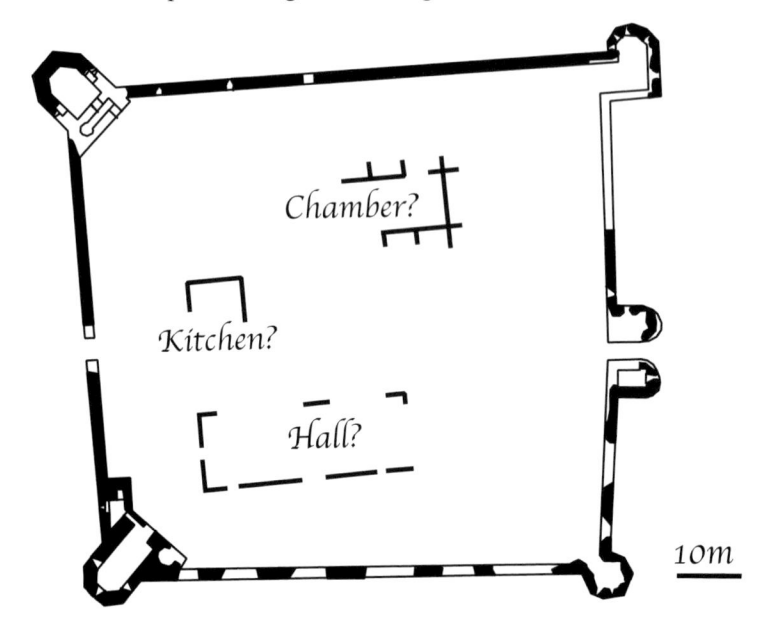

Ballintober Castle, Co. Roscommon: internal buildings

Fig. 8: Ballintober Castle, showing some of the results of resistivity survey (after Brady 2012).
North is approximately at top.

The manner in which these buildings sit inside the curtain wall at Ballintober, not touching it any any point, suggests that they and the enclosing wall are of different dates; were all these elements contemporary with each other, we would expect some physical integration of the domestic accommodation with the curtain wall, based on what we know of castle-design elsewhere in Ireland and in Britain. Given the size of Ballintober, it is difficult to envisage the enclosing walls as anything other than later than the buildings which are enclosed by them. It is worth noting how, in the wording of the inquisition, the "castle" is distinguished somewhat from the "stone wall" around it. At very least, this wording does not undermine the thesis that the wall was built not as integral part of the settlement or "castle" but as a later outer cordon, its shape and size determined by the size of that castle and by a desire to keep a green belt between settlement and boundary. If the geophysical evidence at Ballintober Castle is correctly interpreted here, the claim that the castle was specifically "built to impose [an Anglo-Norman] presence on the O'Conor lands" of north Roscommon[12] must be queried. It may well have intimidated the locals, but it stood Praetorian Guard to a static settlement, looking inwards as much as it looked outwards.

THE DATE OF LISCARROLL CASTLE

The hypothesis that the curtain wall of Liscarroll was built to enclose an existing settlement, à la Ballintober, brings us, finally, to the matter of chronology. A demesne manor of the de Barry family, Liscarroll is located in a district that was settled early in the subinfeudation of Cork. The putative manorial settlement inside the castle enclosure could date from any stage of the 1200s. Although the relative underdevelopment of settlement immediately outside the enclosure and around the church might discourage us from positing a date too early in the century, the size of the enclosure might be related to the longevity of settlement on the site prior to its building.

The date of construction of the towered-enclosure of Liscarroll – the 'castle' as we describe it today – is not recorded. Comparative architectural evidence would suggest a date in the 1270s or later. A date in the 1270s would allow us assign it to David de Barry, who served as justiciar from 1266–8 and who died in 1277, 1278 or 1279, depending on which source one trusts.[13] Its construction may have been in response to the loss of colonial lands on the west side of the Allua river following the defeat in 1261 by the MacCarthaigh king of Desmond of an Anglo-Norman force at the battle of Callann, a battle at which, according to some annalists, David's own father lost his life.[14]

---

1. H.G. Leask, 'Liscarroll Castle, Co. Cork, *JCHAS* 42 (1937), 92-95.
2. Tom McNeill, *Castles in Ireland* (London 1997), 139.
3. David Sweetman, *The Medieval Castles of Ireland* (Cork 1999), 111-114.
4. *Medieval Castles*, 105.
5. Ibid.
6. Gate-buildings of this shape were rarely built between the middle of the thirteenth century and the fifteenth century; Roscrea's gate-building is a rare late (c.1280) example.
7. The literature is vast. See K.J. Conant, 'The after-life of Vitruvius in the Middle Ages', *Journal of the Society of Architectural Historians* 27, 1 (1968), 33-38; for the use of the

Plate 9 Lombard's Castle entrance façade.

Plate 10 View of Buttevant Barracks.

Plate 11 St. John's Church of Ireland, west facade.

Plate 12 Medieval fragments stored in St. John's.

proportional system in the layout of Buttevant town and in Buttevant friary see Chapters 1 and 7 respectively, this volume, and for its use in a post-medieval context local to Buttevant see T. O'Keeffe, 'Lohort Castle, medieval architecture, medievalist imagination', *JCHAS* 118 (2013), 60-70.

8. The significance (especially in terms of reconstruction) of Liscarroll's metrological relationship with Kilbolane requires further reflection.
9. N. Brady, Ballintober Castle, County Roscommon, Roscommon Heritage Poster Series, No. 7, 2012.
10. H.T. Knox, Occupation of Connaught by the Anglo-Normans after A.D. 1237 (Continued), *JRSAI* 33 (1903), 58-74, at 59.
11. Brady, Ballintober Castle, n.p.
12. Ibid.
13. E. Barry, *Barrymore. Records of the Barrys of County Cork from the earliest to the present time, with pedigrees* (Cork, 1902), 22-6.
14. My thanks to Dr Paul MacCotter for discussing these issues with me.

CHAPTER 6

RECONSTRUCTING THE LANDSCAPE OF THE MENDICANTS IN EAST MUNSTER: THE FRANCISCANS

~ ANNE-JULIE LAFAYE ~

The friaries of the mendicant orders were characteristic features of cities and towns of medieval Europe. The rapid development and success they encountered from their appearance at the start of the thirteenth century meant that they had settled in most European countries by the end of that century. Among them the Franciscan friars achieved record numbers of foundations everywhere their order had sent them, and Ireland was no exception.

The impact of the friars on medieval Europe was not confined to their religious and spiritual influence; they naturally chose to settle in towns, where they could reach the crowds who would listen to their sermons and support their community, and research has shown the extent of their material impact on the urban landscape of countries such as Italy and France.[1] But in Ireland, the level of urbanization did not reach that of these countries. Despite the phase of town foundations and urban development brought about by the Anglo-Normans, cities were few and boroughs rarely grew to exceed the size of large villages. One consequence of Ireland's low urbanization is the exceptional survival of mendicant friaries here: in the rest of Europe very little remain of the friars' buildings, while in Ireland the extent of what is left is impressive. It allows us a concrete insight into the mendicant materiality, and makes the attempt to reconstruct their landscape all the more relevant. This paper focuses on a number of sites located in east Muster, an area which is interesting for several reasons. Of course it was a land of colonization, but also a land of contact and borders with the Gaelic Irish. It was therefore a fluid and dynamic landscape. It was a landscape evolving through the strong colonization of the Anglo-Normans with the foundations of numerous boroughs, but it was still a very rural world. How did the Franciscan's settlements fit in this particular landscape, somewhat different to what they had encountered elsewhere?

Over the years, research on the settlements of the mendicants in Ireland has led to the emergence of a historical and architectural model which has also influenced the view on the friaries in the landscape. Scholarly tradition has indeed explained the settlement of the mendicants in Ireland as reflecting ethnic issues, with a first 'wave' of foundations in the thirteenth century, associated with boroughs and Anglo-Norman lords, and a second wave in the fifteenth century,

Plate 13 Buttevant convent of the Sisters of Mercy.

Plate 14 Buttevant Mill as built in the early nineteenth century.

Plate 15   The grotto in the convent grounds, on the site of a medieval nunnery. The worked stones directly below the statue are mouldings from a medieval window.

Plate 16   Buttevant's eighteenth-century market house, on the site of its medieval forerunner. The park in the foreground was the medieval market square.

associated with observance, Gaelic recovery and lords, and the rural west, supposedly remote from English influence. If this does reflect some factual truth, it also expresses a very static and definite (and I believe superficial), black and white view of things, about objects - mendicant friaries- that were certainly not static and fixed in space and time, but were instead constantly subject to change and physical development. This approach also seems to take for granted modern notions that did not necessarily make sense in the Middle Ages when it comes to the perception of a landscape and its significance, and gives too much importance to the role of ethnicity as an explanatory factor in mendicant settlement.

The aim of this paper is therefore to attempt a reconstruction of the landscape of the Franciscan friars of east Munster, in an approach which tries to break from the traditional model and get a clearer and hopefully more objective picture of the settlement of the mendicants in Ireland, including their place in, and impact on, the medieval Irish landscape. The approach will be twofold. First I will try to show how the pattern of the Franciscan occupation fitted into the politics of east Munster, then attempt to analyse the landscape context of the Franciscans in that area and what it meant for the medieval landscape of Ireland in general.

THE FRANCISCANS IN THE POLITICAL GEOGRAPHY OF EAST MUNSTER

To be able to get a picture as detailed as possible and to reconstruct the landscape of the friars, we cannot limit our study to their immediate environment, the friary. Rather, we have to widen our perspective to what they saw as they were leaving to go preach and interact with society: the settlement their friary belonged to, and the countryside around it, in the extent of their *limitatio*. In the first part of this paper I will explore this extended world by looking at the political geography the friars found themselves in, and how it related to their foundations, but not before presenting the friaries of the research area.

Foundations and patronage
There are ten Franciscan foundations in the area covered in my research (Fig. 1). Traditionally the Franciscan friary of Youghal is given as the first foundation of the friars in Ireland, as early as 1224.[2] However the first documentary evidence dates to 1290[3] and some believe 1224 is too early a date, and question the choice of Youghal as a first foundation. Most agree however that Maurice Fitzgerald, then Justiciar of Ireland (1232-45) was the main founder and benefactor of the friary, and he is said to have been buried there in 1257 in the habit of the order.[4] Unfortunately there are no surviving remains of the friary.

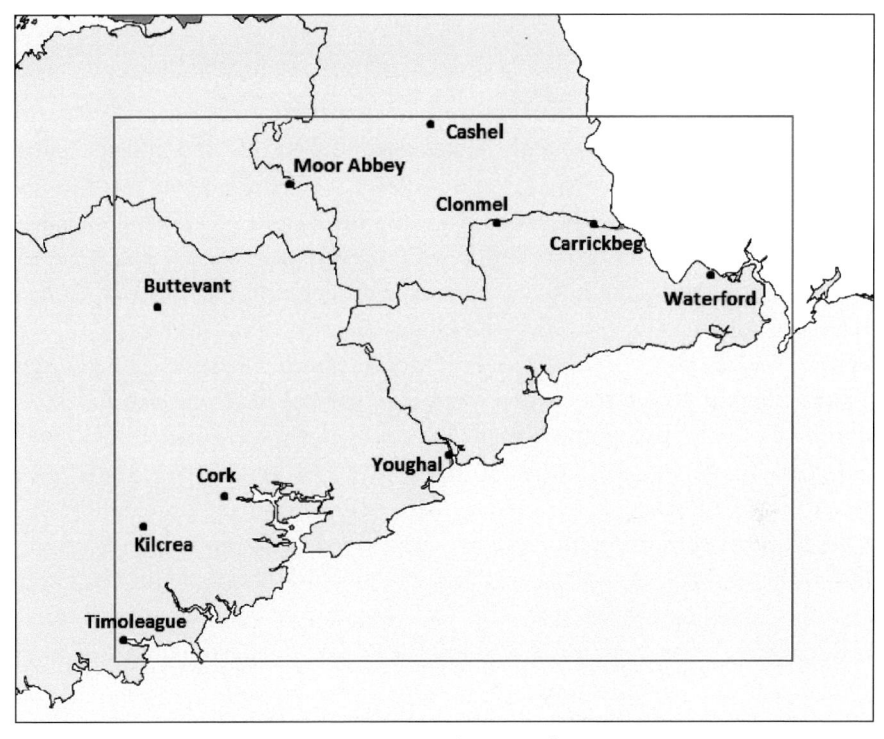

Fig.1: The Franciscan friaries of east Munster

If one accepts that Youghal was first then Cork would have followed it around 1229. Nothing remains of that friary either, and its beginnings are also rather obscure. Both the MacCarthys[5] and the Barrys[6] are associated with the foundation in different sources, and there is also an undated charter from a Philip de Prendergast seemingly confirming the grant of the site to the friars.[7] The Prendergasts were actually associated with the borough of Shandon, which was granted to them by their lord Philip de Barry, and there is also the record of a Dermot MacCarthy having married Dervorgilla Prendergast. The example of Cork is a typical illustration of the lack of certainty when it comes to foundation dates and founders of the friaries. However it also reflects the fact that things were not as straightforward as we might think in any case. A friary rarely had one individual founder, but rather multiple benefactors, and a foundation could have developed over the years, starting with a few friars and a rented house before getting enough funding to build an actual friary. This sort of scenario blurs the standard picture of one founder, one year, one friary. Things can seem a little more straightforward in Waterford, for which all agree that the founder was Hugh Purcell in 1240,[8] and a manuscript listing the burials present in the church names Hugh as founder and places his burial to the left of the altar.[9] Today the remains of the church are still standing and allow for an interesting study of the landscape context of the friary in medieval Waterford, which we will come back to in the second part of this paper.

Another church still standing is of course that of Buttevant. The Franciscans settled there probably around 1251, and not surprisingly the main founder was David de Barry, founder and lord of the borough.[10] Still in Cork, and also in Barry territory, are arguably the most impressive mendicant remains of the whole research area, Timoleague, believed by some to have been founded as early as 1240 by Donal Glas McCarthy. This is what the Annals tell us,[11] and it could be confirmed by some of the thirteenth century architectural features of the church. However an obituary of the friary, now lost, mentions that Margery de Courcy, daughter of Miles de Courcy, lord of Kinsale, was buried there in 1373, alongside her husband William de Barry, and there they are called *primi fundatoris hujus conventus*.[12] Once again this is an example of the foundation of an Irish Franciscan friary being something of a mystery. A detailed study of the architecture of the friary in the course of the research for my doctoral thesis has led me to propose a different, atypical theory. I do not propose to go into the detail of the analysis in this paper. Suffice it to say it suggests that the choir of the church was part of a building which was not originally built for the Franciscans, but was later taken over by them. This analysis introduces a more complex element to Franciscan settlement than traditional scholarship might have suggested. Finally the last Franciscan foundation of County Cork occurred in 1465 in Kilcrea. The founder was undoubtedly Cormac Mac Carthy, lord of Muskerry, who was buried in the habit of the friars after he was murdered by his brother Owen in 1495.[13] Cormac also built a castle, located only a few hundred meters away from the friary, creating a very interesting setting which we will come back to later in this paper.

This quick survey of the Franciscan foundation of east Munster would not be complete without mention of south Tipperary and its four sites. In Cashel the Franciscan friary was apparently founded by a lord William Hackett c.1265,[14] although no documentary evidence can support this statement, and no material remains allow us to get physical evidence of the history of the friary. The Annals of friar Clyn inform us that the friary of Clonmel was founded in 1269. The most likely founder, if the foundation can be attributed to one man, is Otho de Grandison, who was Sheriff of Tipperary in 1267, and who obtained a grant of the junior De Burgh family lands for life. James Ware also explains that others have said before him that the founders were actually the townsmen, or the Geraldines. Only a few miles from Clonmel the friary of Carrickbeg was founded in 1336. The site was given by James, first earl of Ormond, and was located across the river from his borough of Clonmel. Only on the 21 February 1347 was a licence granted to the second earl of Ormond to alienate a messuage and ten acres of land with their appurtenances to the friars for the purpose of erecting a convent thereon.

Finally, and much later, came the friary of Moor abbey, near Galbally, of which the un-aisled church remains, with its tall and slender tower between nave and choir. It was likely to have been founded in 1471 by the O'Briens, although there is a tradition of a thirteenth-century foundation by Donough Cairbreach O'Brien, king of Thomond, who died in 1242. There is however, no record of it. The 1471 foundation is recorded in the Annals of the four Masters, which states in the same entry that it was destroyed only a year after the construction had started.[15] Connor Mor Na-Shrona O'Brien was King of Thomond then (1466-96), and could be at the origin of the foundation.

Political and economic context

In his book *Medieval Ireland, Territorial, political and economic divisions* (2008), Paul MacCotter produced an impressive map based on his reconstruction of the cantreds of medieval Ireland, which illustrates the political and territorial divisions of the time. Looking at a map of the political geography of east Munster based on his work (Fig. 2), some interesting conclusions can be drawn regarding the relation of the foundations to the political context of the area when the friars settled. In Waterford for example one will observe straight away that there is only one foundation for the entire county. Most of the cantreds of the county were part of the royal demesne land, which might explain such a dearth in foundations.

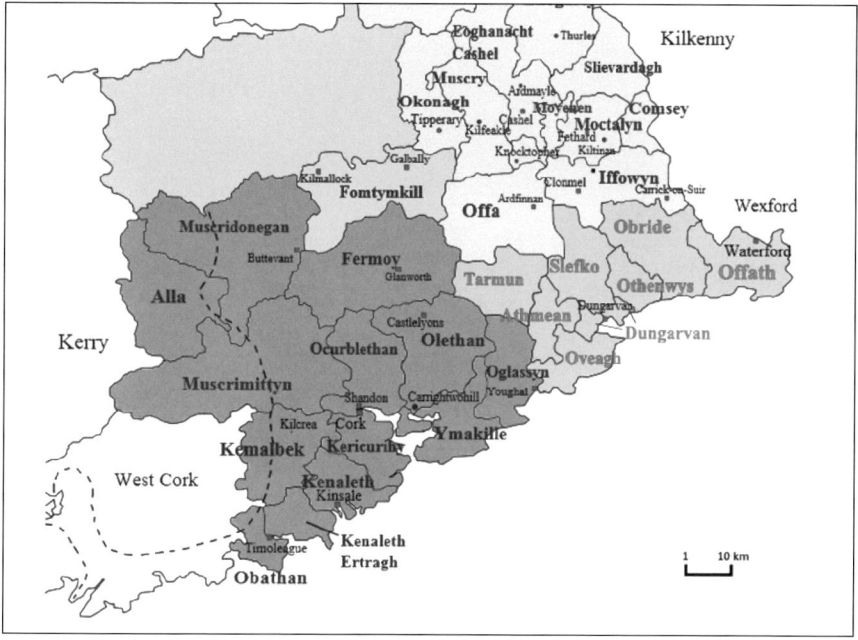

Fig. 2: Political geography of east Munster. The dotted line represents the western limit of Anglo-Norman control in Co. Cork in the late thirteenth-century (based on MacCotter 2008)

In east Cork as we have seen there are four foundations: Youghal, Cork, Timoleague and Kilcrea. Interestingly here, each friary is located within one cantred. As it happened this is a phenomenon that seems to have occurred in most of Ireland, at least for the thirteenth and fourteenth century foundations. The implications of it are not clear, but it certainly seems like there was, to some extent, a conscious approach from both friars and patrons in the distribution of the friaries in the landscape. It could have something to do with the friars' *limitatio*, which was the territory assigned to a friary by the authority of its order, within which the friars would go preach and beg. The cantred might have seemed to the Franciscans the perfect unit for this purpose. Of course the lords who would grant the friars a site on their lands might have had other considerations in mind. East Cork roughly corresponds to the moiety of Desmond granted to Robert fitzStephen in 1177, and one of the main grantees was Philip de Barry, who was given the cantreds of Olethan, Muscridonegan and Killeedy.[16] A junior line of the family later controlled Rathbarry and Timoleague in the barony later known as Barryroe, formerly the cantred of Obathan.[17] Of these four cantreds, three saw the arrival of the mendicant friars, and for all the Barrys are main founders: the Franciscan friaries of Buttevant and Timoleague of course, but also the Carmelite friary of Castlelyons in Olethan.

The Anglo-Norman colonization did not mean, however, that native Irish lordships completely disappeared. The association of the MacCarthys with early mendicant foundations along with the Anglo-Norman lords, as in the case of the Franciscan foundation of Cork, is certainly a sign that despite a weaker position, their attitude towards the colonists was not entirely belligerent. Intermarriage was not unusual, as we have seen with Devorgilla MacCarthy, daughter of a Dermot MacCarthy (possibly the cousin of the Dermot MacCarthy associated with the foundation of the Cork friary), marrying a Prendergast. Before the arrival of Anglo-Normans the MacCarthys had been Kings of Desmond, which roughly covered the modern counties of Cork and Kerry. The thirteenth century marks a period of great contraction of their lordship in Munster, but also the development of alliances and feudal submissions to the colonists. In 1261 the Battle of Callan marked a turning point and the end of the Anglo-Norman expansion in west Cork, and by the time of the Kilcrea Foundation, the MacCarthy lords had recovered an extensive part of the land around Macroom and were even granted land by the English king himself.[18] Their lordship became known as the lordship of Muskerry, and the castle and the friary of Kilcrea were built by Cormac MacCarthy on land he had regained from the Barrett family around 1420. This land became the borders of Cormac's extended lordship of Muskerry, and the building of the castle and the friary are therefore significant.

In Tipperary the situation was peculiar, due to the extent of 'cross-land', or land under the control of the Church. A number of cantreds were under bishopric control which led to the creation and development of episcopal boroughs, such as Cashel. But here again things were not static and the political context evolved significantly over the years. In a similar manner to Kilcrea, the foundation of Moor abbey illustrates the recovery of an Irish lordship. The O'Briens had assumed the kingship of Thomond before the arrival of the Anglo-Normans, but the territories under their control greatly contracted during the conquest. However, by the end of the fourteenth century, as the colony of north Tipperary was lost to unrest and returned under Irish control, the O'Briens regained territories in Thomond, and the foundation of Moor abbey took place in the context of this recovery.[19] Galbally would have been a very strategic location as it afforded a passage from Thomond into Ormond, the Galty Mountains blocking the way to the immediate south of the friary. In the fifteenth century the area was more than ever a border region, between the O'Brien's territory in Thomond and the earldom of Ormond. Could this have been another reason for the construction of the friary? The region also saw the rise of another powerful house from the fourteenth century on: the Earldom of Ormond, associated with the development of the borough of Carrick-on-Suir and the foundation of the Franciscan friary across the river in Carrickbeg.

The friars therefore evolved in a changing and dynamic political context, which resulted in a changing and dynamic landscape. In many cases it might look like the friars were only following the will of powerful lords who brought them to their lands, joining their religious duties to their political ambitions. But the friars had their own agenda, and the places they settled in also served their own interest. The mendicants were primarily urban orders, who needed the crowds of busy towns to preach to, and to benefit from their bequests and alms. In Ireland the Anglo-Norman colonization marked the beginning of an era of significant economic growth, along with the development of towns and the creations of many new boroughs (at least 38 in 1299 in county Cork).[20] Waterford and Cork city, and possibly Youghal, pre-existed the conquest, and were taken over and developed by the newcomers, becoming thriving ports. The new boroughs, often built up from an existing small settlement such as an ecclesiastical site, like in Timoleague, attracted settlers from Wales and England. In Tipperary and Cork in particular, if the multiplication of boroughs and markets was impressive, their creation did not always result in success. Interestingly however, every single settlement where the friars settled has survived to this day in one form or another: could it have been the impact of their presence, or a reflection of their own flair for choosing successful settlements for their foundations?

The friars were certainly attracted to seaport towns, which were already thriving economically when they arrived. Economic expansion paralleled municipal development and demographic growth. It also corresponded to the rise of the wealth and power of the merchant class, who took over the control of government of the towns. All over Europe merchants were generous benefactors to the friars, and it was probably no different in Ireland. There is little documentary evidence surviving of grants or bequests to the friars but there are some clues, some documentary, but also materially, as we will see in the next half of this paper. Seaport towns were connected to an extensive network of inland market towns, and not very surprisingly, every single settlement the friars came to had a market.

Process of foundation and settlement of the Franciscans
Some conclusions can be drawn regarding the conditions of the Franciscans friars' installation in the landscape of east Munster. Multiple patronage appears to have been the rule, rather than the single main founder model favoured by early historians of the orders and some more recent historians. More often than not there is no clear date of either the arrival of the friars to a town, or the actual foundation of the friary, or the constructions of the church and conventual buildings. The fact that very often there is just one friary to a cantred might indicate that the government of the order was monitoring and perhaps influencing the foundations, to realistically serve the best economic and religious interests of the communities. However, the process of foundation and settlement of the Franciscans in east Munster does not seem to have been as clearly organized as that of the Dominicans, whose pattern of settlement followed a complex and codified process, as modern research on the continent has shown.[21]
In Ireland the Dominicans settled in the first few years of their arrival in all the royal cities of the country; in east Munster, this meant of course Waterford and Cork. After that they favoured episcopal boroughs and towns thriving economically, and all at rather distanced but regular intervals, as shown in Fig. 3. The Franciscans on the other hand settled in secondary boroughs from the start and expanded

Franciscans		Dominicans	
		Waterford	1226
Cork	c.1229	Cork	1229
Youghal	1224-1245 ?		
Waterford	1240	Cashel	1243
Buttevant	1251		
Cashel	c.1265	Youghal	1268
Clonmel	1269		
Timoleague	1240-c.1320 ?	Kilmallock	1291

Fig.3: Sequence of the thirteenth century foundations of the Franciscans and the Dominicans

into more important cities later. This I believe followed a pattern similar to that in England, where in the first few years of their arrival two or three friars would establish a foundation simply by renting a house, before a friary was built and a community formed. In Ireland, like elsewhere in Europe the Franciscan foundations are more numerous than those of the Dominicans, probably because of those very different approaches to choosing settlement sites.

This seemingly less strict pattern did not mean however a lesser interest of the Franciscans for wealthy and powerful patrons, or vice versa. The association of the great families of the region with several friaries, and the relation of the friars with the merchants who ruled the cities of medieval Munster hint at the collaboration between the friars and their patrons to insure the realization of their respective interests, be it political, economic or religious and material. In what ways does the political and economic context of installation of the friars relates to the landscape context of their friaries?

LANDSCAPE CONTEXT OF THE FRIARIES

Problems of identification
Apart from Kilcrea all the Franciscan friaries in the research area are associated with some form of nucleated settlement. Of course these cover a number of types of settlement, clearly identifiable in the modern landscape. Some are villages, some are small towns, some are bigger towns, and some are cities, all of which existed when the friars arrived. However it is not always easy to know for certain what these places looked like or what was their status in the Middle Ages. This is an important aspect of the study of the settlement of the friars in Ireland: what was the medieval landscape in which the friars settled?

It is rather obvious for cities such as Waterford and Cork. But even in the latter, the friaries were located outside of the city walls, and at least for the Franciscans, in a separate borough, in what were not necessarily very urbanized areas. In other cases, we know the town they settled was a thriving borough, like Youghal or Clonmel. But sometimes, it is not known what was the exact status of a settlement in the Middle Ages and it therefore makes it a little more difficult to reconstruct the landscape of a mendicant house. Let's take the example of Moor abbey. Nowadays it is an apparently remote site, surrounded by fields and with the Galty Mountains in the background. However almost directly opposite to the west doorway of the church is a road which leads to the oldest part of the village of Galbally, which is believed to have been a borough founded in the early thirteenth century (see Plate 6). Nearby is the site of a castle of which nothing remains, as well as a much ruined and unusually long medieval church, which looks like it could have supported a population more important than one may think looking at the village nowadays. In Ireland a borough was not necessarily a large settlement, with a properly urbanized state such as we associate with a modern town. And an apparently remote site nowadays was not necessarily considered in such light in the medieval times.

It seems that we cannot think about mendicants and landscape in the same way in Ireland as in other countries such as France or Italy, where things were more definite in matters of urban/rural landscape, but instead we might need to put aside these urban/rural/remote distinctions, and focus on the significance that particular landscapes had in the middle ages, on the way areas were perceived then by the people living in them, and try to determine how the friaries fit into these: what were the bearings that medieval Ireland's particular landscape had on the settlements of the friars?

Location of the friaries
As with many aspects of the mendicant friaries, there is a traditional model of their general location in the landscape. In all European countries similar characteristics are noted: a peripheral position, outside the walls of a town.[22] As a matter of fact Buttevant friary does not fit with this model. As Eamonn Cotter has shown (Chapter 1), the Franciscan friary had a very central position in the borough, though the borough may have developed around it. Clearly things are not always straight forward when it comes to the friaries in Ireland.

Regarding the walled towns of our research area, a very common location was near the town walls, inside or out, and often close to a gate. This is also the case all across Europe. This is a logical location given their need to get in and out of town often to complete their preaching activities; indeed, the friars would preach in the public places of the walled city, but to the populations of growing suburbs. Likewise if the friary was inside the walls, a site near a gate, and the securing of its control, would greatly facilitate the friars' coming and going. It also meant a constant contact with the townspeople who had no choice but to use those gates. In 1317 for example, the Cork Dominicans, whose friary was located outside the South gate of the city, were conferred the custody of the key to the gate by Sir Roger Mortimer, then Lord Lieutenant of Ireland.

There are three examples of Franciscan friaries located inside the walls of boroughs in our research area: Buttevant, Clonmel, and Waterford. But even when outside, the friary remained close to the walls, as in Cashel. There is an interesting parallel between Cashel and Clonmel, for both of which records tell us that murage grants started after the arrival of the friars, which means that the two boroughs were most likely not walled then. In Cashel however the friary was not included in the walled area, while in Clonmel it was (see Plate 4). In both cases when the walls were built a gate was positioned so that it connected the friaries either directly to the town in the case of Cashel, or to the exterior in the case of Clonmel. In Cashel this led to the gate being named after the friars. In Waterford also the street along the friary precinct led directly to a gate giving access to the quays which they might have had possession of.

The three friaries of Clonmel, Cashel and Waterford also tell about their relation to other religious buildings in Irish boroughs, with the interesting proximity to the Cathedral in Waterford, and to the parish church in Cashel, while in Clonmel the location of St Mary's church in the opposite corner of the town presented an interesting symmetry, which certainly raises the question of the relation of the friaries to wider issues of borough development and urbanization.

Regarding the relation of the friaries to geographical features, the most obvious occurrence is certainly the proximity of water, as it is apparent in the examples of Waterford and Clonmel. The obvious reason for this is the need of a water supply for the friary, as well as fishing. Obviously seaport towns are the perfect choice to cover both of these needs, and it is not a surprise to find Franciscan friaries in the majority of cases close to the harbour and ports of these towns, like in Waterford, Youghal, Timoleague, and Cork. There is evidence for the friars owning fishing weirs and pools in the three friaries in Cork: None are mentioned in the extent of the Franciscans' possessions, but in the 1240 grant from Philip de Prendergast he gives them a fishery, and it is confirmed in 1341 and 1520.[23] Inland friaries are located on river banks, like in Carrickbeg, Clonmel, and of course Buttevant, or at a short distance from them, like in Kilcrea and Moor abbey. For all of these, it is almost certain that access to the river was included in the land attached to the friary, and often a place name still relates the friary to the water source to this day, such as the sites of St Francis Well near Moor abbey. The only Franciscan friary of our research area not located near water is the Cashel foundation.

Settlement planning and impact on the medieval landscape
Because of the smaller size of the Irish towns, the mendicant friaries must have had a greater impact on their landscape than in other countries. The friars' houses must have defined the landscape of the Irish boroughs as much as did castles, parish churches and walls, rather than just being a feature among many others as they were in larger cities. This was also influenced by the fact that Irish friaries very rarely moved from their original positions, probably quite simply because there was no need to: the size of the town meant that even a suburban position still meant being closer to the 'centre' of the boroughs.

Moreover, the study of the position of the friaries in the boroughs of east Munster reveals more than just a material impact, but also the possible collaboration between the friars and the lords of the boroughs they settled in, in regards to the decision of where the friary site should be located. Indeed in Waterford, Youghal and Cork, there is an interesting parallel in the position of the Franciscan and Dominican friaries (Plate 5). In Waterford this hypothesis can even be linked to the relationship of the friars with the city's powerful rulers, i.e. the merchants. Indeed the positions of the friaries at each end of the quays, controlled by a few merchant families, makes attractive the theory that the latter would have used the friars to help them keep control of the quays.

The relationship between urban growth and the coming of the friars has been studied extensively in Italy and France. A major characteristic of Ireland is that here boroughs developed around the same time as the friars arrived, whereas elsewhere towns were already in an advanced stage of urbanization. As a result, some interesting parallels can be drawn which might indicate a direct link between the development of new boroughs in the wake of the Anglo-Norman colonization and the foundation and building of the friaries. Boroughs were of course a way for lords to make their land profitable, but they also represented an expression of their authority and control over that land. Burgesses might have been given rights and freedom unlikely to be found elsewhere, but the borough itself was planned out by the lord. Some key features were common to most seigneurial boroughs, such as a castle, a parish church, a main street with burgages along it, a market, very often a river or a harbour, and of course sometimes a friary, the positions of all of which might not have been left to chance. In east Munster, the settlements of Buttevant, Timoleague, and Moor abbey/Galbally illustrate this phenomenon in different manners (Plate 6). We know from the study of Buttevant presented by Eamonn Cotter (this volume) that it was a planned borough. The central position of the Franciscan friary could indicate that it was part of the plan from the very start. Similarly in Galbally and Timoleague, if things might not have been as geometrically planned, it seems that the position of the friaries was not merely coincidental.

There is no doubt that the friaries, through their sheer size and the extent of their occupation in small Irish towns, had a significant impact on the medieval landscape. In the course of my research I have tried to reconstruct the extent of the two friaries of Waterford (Plate 5). Located at each end of the old walled town their precinct would have covered a rather large portion of this very contained urban area. The height of their walls and towers would have dominated the landscape of the port side of the city, and they would have been quite a sight for the boats coming onto the quays.

Similarly the friaries of Timoleague and Buttevant, with their impressive size would have been one of the foci of these rather small boroughs. And in apparently more remote areas friaries would have been even more striking in the landscape. In fact their conspicuous nature might have been part of the reason why lords such as the MacCarthys, the Barrys or the O'Briens built them, as a physical actor in the construction of a political/strategic landscape in their lordship, be it Anglo-Norman or Gaelic Irish. The example of Kilcrea is a case in point, with its striking friary-castle association (Fig. 4). As we saw in the first part of this paper, the area was an important borderland recovered by the MacCarthys from both Anglo-Norman and Gaelic lords.[24] I believe the construction of this friary and castle is about lordship, and the expression of authority and control over land the same way boroughs like Timoleague have been, and in both cases, the friaries were very much a part of this

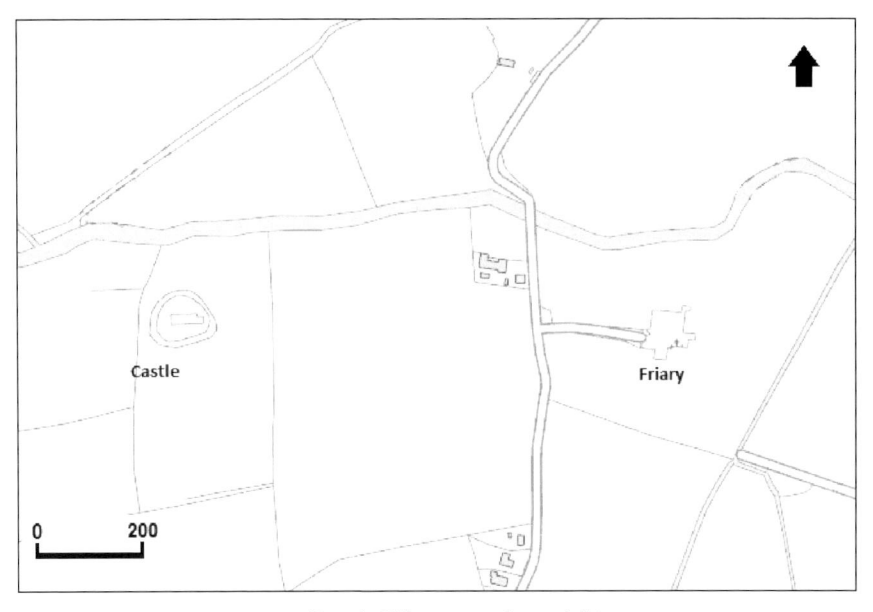

Fig.4: Kilcrea castle and friary

CONCLUSION

In order to reconstruct the Franciscan landscape of east Munster, this paper has established the political and economic conditions of the installation of the friars, with the pattern of their settlement in the political geography of the area and what it meant: we have seen that it had to do with both the interests of powerful and wealthy patrons, and of the Franciscans themselves.

Then we tackled the question of the physical and material landscape context of the friars in relation to that political geography. We saw that a major difference between Ireland and England and continental Europe was that in Ireland the thirteenth century witnessed a situation in which the arrival of the friars was following the creation and development of boroughs, which were at the same time much smaller and less urbanized than their English and continental counterparts. This resulted in a very different place of the mendicant settlements in the landscape, with a more important physical presence of the friaries relative to the size of the boroughs, but also with their having possibly been part of the actual planning of these boroughs. The friaries were one of the main foci of the settlement, not encased in the urbanization of a large city as could be the case in France or Italy.

Another characteristic of mendicant settlement in Ireland is the remoteness of certain sites, traditionally explained by the Irish context of ethnic division between the English colonists and the Gaelic Irish. The examples of the

Franciscan friary of Galbally and Kilcrea in east Munster illustrate that the landscape in which they were placed was not necessarily seen as remote and isolated at the time, and moreover that their locations had to do with issues of lordship and power, not of ethnicity, and that the mendicant friaries found their place in the creation of a political landscape expressed in a physical and material one.

---

1. E. Guidoni, 'Città e ordini mendicanti. Il ruolo dei conventi nella crescita e nella progettazione urbana del XIII e XIV secolo' *Quaderni Medievali* 4 (1977), 69-106; P. Volti *Les couvents mendiants et leur environnement à la fin du Moyen Age*, (Paris 2003).
2. J. O Donovan, (ed) *Annála ríoghachta Éireann: annals of the kingdom of Ireland by the Four Masters, from the earliest period to the year 1616*, 7 vols, (Dublin 1851), (henceforth *AFM*) iii, 217; *Archivium Hibernicum* (1912-), (henceforth *AH*) 6 ii, 144-5.
3. H.S. Sweetman & G.F. Handcock (eds) *Calendar of documents relating to Ireland, 1171-1307,* 5 vols, (PRO, London1875-86) (henceforth *CDI*), iii, 320.
4. J. Ware, *De Hibernia et Antiquitatibus ejus Disquisitions*, (London 1654).
5. *AH* 6 ii & iii, 197; *AFM* iii, 251; L. Wadding et al., *Annales Ordinis Minorum,* 32 vols, (Quarrachi, 1931-64), ii, 275.
6. *AH* 6 ii, 145.
7. Ware 1654; A. Gwynn & N. Hadcock (eds) *Medieval Religious Houses: Ireland*, (Dublin1970), 246.
8. Wadding ii, 47-9; *AFM* iii, 299.
9. J. C. Walton, 'A list of early burials in the French church, Waterford' in *JRSAI* 103 (1973), 70-7.
10. *AFM* iii, 341.
11. *AFM* iii, 301.
12. E. B. Fitzmaurice & A. G. Little, *Material for the History of the Franciscan Province*, (Manchester 1920), 155-6; M. Archdall, *Monasticon Hibernicum*, (1786), 78.
13. *AH* 6 iii, 199.
14. Ware 1654, 237; Gwynn & Hadcock 1970, 244.
15. AFM iv, 1071.
16. P. MacCotter, 'The sub-infeudation and descent of the Carews/Fitzstephen moiety of Desmond' in *JCHAS* 101 (1996), 64-80, & 102 (1997), 89-106 1997.
17. *AH* 1972, 113-19.
18. K. W. Nicholls, *Gaelic and Gaelicized Ireland in the Middle Ages*, 2nd ed., (Dublin 2003), 188-9.
19. Nicholls 2003, 185.
20. J. Mill et al. (eds) *Calendar of the justiciary rolls of Ireland*, 3 vols, (Dublin 1905-56) 1295-1303, 265; K. W. Nicholls, 'The development of Lordship in County Cork, 1300–1600' in O Flanagan, P. & Buttimer, C. G. (eds) *Cork: History and Society*, (Dublin 1993). 157-211, map, p. 161
21. M. H. Vicaire, 'Le développement de la province dominicaine de Provence (1215-1295)' in *Annales. Économies, Sociétés, Civilisations* 28 (1973), 4, 1017-41.
22. J. Le Goff, 'Ordres mendiants et urbanization dans la France médiévale. Etat de l'enquête' *Annales ESC* 4 (1970), 924-946; H. Martin, *Les ordres mendiants en Bretagne, vers 1230-vers 1530, pauvreté volontaire et prédication á la fin du Moyen Age*, (Paris 1975).
23. A. E. J. Went 'Historical notes on the fisheries of the Bandon River' in *JCHAS* 65 (1960), 116-126
24. Nicholls 2003, 190.

CHAPTER 7

THE SEQUENCE OF CONSTRUCTION OF BUTTEVANT FRIARY CHURCH IN THE THIRTEENTH CENTURY

~ TADHG O'KEEFFE ~

Military power features very prominently in popular perceptions of the establishment of Anglo-Norman lordship in Ireland during the 1200s. The town of Buttevant sits squarely in a district where the archaeological evidence seems to prove the validity of that perception. One of a row of medieval settlements peppering the western extremity of the fertile lowlands of central Cork and east Limerick, its thirteenth-century castle and now-missing town wall, as well its proximity to Liscarroll Castle, perhaps the most grimly militaristic castle of Anglo-Norman Ireland, create an abiding sense of a 'frontier' community on permanent orange alert. But life for Anglo-Norman colonists around Buttevant did not always revolve around hostilities, or even the anticipation of hostilities, with the Gaelic-Irish. It is inconceivable that market towns like Buttevant, or Dunmore, Co. Galway, to chose an example from contemporary Connacht, did not benefit economically from the proximity of Gaelic-Irish communities. Indeed, one could posit that towns of their ilk which were founded in such 'frontier' locations were not so much agents of local colonisation as places in which the Anglo-Norman economy could plug into the indigenous economy. The apparent testimony of Liscarroll notwithstanding, conditions in the later thirteenth century were settled enough for English settlers to farm the rural hinterland of Buttevant, their moated sites offering them the sort of low-level protection from wild animals and passing brigands which sufficed for contemporaries in England.

The Franciscans who came to Buttevant in 1251 at the invitation of David de Barry are unlikely to have perceived constant danger, even if they were provided with a site in the bosom of the walled town (Fig. 1).[1] As mendicants, they had no potential pastoral functions in the town or hinterland, unlike the Augustinian priors of Ballybeg, the previous object of local de Barry patronage. Their invitation, and presumably also their acceptance of the invitation, reflects a certain confidence that Buttevant would prosper, and the very fine friary which they possessed in the heart of the town testifies to that confidence.

Buttevant friary was the subject of an architectural survey by Robert Cochrane in the first decade of the last century.[2] He by-passed the problems of chronology, highlighting only the distinction between its thirteenth-century and fifteenth-century parts. In this paper I want to consider the thirteenth-century architecture of the church, the complexity of which has long been apparent. The friary is undergoing conservation, so what follows is based on pre-conservation visits (none made for the specific purpose of attempting an architecural history) and is to a degree preliminary, but it offers a scheme which can be tested by closer examination of the fabric than was possible for this paper.

On the whole, there seems to be four main phases of construction between the middle (or even the early) thirteenth century and the start of the fourteenth century. These are described here as Phases rather than Periods, since Phases 2, 3 and 4 were all compressed into a narrow time-span suggestive of overlap, as perhaps was Phase 1 as well.

PHASE 1: PRE-1250?

The most unusual feature of the church is the crypt beneath its east end. This was was the subject of a short article last year[3] so a summary will suffice here. It is a two-storeyed structure, with inserted barrel vaults at both levels. It is entered today by a flight of steps descending from the south end of the east range of the cloister. These steps lead to the upper level of the crypt, a space which has a central pillar carved with corner rolls and topped with a capital decorated with 'stiff-leaf' ornament (Fig. 2). A second flight of steps descends to the lower storey, also centrally partitioned but plainer in appointment. Was there another way into the crypt? By right there should have been: crypts were generally designed for circulation, so one stairs allowed access and another egress. The normal position of a stairs would be in the church, but even though there seems to have been some rebuilding of the crypt's west wall, there is no certain evidence that it was ever accessible from the church.

Medieval crypts are not common in Ireland and are certainly not to be expected in mendicant churches. So, how do we explain this one? Four options are reviewed in the earlier paper. The first option is structural. The friary stands on the terrace of the Awbeg river, and the crypt was needed to carry the choir over the scarp. I would rule this out on two grounds: first, the crypt is rather too elaborate for such a function, and second, it seems unlikely that the friary's patron, David de Barry, would burden the friars with a site that needed such remedial action before construction. The second option, less firmly rejected though rejected nonetheless, is that it fulfilled a function – a parlour, a sacristy, or even accommodation for an anchorite or two – that would normally have dedicated space elsewhere in a monastic context. There is no reason why the Franciscans at Buttevant would have broken so radically from convention. The third explanation, also rejected, is the obvious one: medieval crypts were liturgical spaces, designed to contain and to permit veneration of objects of great sanctity, such as blessed relics. The absence of evidence that the crypt could be accessed from the church would seem to rule out this explanation, but we could not rule out the possibility that deceased members of the de Barry family – objects of veneration in their own right – were interred here, including David Óg de Barry in the late 1170s.

The final suggestion seems at first the least favourable but is certainly worth a punt, and explains why Phase 1 of the friary is tentatively dated here to *before* the friary's actual date of foundation! On the north side of the church the exterior walls of the crypt and the choir are not precisely flush with each other, suggesting they were built as two different entities in two different episodes. That impression is strengthened considerably by looking at the exterior east wall of the friary church (Fig. 3): the crypt, comprised of the lower, buttressed part of the wall, from the putlog holes down to the ground, appears to be a different building, with the choir intruding onto it from an entirely different architectural conversation. I suggest that we are looking at two *periods* of construction rather than two *phases* of construction, with the crypt starting as a building in its own right, possibly as a secular structure, maybe even a castle. If so, Buttevant would join the ranks of friaries known or believed to have been built on top of older castles: Carrickbeg, Co. Waterford, Banada, Co. Sligo, and Quin, Co. Clare.

PHASE 2: 1250s

The earliest phase of the church above the crypt is represented by a series of very wide arches along its south side. There are three of these close to the east end of the choir, all slightly segmental-arched (especially that furthest east), with a fourth, properly round-arched example, in the nave, close to its west gable (Figs. 4, 5). Presumably two more were removed when the transept was built. These arches were not relieving arches for the windows beneath them, although they appear externally to fulfill that function (see, for example, the smaller but broadly comparable arches in Rathfran Dominican friary in Co. Mayo), but pre-date those windows. They opened with splayed jambs and arches from the interior, suggesting they were to be filled from ground level with masonry containing their own, now-lost, windows. The obvious parallel is with Timoleague (Figs 6, 7), though in that church the large arches are confined to what was the choir prior to the insertion of the bell-tower.

Cochrane shows both the eastern jamb, extending fully to ground level on the outside, and the east-side springing of another arch further to the west end in the church (Fig. 8). It is not there today. If his drawing is correct – and he did draw it with some conviction – we must conclude that the present west wall of the church is not original and assign it to a 1260s truncation (Phase 3) of a longer building. It was presumably the last such arch at the west end of the church. The doorway still visible (though blocked) between the last surviving arch and

Cochrane's now-missing arch would suggest only one arched bay is missing: doorways at west ends of south walls in thirteenth-century churches tended to have just single bays on their west sides.

A longer church than we see has implications for our reconstruction of Buttevant's metrology. As is well-documented, church buildings were frequently laid-out using the ratio of 1:√2 (1:1.4142), a ratio recommended by Vitruvius, a first-century BC Roman architect and engineer[4]. The ratio was achieved by builders on the ground by simply marking out a square and using its diagonal to form a rectangle. At Buttevant, an informing square (25ft or 7.62m wide) was used to mark out the presbytery, which was normal practise, and a rectangle based on its diagonal (measuring 35ft 4in x 25ft, or 10.78m x 7.62m), or was used to mark out the choir. The original division between the nave and choir may have been a simple floor-step with a screen. The interior east wall of the Phase 4 bell-tower was inserted on the line of this simple division. The original church seems to have been laid out with three more 1:√2 rectangles, giving a full interior length of 115ft 6in (or 45.75m). In this reconstruction, the original interior west wall was 15ft 6in (or 4.72m) west of the present west wall, allowing room for us to reconstruct, as expected, room for one large arch and a buttress on the south face of the nave (Fig. 9). When the church was shortened in Phase 3, the builders actually returned to proportional thinking, remeasuring the church to give a new metrological logic: its new Phase 3 length of 150ft (59m) was exactly six times its width, and the builders in Phase 4 simply split this length to position the west-facing wall of the new bell-tower (Fig. 9).

Phase 2 is the foundational phase of the friary. The architectural detail is too meagre to claim that it matches the historical evidence of foundation just after 1250 but, with evidence of changes made to the church in the succeeding decades of the century, a date of *c.*1250 prevents too much crowding of the architectural chronology. David de Barry, then, oversaw the building of a long, peculiarly-lit, church (and presumably of the earliest cloister and associated claustral ranges too, though the remains on the north side of the church are too meagre for close dating).

PHASE 3: POST-1260?

The first significant alteration to the church dates from the period after 1261 when David Óg de Barry becomes the Lord of Buttevant in succession to his father who apparently lost his life at the battle of Callann in that year[5]. The alteration in question is the insertion of lancets at equal intervals along the south wall of the nave and choir, breaking the rythym of the large arches. It is not an early alteration that can be dated stylistically, but it must be adjudged early since the east window has remains of lancets of this type (Fig. 10), and it is difficult to conceive of a window of different design being here and removed between 1251 and 1261.

The pair of new lancets in warm sandstone at the west end of the church (Fig. 11) is the best preserved; only fragments, mainly of the rubble arches above the cut stonework, remain along the side of the choir, and they need to be looked for carefully since their place was taken by shorter and better-preserved lancets, probably in Phase 4. The church seems to have been truncated in Phase 3: the westernmost large arch of the original church was sliced off at this time and the west wall of the church was brought back about 5m to the east. We can say this because the outlines of the Phase 3 lancets, later filled with pairs of cusped-ogees and new mullions, can be seen on both external (Fig. 12) and internal (Fig. 13) faces of the new gable wall.

PHASE 4: 1270s OR EARLY 1280s

Substantial additions were made to the friary church at a slightly later date, possibly by David Óg de Barry, or possibly after his death and burial in the church late 1270s. We should not push these changes too late in date, although there is no reason why some could not have been c.1300 or even into the early 1300s. David Óg is the type of high-profile patron – he served as justiciar for two years – whom we might imagine investing time and energy in his family's new dynastic church.

The two most significant changes were the insertion of a bell-tower halfway along the church's length, and of a new transept off the south side of the nave. The only alteration made to the north wall was the (1280s more than 1270s?) insertion – replacement – of a window (Fig. 14) halfway along its length and probably overlooking the roof of the west walk of the cloister.

The bell-tower is now lost, apart from a small portion of its lower part on the south side which shows that it was flanked on the this side at least (but probably on the north as well) by a recessed altar accompanied by a piscina (Fig. 15). The view from the nave to the choir would have been obstructed by a screen at this point, but lay penitents in the nave, who entered the church through a west door that was replaced by the present west door in the fifteenth century, would have heard the liturgies and chanting in the choir. Apart from occasions when some public procession through the church may have been in order, the mendicant community itself generally entered their end of the church – the choir – through a doorway off the south cloister, walking into the north side of the tower and turning left into the choir. The vaulting which we assume to have covered the lower part of the tower, the point of entry, was normally elaborated to capture the liminal experience of entry into sanctified space. Corner shafts in the surviving lower part of the tower suggest a structure of considerable elaboration, and this is confirmed by trustworthy depictions of the full tower *in situ*, including a fine lithograph of *c*.1750 (Fig. 16). The loss of this tower is a great pity; aside from being one of the earliest, modelled perhaps on the tower of Youghal's fully-demolished Franciscan friary, it was a structure of some beauty.

The second great addition was a transept immediately west of the new tower. New walling was needed to accommodate the entry from the church, and so original fenestration of both Phases 2 and 3 was removed and replaced by a blank wall perforated by a double arch (Fig. 17). Two windows facing westwards are symptomatic of the problem of precise dating of this transept: the better preserved of the two (Fig. 18) had a quatrefoil over two round arches (as the other might also have had), which is a general middle- to second-half of the thirteenth century type, but the jambs of it and its partner window have a mixture of moulding types, both thirteenth-century but only one of them – presumably the more complex one, with roll-moulding – actually contemporary with the elaborate window heads. The interiors of the windows (Fig. 19) are contained in fine arches, elaborated with capitals with fine but somewhat generic floral motifs (Fig. 20), thirteenth-century in design but not of any particular condensed period within that century. We cannot identify the benefactor whose tomb occupies the projecting chapel on its east side (Fig. 21); tempting as it is to suggest it may be David Óg de Barry himself given its sumptuous surrounding, the fact that a similar tomb design is found more modestly enframed in the north wall of the nave opposite the transept (Fig. 22) would seem to rule this out.

CODA: THE FRIARY IN THE FIFTEENTH CENTURY

Cochrane compressed the later medieval alterations to the friary into a single fifteenth-century phase, just as he did the complex thirteenth-century alterations, and I am following suit, though perhaps a little more knowingly. The east and west windows were reduced in size through the insertion of typical later medieval twin-light designs, a fine reticulated-traceried window was inserted into the south wall of the choir, replacing one-and-a-half late (Phase 3) thirteenth-century lancets, and the upper part of the tower may have been built at this time, judging by the depictions of it pre-destruction.

The major alteration of the late middle ages was the encasing of the south end of the transept in new masonry, distinguished by a great archway (Fig. 23) facing – not insignificantly, perhaps – in the direction of the castle. The obvious progenitor for this design is Bunratty Castle, but there were other castles in Munster – Redwood and Drumnamahane, Co. Tipperary, and Listowel, Co. Kerry (Fig. 24) – where a similar arch spanned the top of two turreted projections. The arch-type could be described as triumphal, and it is not implausible that the concept came via a circuitous route from eleventh- and twelfth-century triumphal arches in great churches and castles, themselves the inheritors of the concept from the Classical past, via Charlemagne's palace chapel in Aachen[6].

If the later medieval modifications to the church, other than the triumphal-arch encasing of the transept's south wall, seem modest, a quick perusal of the fragments of the cloister embedded in the north wall of the church (Fig. 25) should dissuade us from thinking the later medieval friary an impoverished-looking place next to its opulent predecessor built at the height of local de Barry power in the later 1200s.

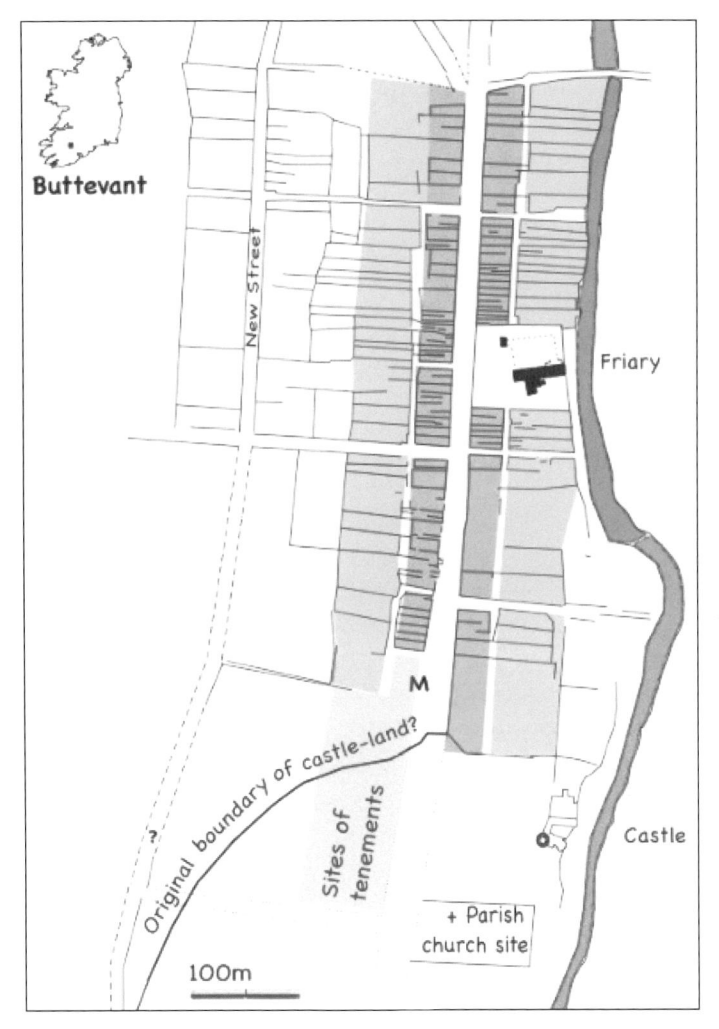

Fig. 1: Buttevant in the thirteenth century: a suggested reconstruction of the town-plan.

Fig. 2: The pillar in the upper part of Buttevant crypt (photo: E. Cotter).

Fig. 3: The east end of Buttevant friary (photo: E. Cotter).

Fig. 4: The south wall of the friary church choir (photo: E. Cotter).

Fig. 5: The south wall of the friary church nave (photo: E. Cotter).

Fig. 6: Timoleague friary, north wall of choir.

Fig. 7: Timoleague friary, interior north wall of choir at junction of east wall.

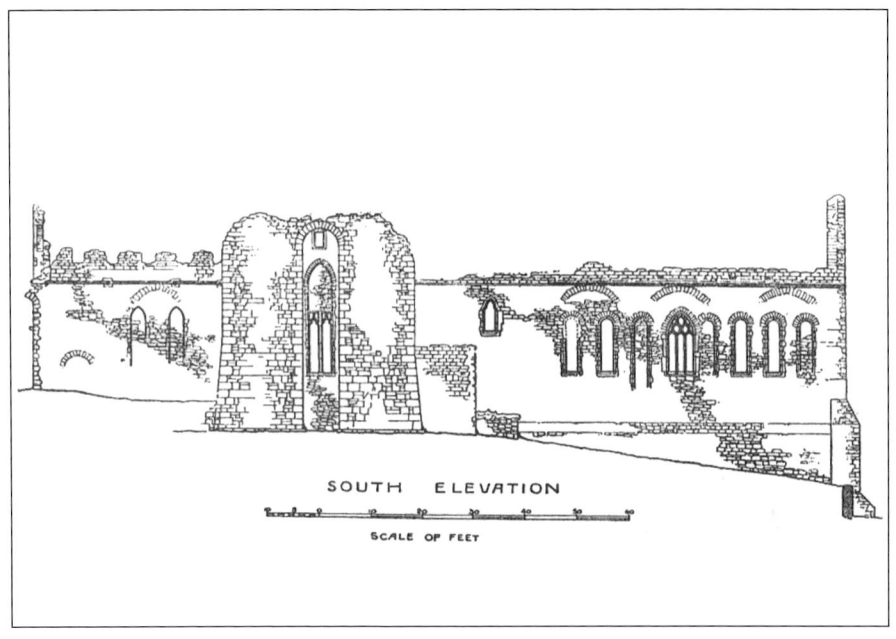

Fig. 8: Robert Cochrane's drawing of Buttevant friary's south elevation.

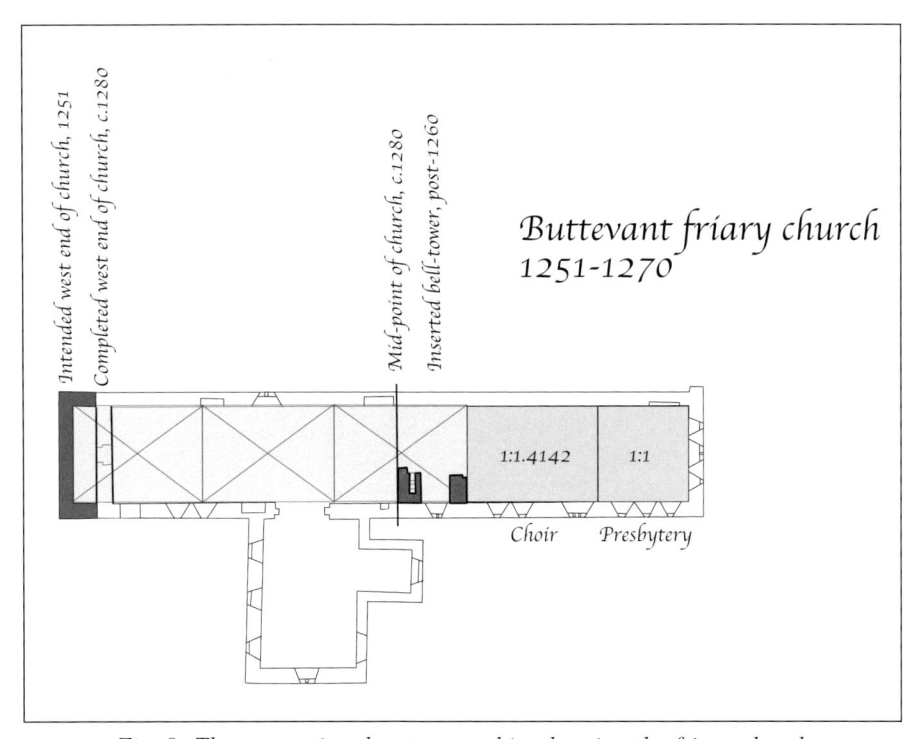

Fig. 9: The proportional system used in planning the friary church.

Fig. 10: The east end of the friary church.

Fig. 11: The south wall of the friary church nave showing the Phase 3 lancets.

Fig. 12: The west wall of the friary church, exterior.

Fig. 13: The west wall of the friary church, interior.

Fig. 14: The north wall of the nave of the friary church, exterior (photo: E. Cotter).

Fig. 15: The remains of the tower, looking east.

Fig. 16: Buttevant friary, c.1750.

Fig. 17: The arched entrance into the new, Phase 4, transept, from the south.

Fig. 18: The exterior of the south window in the west wall of the transept.

Fig. 19: The interiors of the two windows in the west wall of the transept.

Fig. 20: A rear-arch capital in the west wall of the transept (photo: E. Cotter).

Fig. 21: A view into the east-facing transeptal chapel.

Fig. 22: The tomb recess on the north wall of the nave.

Fig. 23: The enframed south wall of the transept showing the triumphal arch (photo: E. Cotter).

Fig. 24: Listowel Castle.

Fig. 25: Fragments of the cloister arcade (and of other features, such as tombs) 'preserved' in the rebuilt north wall of the friary church.

---

1. Drawing from T. O'Keeffe, 'Landscapes, castles and towns of Edward I in Wales and Ireland: some comparisons and connections', *Landscapes* 11, 2, 60-72, Fig. 5.
2. *Seventy-Seventh Annual Report of the Commissioners of Public Works in Ireland, 1908-1909* (Dublin 1909), at 25-30
3. T. O'Keeffe, Buttevant friary and its crypt, *Archaeology Ireland* 26, 3 (2012), 23-25
4. See 'Liscarroll Castle', Chapter 7, this volume.
5. Ibid.
6. T. O'Keeffe, *Romanesque Ireland* (Dublin 2003), 23-25.

Chapter 8

Denny Muschamp and The Ploughlands of Grange

~ JAMES O'BRIEN ~

The townlands of Grange, east and west, are situated in the parish of Buttevant, barony of Orrery and Kilmore, in the county of Cork. Officially, the former consists of 513 acres, 1 rood and 4 perches and the latter of 425 acres, 0 roods and 20 perches. In general terms, both townlands reflect the average area of other adjacent townlands which tend to consist of parcels of land of between 4 to 6 medieval ploughlands.[1] The *General Valuation of Rateable Property in Ireland*, otherwise Griffith's Valuation,[2] records that the townland of Grange East was occupied by 5 tenants (Wm. Linehan, James Sullivan, George Green, William Green and John Madden), a fox cover reserved to the proprietors, and the line of the Great Southern and Western Railway. It had a total valuation of £360-2-0. Its counterpart, Grange West, was occupied by 5 tenants (Christopher Crofts, James Roche, Thomas Leahy, Patrick Corbett and William Burke) and the line of the Great Southern and Western railway. It had a total rateable valuation of £330-2-0.

Griffith lists the Honourable Catherine Nugent (1812-1882) and John Thomas Vesey (1815-1881) as the proprietors of the townlands. This is a peculiarity in the proprietorship of the parish of Buttevant since most of it was owned either by Viscount Doneraile or the Earl Egmont as successors to the Barrymore estate. At first view, neither Catherine Nugent nor John Thomas Vesey had any immediate connections with the parish, nor indeed with the county. As it transpires, both owners were first cousins and scions of the Viscounts de Vesci of Abbeyleix. They would more naturally have been associated with the county of Laois and south county Dublin, where much of the de Vesci estate was located.

The Honourable Catherine Nugent was the daughter of John, second Viscount de Vesci (1771- 1855), and his wife Frances Laetitia Brownlow of Lurgan, Co. Armagh. In 1833 she married her first cousin, Patrick John Nugent (1805-1857) of Portaferry House, Portaferry, Co. Down. Her ownership of Grange derives from the marriage settlement made on her in 1833 when she received from her father that portion of the Cork estates of Viscount de Vesci situated in those townlands.[3]

The other joint proprietor, John Thomas Vesey, was the son of the Reverend the Honourable Arthur Vesey (1773-1832), and his wife Sydney Johnstone of Woodpark House, Co. Armagh. Arthur Vesey was the second son of Thomas Vesey, first Viscount de Vesci and Selina Brooke, and brother to John, second Viscount, the father of Catherine. Arthur held the position of rector of Abbeyleix. In 1804, John reached a settlement with his brothers Arthur and Charles (1784-1826) for their interest in the de Vesci estates by which both signed releases to John. While Arthur received a cash settlement, Charles received, as his portion of the estates, a proprietorial interest in the lands of East and West Grange as well as in the de Vesci estate in the Barony of Kerrycurrihy, in the County of Cork, and on Kyle's Quay in the City of Cork.[4] In 1826, Charles died without issue and his interest in Grange appears to have passed, either directly or indirectly, to his nephew John Thomas Vesey, son of Arthur. John Thomas also held an estate in the Barony of St. Mullins in the County of Carlow.[5]

GRANGE, LORD BARRYMORE AND THE EARL OF CORK

David Barry (1604-1642), Lord Barrymore, his eldest brother being deaf and dumb, succeeded to the de Barry estates on the death of his grandfather on 16 April 1617.[6] He was thirteen years old. From the outset, he was entangled in a dispute between his mother and his aunt, the Countess of Ormonde, for control of his guardianship and the administration of the Barrymore estates which, along with much more, included the manor of Buttevant and the ploughlands of Grange. He was left roofless and practically destitute. In desperation, his mother, Lady Elizabeth Barrymore, turned to Richard Boyle, Earl of Cork, for support in pressing her claims. As ever, seeing a business opportunity, Boyle agreed to assist her under certain conditions.

According to the agreement reached between the Lady Barrymore and the Earl of Cork, the young Lord Barrymore would marry Alice Boyle, his eldest daughter, and the Earl, in turn, would reduce the debts accruing to the young Lord Barrymore to a sum not in excess of £3,000. It was also agreed that the education of the boy would be vested in the Earl of Cork who promptly despatched him to Eton and continued to cover his debts. The marriage between David, Lord Barrymore, and Alice Boyle was eventually solemnised by Michael Boyle, Bishop of Waterford, at Lismore castle on 9 July 1621.[7]

Lord Barrymore took up residence in the family castle at Castlelyons which he rebuilt at great expense with much of the funds lent to him by his father-in-law in exchange for mortgages on the Barrymore estate at Castlelyons, Carrigtwohill, the Great Island and at Fermoy. Dorothea Townshend recounts that 'Fond as the Earl of Cork was of his eldest daughter's husband, he could not always suppress a grumble at the amount of money he was asked to lend to the poor and proud head of the Barry clan, but Alice could generally manage to persuade her father to open his purse-strings'. Things came to a head in 1637: 'A serious appeal for money came in the year 1637, when Lord Barry heard a report that the Duke of Buckingham had promised to support Viscount Gormanston's claims to take precedence of Viscount Buttevant, and he flew in great agitation to implore Lord Cork to save him this humiliation, by bidding higher in the market for titles and buying him an earl's coronet! The thousand pounds at which Buckingham priced the title was of course advanced by Lord Cork, secured on lands which his son-in-law let to him at a peppercorn rent. The Earl of Barrymore also had to pay £243 8s. 8d. in fees, and then was for ever secure from the pretensions of mere viscounts'.[8]

Following these advances, the Earl of Cork consolidated his loans (by now in excess of £7,000) to Lord Barrymore by deed made on 1 April 1638 and, in exchange for perpetual leases at peppercorn rent, the Earl of Cork acquired possession of 'lands in the manor of Buttevant...consisting of seven ploughlands of Grange; and the lands of Boherscrob, Barryshill, Croganes, Ardprior, the profits of the manor court of Buttevant, and various chief rents; the lands of Ardlombard, Castlelombard, Gortnefowlue, Baneminny, Baultane and Farrenweston'.[9] By the same deed, Boyle vested this interest in his youngest son Robert (the scientist who formulated Boyle's law), as a feoffee in trust. By the time of his death in 1691, the extent of Robert Boyle's interest in the manor of Buttevant amounted to 'nine ploughlands and a half of Buttevant, and the moiety of the lands called Buttevant and Rice's Lands'.[10]

THE VESEY AND MUSCHAMP FAMILIES

In the reign of Elizabeth I William Vesey, a scion of the house of de Vescy in Cumberland, was the first of his family to settle in Ireland, with various members of the family occupying ecclesiastical offices. His son, Thomas Vesey, was rector of Ballinscullen and Maghera in the diocese of Derry in 1629. Thomas transferred to Coleraine in 1635 and eventually became Archdeacon of Armagh (1655-62). His son John (1638-1716) became chaplain to the Irish House of Commons in 1661 and in June of the same year obtained the rectories of Ighturmurrow and Shandrum in the diocese of Cloyne, together with the vicarage of Rathgoggin, *alias* Charleville, evidently through the influence of the Boyle family. In October 1662 John was appointed archdeacon of Armagh, but was succeeded by his father in May 1663. On 3 February 1667, he was created dean of Cork and treasurer of Cloyne, and from there he was advanced to the joint bishoprics of Limerick, Ardfert, and Aghadoe on 11 January 1673. He was consecrated the following day in Christ Church, Dublin, by Michael Boyle, protestant archbishop of Dublin, assisted by the archbishop of Armagh and the bishops of Killaloe and Ossory. Five years later, he was advanced to the

Archbishopric of Tuam. In addition to his ecclesiastical offices, John Vesey was a member of the Privy Council for Ireland and a Lord Justice of Ireland.

The key to unravelling the de Vesci connection with the parish of Buttevant and the townlands of Grange is not, however, to be found in the immediate Vesey family. For this we have to turn to the Muschamp family, and particularly to Denny Muschamp (c.1637–99), whose heirs were the descendants of Sir Thomas Vesey (c.1668-1730) in virtue of the latter's marriage in 1698 to Muschamp's only daughter, Mary.

The Muschamp family had originally come from Godalming in Surrey. Through the strategic marriage of William Muschamp (c.1546-1601) to Mary Agmondsham (c.1548-1620), they had come into possession of the property of the Agmondsham family which consisted of the manors of Rowbarnes and Christ Church at East Horsley, also in Surrey. The Agmondshams had held Rowbarnes at least since the thirteenth century,[11] and Christ Church (which had, up to the dissolution of the monasteries, pertained to the monks of Christchurch in Canterbury) since 1560, when it was granted by Elizabeth I to John Agmondsham.[12] A third manor in the same parish, East Horsley Episcopi, which belonged to the bishops of Exeter prior to the reformation, was acquired in May 1698 by Denny Muschamp and integrated into the Muschamp interest at East Horsley.[13]

The eldest son of the Muschamp/Agmondsham marriage, Agmondsham (I) Muschamp (c.1568-1642) succeeded his mother in the manors of East Horsley in 1620. In 1593, he married Mary Bellingham (1568-1632), the daughter of Richard Bellingham and Mary Whalley of Newtimbers Place, West Sussex.[14] Seven children were born of this marriage among them William (1593-1660) and Agmondsham (II) Muschamp (1598-1658). Being the eldest son, William succeeded to the manors of East Horsley.[15]

As a second son, Agmondsham (II) had small prospect of succession to the estates in East Horsley held by his family. Rather, he sought his fortune by turning to the army, rising eventually to the rank of Lieutenant Colonel, and to Ireland. His initial contact with Cork is uncertain but it is known that he was actively engaged with the expeditionary force led by Sir Charles Vavasour which landed in Youghal in February 1642. It is also documented that he was in contact with Richard Boyle, Earl of Cork, from that time.[16] Although he sided with Cromwell in the civil war, nevertheless, in 1653 he obtained a 31 year lease of those lands in the manor of Buttevant which, as shown above, had been acquired from Lord Barrymore by the Earl of Cork and vested by him in his youngest son Robert Boyle.[17] Agmondsham Muschamp also amassed a significant amount of property in the city of Cork, particularly in the area of Kyle's Quay, and at Ballybricken, near Carrigaline, in the barony of Kerrycurrihy, in the county of Cork. Around 1637, he married Anne Denny and by her had at least four children: Denny, Anne, Martha (d.1726), and John (1650-75). Anne Muschamp married, as his second wife, Archbishop John Vesey of Tuam whose ecclesiastical career depended totally on the favour of the Boyle family. Martha Muschamp married Joseph Cuffe of Castle Inch, Co. Kilkenny.[18] Agmondsham Muschamp died in 1658.

Agmondsham's eldest son Denny Muschamp was born at East Horsley in Surrey in 1637. His mother was Ann Denny, a member of the Denny family which had acquired the confiscated estates of the Earl of Desmond situated in the vicinity of Tralee. A civil servant in the Irish administration, he became a large scale property speculator who, in the political upheaval of the mid-seventeenth century, amassed very considerable land holdings in Ireland and England. It would appear that his career was due to the promotion and influence of the Boyle family and was consolidated by a series of inter-marriages with them and with other client families of the Earl of Cork, many of whom occupied significant positions in the Irish administration – not least of whom was the Earl of Cork's grandson, Richard Jones (1641-1712), first earl of Ranelagh, who operated a tax farm on Irish revenues.[19]

Sometime prior to 1664, Muschamp made an advantageous marriage with Elizabeth Boyle, daughter of Michael Boyle, then Archbishop of Dublin. At least three children were born to this marriage, the only surviving one of whom, Mary Muschamp, married, in 1698, her cousin Thomas Vesey, son of John Vesey, Archbishop of Tuam and Anne Muschamp. After the death of his first wife, Denny Muschamp married, in 1692, Frances, Viscountess Lanesborough (d.1722), widow of George Lane, 1st Viscount Lanesborough. She was the youngest daughter of Richard Sackville, 5th earl of Dorset, and his wife, Frances Cranfield.[20]

Denny Muschamp entered the Irish Commons in 1665 representing Swords, a seat controlled by his father-in-law, Michael Boyle. At about this time, he was appointed to the influential position of secretary and agent to Boyle and retained this office throughout the period in which Boyle held the sees of Dublin and Armagh and the office of Lord High Chancellor. In 1665, he became a commissioner of the revenue, and in 1677 clerk of the crown and peace for Ulster. Throughout the next thirty years, he continued to acquire further public offices including those of muster-master general in 1677 which gave him responsibility for the payment and procurement of the army in Ireland; constable of Maryborough in 1679; registrar to the commission for defective titles in 1684; and, in 1695, election to the borough of Blessington which again was controlled by Michael Boyle.[21]

THE MUSCHAMP INTEREST IN THE MANOR OF BUTTEVANT

The first recorded interest of the Muschamp family in the manor of Buttevant is a lease granted by Robert Boyle, and dated 18 March 1653, by which Agmondsham (II) Muschamp obtained the manor for a period of 31 years at an annual rent of £120.[22] It is clear that Muschamp held this as a head rent and sub-leased the various portions of the manor to his own tenants. Following Muschamp's death in 1658, his interest in the manor of Buttevant passed to his widow, Anne Denny, who, for a consideration, subsequently released it to her son Denny Muschamp.

On 3 July 1669, Denny Muschamp obtained a further lease from Robert Boyle for his Buttevant interests. According to the terms of the 1669 lease, Muschamp acquired a 99 year interest in the manor of Buttevant to run from the date on which the lease of 1653 fell in, at an annual rent of £160. In theory, the new lease would run from 1684 to 1783. By deed dated 20 June 1670, Denny Munschamp sub-leased his interest in east and west Grange on three lives at a rental of £80 per annum to Robert Cuffe[23] of Killeagh, Co. Cork, who appears to have retained an interest in the property until at least 1725 when the Cuffe title was contested in a law suit brought by Sir Thomas Vesey, Denny Muschamp's son-in-law, and by Sir John Denny Vesey, 2nd Baronet, 1st Lord Knapton, Muschamp's grand-son.

Following on the death of the Honourable Robert Boyle on 30 December 1691, his interest in the manor of Buttevant was to be sold and the proceeds divided between his surviving brothers and a number of charitable bequests which he had made. At this sale, Denny Muschamp acquired the fee simple of those parts of the manor of Buttevant which had devolved on Robert Boyle in 1638 when they had been effectively alienated by Lord Barrymore. In 1693 he closed the deal for Robert Boyle's interest by payment of £300 and by a further payment of £1,200 which he borrowed from his brother-in-law, John Vesey, Archbishop of Tuam, whom he repaid in the following year.

Denny Muschamp, however, did not personally retain his interest in the manor of Buttevant. In 1692 his interests in the manors of Abbey Leix and Buttevant formed part of the lands devised on his new wife, the Viscountess Lanesborough, as part of her marriage settlement. This arrangement continued until 1699 when Muschamp's only surviving daughter by his first marriage, Mary, married her cousin Sir Thomas Vesey. In 1698, as her marriage portion, Mary received from her father and her step-mother those properties which had been settled on the Viscountess in 1692. While retaining a life interest in them, the Viscountess effectively devised the manors of Abbey Leix and the Muschamp interest in the manor of Buttevant including the ploughlands of East and West Grange on Mary Muschamp. In her will of 1721, she further devised on her step-daughter all of her remaining interest in these estates together with all of Denny

Muschamp's Irish estates held by her. In what was obviously a family re-organisation of property title, in exchange for her interests in the manors of Abbey Leix and Buttevant, Denny Muschamp ceded to his wife his East Horsley interests in Surrey which included the manors of Rowbarnes, Christ Church and East Horsley Episcopi. Following her husband's death, the Viscountess Lanesborough took up residence in England where she died in 1721. She was buried in St. Michael's Church, Withyam, Sussex. Shortly before ceding her Buttevant properties, Vicountess Lanesborough made a gift of a communion cup to the Protestant parish of Buttevant and founded an endowed school which continued to function until 1818 when the leases of the endowment expired and were not renewed.[24]

Mary Muschamp's marriage portion effectively laid the foundations for the de Vesci estate and assured that her husband had the possibility of being raised to the peerage. Through her, the ploughlands of east and west Grange came to the de Vesci family and continued in it until May 1860 when they were advertised for sale.[25] After a period of more than two hundred years, the ploughlands of east and west Grange were re-integrated into the manor of Buttevant when they were acquired by Lord Doneraile[26] who retained them until their sale under the land acts of the late nineteenth century.

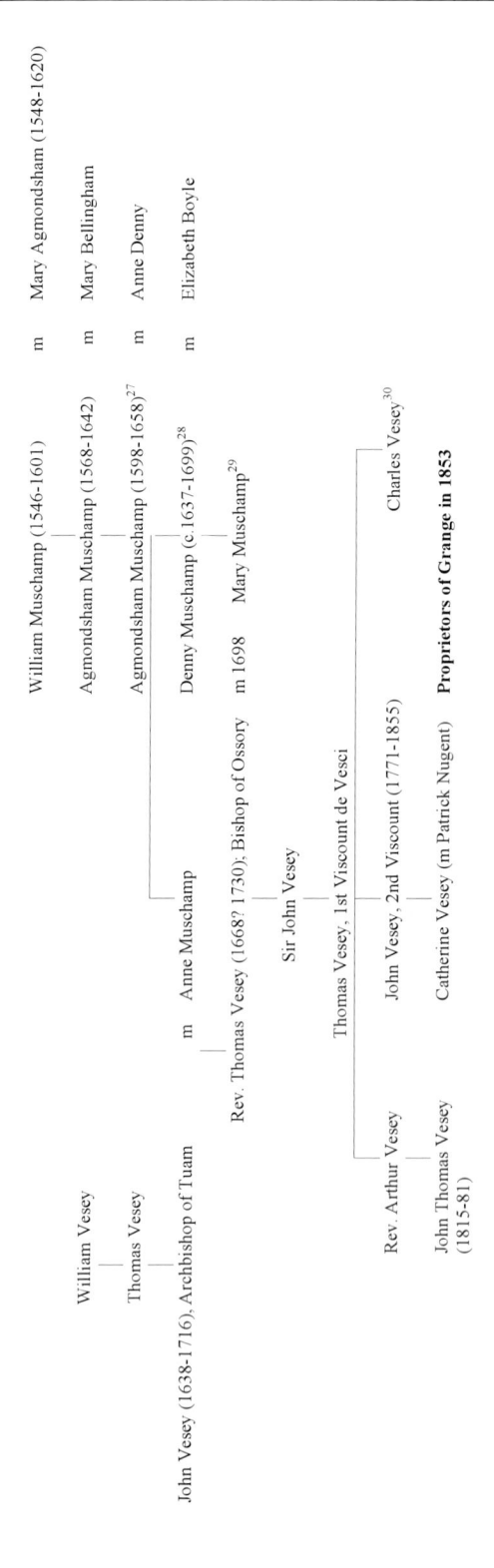

```
                                                William Muschamp (1546-1601)      m    Mary Agmondsham (1548-1620)

                                                Agmondsham Muschamp (1568-1642)   m    Mary Bellingham

                                                Agmondsham Muschamp (1598-1658)[27] m  Anne Denny

William Vesey                                   Denny Muschamp (c.1637-1699)[28]  m    Elizabeth Boyle
     |
Thomas Vesey                                                    m 1698    Mary Muschamp[29]
     |
John Vesey (1638-1716), Archbishop of Tuam        m  Anne Muschamp
                        |
                        Rev. Thomas Vesey (1668? 1730); Bishop of Ossory             Charles Vesey[30]
                                        |
                                        Sir John Vesey                               **Proprietors of Grange in 1853**
                                        |
                                        Thomas Vesey, 1st Viscount de Vesci
                                        |
                                        John Vesey, 2nd Viscount (1771-1855)
                                        |
                         ───────────────┴───────────────
                         |                             |
                Rev. Arthur Vesey              Catherine Vesey (m Patrick Nugent)
                         |
                John Thomas Vesey
                    (1815-81)
```

Fig 1. Family tree of the Muschamp and Vesey families.

Fig 1. Family tree of the Muschamp and Vesey families.

1. A ploughland is generally reckoned as approximately 120 acres. The combined acreage of East and West Grange would represent approximately 8 ploughlands.
2. Completed for the county of Cork on 23 July 1853.
3. National Library of Ireland, de Vesci papers, MS 38,751/9'
4. de Vesci papers, MS 38,751/3'
5. National Library of Ireland, Doyne papers, MS 29,770/100.
6. David Barry, first Earl of Barrymore, sixth Viscount Buttevant and twentieth Baron Barry died on 29 September 1642 of wounds received at the Battle of Liscarroll. He was interred in the Boyle vault in St. Mary's, Youghal.
7. Dorothea Townshend, *The Life and Letters of the Great Earl of Cork* (London, 1904), p. 145 and 148; quoting the diary of the earl of Cork: 'On this day I agreed with Sir Lawrence Esmond, Mr. Patrick Sherlock, and Mr. Barry and his sons on behalf of my lord Barry, to redeem all his mortgages so that they exceeded not £3000, and to have ten in the hundred for the use of my money, the surplus of the rent to be disposed of for the young lord's maintainence. And I am to give Alice the rents of the Abbey of Castle Lyons to buy her pins, and I to have the breeding of the young Lord Barry.'
8. Townshend, *Life and Letters* p. 150; de Vesci papers, MS 38,856/1-4.
9. de Vesci papers, MS 38,856/1-4; Townshend, p.150
10. See James Grove White, *Historical and topographical notes, etc. on Buttevant, Castletownroche, Doneraile, Mallow and places in their vicinity,* vol. 1, (Cork, 1908) sub Buttevant for a transcript of the will of Robert Boyle which is taken from Smith's history of Cork. A copy of the will together with instruments authorizing John Vesey, Archbishop of Tuam, to discharge its charitable provisions is contained in the de Vesci papers MS 38,746/8.
11. See H.E. Malden, *A History of the County of Surrey*, vol. 3, (1911), pp. 349-352. Since the time of Elizabeth I the manors of Christ Church and Rowbarnes were united in the Agmondsham family.
12. See E.W. Brayley, *A Topographical History of Surrey* (London, 1841), p. 63; For the Agmondsham and Muschamp holdings in East Horsley see Surrey County Council Archives, Properties in East Horsley, Wonersh, Bramley and Other Surrey Parishes: Deeds, 1427-1831, G92/1/2a-6; 3; 4; 5; 18; 23a-d; 26; 27 a-b; 29; 30/1/2; 36; 37/1; 39; 40a-b; 41; 43; 44; 45 and 48. According to Brayley, John Agmondsham was succeeded by his son, John, a barrister of the Middle Temple in 1564. He died without issue in 1598 and the manors of Christ Church and Rowbarnes in East Horsley eventually passed to his sister, Mary, the wife of William Muschamp of Godalming.
13. Brayley, *A Topographical History*; Sir Bernard Burke, *A Genealogical and Heraldic History of the Commoners of Great Britain and Ireland*, vol. 2, (London, 1835) p. 493: Denny Muschamp conveyed all three manors to his wife the Viscountess of Lanesborough who in 1722 devised them on her grandson (by her first marriage to George Lane, Viscount Lanesborough) James Fox with a remainder to her youngest grandson Sackville Fox.
14. William Berry, *County Genealogies: Pedigrees of the families in the county of Sussex*, (London 1830), p. 191.
15. The manors passed in turn to his son William by Frances Lisle, then to his grandson, William, and finally to his great-grandson Ambrose Muschamp (1652-1701). In his will of 1701, Ambrose Muschamp devised the manors of East Horsley on the Viscountess Lanesborough, the widow of his cousin Denny Muschamp.
16. Townshend, *Life and letters*, p. 408.
17. Townshend, pp 481ff; Grove White, *Historical and topographical notes*, etc., p. 335; de

Vesci papers, MS 38,856/1-4.
18. Joseph Cuffe was born at Ennis, Co. Clare c. 1626 and died at Castle Inch, Co. Kilkenny, 1679. Joseph Cuffe and Martha Muschamp were the grandparents of John Cuffe, first Baron Desart. Joseph Cuffe was a Cromwellian and received a grant of 5,000 acres in the Barony of Shillelogher in Kilkenny.
19. Ranelagh was eventually expelled from Parliament in 1703 when discrepancies in the amount of £900,000 were discovered in his accounts as Paymaster
20. Her elder sister Lady Mary Sackville (1646-1710) married 1664/5 Roger Boyle, 2nd Earl of Orrery, grand-son of the Earl of Cork.
21. See Muschamp, Denny, entry by John Bergin in James McGuire and James Quinn (eds), *Dictionary of Irish Biography*, (Cambridge, 2009).
22. de Vesci papers, MS 38, 856/1-4 contains a statement of Denny Muschamp's interest in the lands of the manor of Buttevant dated 1670.
23. Robert Cuffe appears to be a nephew of Denny Muschamp and the son of Joseph Cuffe and Martha Muschamp.
24. William Maziere-Brady, *Clerical and Parochial Records of Cork, Cloyne, and Ross* (London, 1864), vol. 2, p. 59: 'On a chalice now (1863) in use in Buttevant Church, is this legend: "This, with the cover, was given to ye Parish Church of Buttevant by ye Viscountess Lanesborough, wife to Denny Muschanp, esq., 1698, February." The chalice and cover are silver, gilt, and weigh about 20 oz. The same lady endowed a school at Buttevant with £20 per an., a house, and half an acre of land. But this bequest ceased in 1818, when the interest of her heirs in the lands on which the annuity was charged expired"; for a photograph of the communion cup see Charles Alexander Webster, *The Church Plate of the Diocese of Cork, Cloyne and Ross* (Cork, 1909), p.87.
25. University College Galway, Landed Estates Database: http://landedestates.nuigalway.ie:8080/LandedEstates/jsp/estate-show.jsp?id=2756 (accessed 24 March 2012).
26. Register of Fixed Rents (1881), no. 1379, between Lord Viscount Doneraile and John Madden of Grange.

Notes to Fig. 1
27. This Agmondsham was in Ireland with Vavasour in 1642; obtained lease of the Grange lands from Boyle, who had acquired them from Lord Barrymore.
28. Denny Muschamp acquired the fee simple in the Grange lands.
29. Mary inherited the Grange lands, bringing them to the Vesey family.
30. Charles acquired an interest in the Grange lands from his brother John. Having died without issue his interest passed to his nephew John Thomas. John's interest passed to his daughter Catherine.

CHAPTER 9

THE REVIVAL OF THE MIDDLE AGES: BUTTEVANT IN THE 19TH CENTURY[1]

~ DAGMAR Ó RIAIN-RAEDEL ~

In spite of its undoubted significance during the Middle Ages, Buttevant's fortunes subsequently suffered serious set-backs, and later commentators felt obliged to note this decline, summed up by the authors of the 1962 *Shell Guide to Ireland* who stated: 'in 1691 the Williamites burned the town [of Buttevant] and it has never wholly recovered.'[2] Previous comments had been equally uncomplimentary. The 1731 'Abstract of the state of Popery in the Diocese of Cloyne, humbly laid before the Lords' Committees appointed to inquire into the state of Popery in this Kingdom' found Buttevant at what must have been its lowest ebb: 'Parish of Buttevant: one mass-house; one Popish priest, a thatched house within the precincts of the old Abbey, wherein one or two old Friars have dwelt some time past, one of these lately dead. No Popish school.'[3]

The Cornish antiquarian, William Borlase (1696-1772), as cited by Thomas Crofton Croker in his *Researches in the South of Ireland* (1824), described Buttevant as 'an old nest of abbots, priests, and friars', …, which 'though formerly a town of importance and opulence, is now a poor place…It was walled, and governed by a corporation, and traces of its consequence may still be seen in the solid old walls and ruins scattered amongst the mean houses of which it is at present composed.'[4] Much later, at the beginning of the twentieth century, Colonel James Grove White of Kilbyrne, not far from Buttevant, could still write that 'this whole town formerly seems to have been an assemblage of churches and religious houses, which, being dissolved, consequently went with them to ruin…'[5]

As will be seen, however, some early accounts of the town also contained a note of optimism. Thus, while the 1824 Pigot & Co.'s Directory expressed the view that the ancient town of Buttevant had formerly been 'a place of very great note', and that 'its present wretchedness still exhibited some vestiges of its religious buildings, which sadly now were nothing more than a heap of ruins, it added that 'the castle has been repaired by its present owner, Sir John Anderson, and has become 'an elegant and respectable mansion.'[6]

Similarly, some forty years later, Charles Bernard Gibson, although commenting that 'the old town is little more than a Golgotha, or place of skulls', 'where nothing seems to have grown or flourished for centuries', went on to remark that this gloomy outlook did not take account of the new Catholic church.[7]

The last two notices strike a more optimistic and encouraging note on the strength of new developments which took place in the course the nineteenth century. Gibson referred to the new Catholic church of St Mary's, while Pigot's Directory pointed to the person of John Anderson, arguably the man who, together with his son, James Caleb, can be credited with the revival of Buttevant. While both notices may appear unconnected, they form part of a pattern signalling the manner in which the town was attempting to regain some of its former glory. Furthermore, the Middle Ages, which had seen Buttevant's heyday, were to provide some of the inspiration and direction towards a 'second flowering' of the town.

BUTTEVANT'S NEW ENTREPRENEURS:
John Anderson (1747–1820) and James Caleb Anderson (1792–1861)[8]

A French emigrant aristocrat who travelled through Ireland in the aftermath of the French Revolution described Cork as 'one of the richest and most commercial cities of Europe. The principal merchants are nearly all foreigners, Scotch for the most part, and in the short period of ten years are able sometimes to make large fortunes.'[9] He may well have been speaking of John Anderson, a Scottish emigrant who settled in Cork city c.1780, and who in the space of a few years had built up his malting and warehouse complexes on Lapp's Island, in the vicinity of the present Anderson's Quay, which is named after him. Soon, his fortunes had improved sufficiently to have him appointed to the city's prestigious and influential Committee of Merchants and to be made a Freeman of the city in 1787.[10] But what ultimately secured Anderson's fame and fortune was his foray into the provision of mail-coaches in Ireland. Originally set up to provide the means for carrying mail more securely and swiftly, the coach system evolved into a revolutionary mode of passenger transport. However, it soon emerged that the undertaking proved more complex than anticipated and Anderson noted:

> The proposal being moderate, it was readily accepted under the stipulation that the whole responsibility was to rest with myself; that the coaches, horses, harness etca were to be all provided at my own expense, and that I was also to find what further means, besides the tolls, might be necessary, for having the roads put in proper repair, and changed when required, and also to make new lines of road where the old ones would not answer the purpose.[11]

Clearly, Anderson did not shy away from courageous business decisions, which, at least initially, were to pay off handsomely, enabling him to move into politics, and to become a staunch pro-Union supporter and agitator in the process. Having secured the franchise from the Post Office to provide a mail service from Dublin to Cork in 1789, and from Cork to Dublin in 1793, he proceeded to set in place an extensive infrastructure of roads, bridges, inns and staging coaches, and this was followed by the development of further routes within Ireland.

The Founding of Fermoy

Great as his contribution to the city of Cork and the national transport system may have been, it was in Fermoy that John Anderson was to leave his most enduring legacy. Strategically located on the Cork to Dublin road, at a crossing point of the river Blackwater, Fermoy had many advantages. Anderson resolved to make a town of the place, and succeeded in 'constructing the handsomest country town in Ireland.'[12]

When the Fermoy estate of the Forward family became available in 1791, Anderson purchased the larger part of it, even though it meant having to borrow heavily; all his earlier profits had been invested in the mail coach enterprise. Nonetheless, by 1800, Anderson could announce his progress in providing the infrastructure for industrial and residential enterprises in Fermoy. In addition, he widened the existing bridge over the Blackwater, laid out the handsome new town alluded to above, contributed financially to the building of the churches of both denominations and of a hospital, set up an Agricultural Society and a bank to provide finance for both industry and agriculture.[13] Indeed, just before his bankruptcy, he provided a generous lease for the site of the Catholic church. All of these achievements he could observe from his newly built Palladian-style Fermoy House, situated on the northern bank of the river. More importantly, he also responded to a British government demand for military barracks by offering to provide not only suitable lands without rent, but also to construct the buildings within a three-year period.

Although already heavily in debt, Anderson then proceeded to purchase the lands of Henry, eighth earl of Barrymore, amounting to some 2,600 acres, and including 'the Barry town, castle and manor of Buttevant.'[14] Being obliged to provide equity for the heavily mortgaged estate, in addition to a life annuity for the earl and countess, proved very costly and, by 1816, Anderson had to declare bankruptcy. A meeting of creditors, which included most of the nobility of Co Cork, all of whom had been close friends and colleagues, was unable to reverse the position. Anderson's appeal to the Chief Secretary of Ireland, Robert Peel, for a government loan of £150,000, surely an outrageously excessive sum at that time, proved unsuccessful, and even the support of his close friends, the Earl of Listowel, Lord Shannon, Lord Donoughmore and the Earl of Bandon, could not save him. In his appeal, Anderson blamed the 'combination of losses and disappointments mainly connected with my unfortunate purchase of the Barrymore Estate' for his financial embarrassment and feared that if a loan was not forthcoming and his properties were forced from him, they could 'fall into the hands of some rich Catholics, which might make an essential difference against government in the future management of this country.'[15] However, his 'unlucky purchase of the Barrymore estate', as he termed it, in conjunction with a general financial depression in the wake of the end of the Napoleonic Wars, was to bring to a miserable end, in his own words, 'his feeble efforts towards civilising and improving the south of Ireland.'[16] He died in 1820 on a stay in London where he had travelled to plead with King George IV. It was to be a sad twist of fate that his son, James Caleb, whose new inventions were to supersede the mail coach system inaugurated by his father, was also to find himself having to declare bankruptcy. By then, however, both he and his father had left their mark on Buttevant, beginning with the provision of barracks.

Buttevant Barracks
As he had done in Fermoy, John Anderson provided land free of rent for the setting up of army barracks in Buttevant, no doubt hoping, for the town and for himself, to reap the benefits inherent in such an investment. Originally on 14 acres, the barracks, later extended to some 23 acres, were built around two squares, divided by a central range, providing enough space to accommodate three regiments (Fig.1 and Plate 10).[17] Now the home of the local GAA club, only some walls and the entrance gate are still standing. The north-western part of the town grew to accommodate officers' quarters, married quarters and hotels, in the process providing a separate new focus within the town.

Though never planned on a scale as large as that in Fermoy, the barracks were nevertheless strategically placed near to the Cork-Limerick road, where Anderson himself had initiated a mail coach scheme and, from 1849 onwards, they were within easy reach of the now disused and derelict Buttevant/Doneraile railway station. The latter was to prove of special importance,

> as this [southern] half of Ireland, the most disposed to domestic disorders and agitation, and to foreign invasion, possesses already very rapid means of communication with Dublin in every direction, and the barracks on these lines should in general be maintained.[18]

As in Fermoy, the troops were very active during the agrarian disturbances of the early nineteenth century, during which time many of them were also stationed in the private residences of the area.[19]

Buttevant benefitted commercially from the barracks which were capable of accommodating 1,126 men and, as in other Irish towns, were 'a place of civilian as well as military employment.'[20] Commercial activity in the town increased considerably and, no doubt, social occasions would have involved the local gentry. Although the barracks had a chapel of its own, the officers were known to have frequented St John's Church of Ireland church, where the west gallery had been reserved for them. Though there was seemingly no effort on the part of Anderson to lay out the town in the style of Fermoy, building activity nevertheless increased and the main street, connecting the barracks with the southern castle complex, assumed its present nineteenth-century look. Although probably going back to medieval times, the so-called 'New Street', running parallel to Main Street, may also have received improvements to allow for direct access to the barracks.

Fig. 1: Barracks, Buttevant, Co Cork.

The restoration of Buttevant's past: The Castle
While the barracks developed a life of their own at the northern side of the town, Anderson had secured for himself the castle complex situated on the opposite end of the main street, which became available when Richard, 7th Earl Barrymore (1769-1793), who had begun to tackle his debts, shot himself accidently. His brother Henry proceeded to sell the lands and castle in Buttevant. As at Fermoy, the *parvenu* Anderson was again able to take advantage of the break-up of hereditary estates, although the purchase of the Barry estate was eventually to contribute to his own downfall. However, with the purchase of the castle complex, Anderson could finally put an aristocratic veneer on his family, and his eldest son, James Caleb, who took up residence in the castle, was no doubt aware that it was here that Buttevant had first evolved. The castle of the Barrys, originally built in the thirteenth century, had formed the centerpiece of a demesne which also incorporated the manorial or parish church. Furthermore, it was

neatly book-ended by the two religious foundations the Barry family had provided for, the Augustinian priory at Ballybeg and the Franciscan friary, both dedicated to St Thomas à Becket. The castle was thus at the centre of an ecclesiastical and administrative complex, which was further marked by a market house and fair green. Anderson defined this area further by changing the outline of the southern approach to the town. Keeping the streetscape of the town centre intact, he changed the road which ran from Ballybeg past the Church of Ireland building before becoming the main street just south of the friary, and thereby traversing his estate, so that it would skirt the demesne, thus providing the southern approach with the elegant curve that is still there today.

The manor of Buttevant had not been simply an ensemble of historic buildings, it had also been a Seneschal's court, which presumably provided the lord of the manor with particular power. For a *parvenu* like John Anderson, this historical dimension to the castle and its environs represented an opportunity to lend himself and his family some *gravitas*, and enabled him to reinvent himself and his family as successors of nobility. Ironically, John Anderson did not himself accept what would have been the ultimate crowning of his status, namely the granting of a baronetcy. Instead, he had the honour bestowed on his eldest son, James Caleb, who was created a baronet when he came of age in 1813, in recognition of the great services rendered by his father.

Both father, and later, his eldest son, who lived in Buttevant permanently, apparently took to the idea of the medieval manor in an enthusiastic manner. Having secured the prosperity of the town by attracting the military, they occupied themselves with the development of the castle complex at the opposite end of the town, its castle, parish church, market, fair green, mill and bridge, which also already existed in medieval times.[21] Built on a vantage point over the river Awbeg, the thirteenth-century Barry castle was converted by the Andersons, possibly under the supervision of the Pain architects, into an extensive, castellated, three-storey mansion, replete with corner turrets (Plates 1 and 2). Taking their cue from what may have been the castle's original style, they added an impressive ogee-arched entrance with label mouldings, flanked by two narrow loopholes.[22] Writing in 1837, Samuel Lewis suggested that 'Buttevant Castle, the residence of Sir J. Caleb Anderson, Bart., was originally called King John's Castle, and formed one of the angles of the ancient fortifications of the town.' Interestingly, he was also of the opinion that 'it was considerably enlarged and modernised by the late Mr. Anderson, and has lost much of its antique appearance.' While it may be assumed that Lewis was referring to the newly constructed mansion, he does not take into account that the Andersons actually put a more antique appearance on the castle than this may have possessed during the residence there of the Barry family. He was, however, perfectly right when he commented that the castle was 'beautifully situated on a rocky eminence on the margin of the river, of which it commands a fine view; within the demesne is the church, the spire of which combining with other features of the scenery adds much to the beauty of the landscape.'[23]

Lewis had probably taken over the sentiments expressed in 1830 by Robert O'Callaghan Newenham in conjunction with his drawing of the castle; Newenham wrote: 'This Castle is boldly situated on a rock above the Awbeg and close to the town of Buttevant. Sir John Anderson, to whom it belongs, has fitted it up with skill and good taste, so as to preserve, in some degree, the character of the building, and render the Castle a striking ornament in the country.'[24] Although no longer to be seen, the Andersons may also have added an antiquated look to an existing bridge near the castle. Moreover, judging by the peculiar model adopted for their mill, they were determined to put the final touches to the medieval precinct they could now call their own.

The Mill
Not content with the newly recreated medieval appearance of his castle, Anderson also arranged for his mill to display a similar design. Standing six storeys high, the mill, which probably had previously possessed a pitch roof, continues to impress to this day (Plate 14). It was here that Anderson introduced the most advanced milling machinery known at the time, in the process increasing the annual output of flour by hitherto unknown quantities. However, it was not the milling business that was to decide his future but his work as an inventor, which allowed him to take out various patents. Thus, in 1831, he lodged specifications for 'improvements in machinery for propelling vessels on water', followed, in 1837, by 'improvements in locomotive engines', and, in 1846 by 'certain improvements in obtaining motive power, and in applying it to propel carriages and vessels, and to the driving of machinery.'[25] He established the Steam Carriage and Wagon Company, and, although the engines were to be produced in England, he hoped to make good use of the improvements his father had made to the Irish road system. The *Engineers and Mechanics Encyclopedia* for 1839 could announce that a patent had been granted to Sir James C. Anderson, Bart. of Buttevant Castle:

> for a very judicious arrangement of mechanism for propelling carriages by manual labour. This gentleman designed a carriage, in which as many as twenty-four men were arranged on seats, in the manner of rowers in a boat, but in two tiers, one above the other; the action was nearly the same as the pulling of oars, the only difference being, that by Sir James's plan, all the men sitting on one seat pulled at one horizontal cross bar, each extremity of which was furnished with an anti-friction roller, that ran between guide rails on the opposite sides of the carriage. The ends of each of these

horizontal bars were connected to reciprocating rods, that gave motion to a crank shaft, on which were mounted spur gear, that actuated similar gear on the axis of the running wheels of the carriage; so that by sliding the gear on the axis of the latter, any required velocity could be communicated to the carriage, or a sudden stop made.

A carriage of this kind it was proposed to employ as a drag, to draw one or more carriages containing passengers after it. The worthy Baronet informed us, that he had chiefly in view the movement of troops by this method, which would enable them to effect their marches with greater facility and dispatch; hence he justly considered that there might be a great diminution of the peace establishment, without detriment to the service. [26]

But, as the writer recorded: 'We are not sure that a carriage was ever built in accordance with the patented plans of 1832, as Sir James Anderson appears to have fallen into pecuniary difficulties about this time.' Nevertheless, Anderson continued in his efforts and, in 1838, a fellow North Cork resident reported in the *Farmers Magazine* that:

> though living within twenty miles of Sir James's seat, Buttevant Castle - we, like the rest of the world, were left almost in ignorance of the final accomplishment of an undertaking to which he had given the greater part of his life, and sacrificed a fortune, now, we feel convinced, to be amply refunded. He worked in silence, and oft, perhaps, in sorrow, until his task was done - and ere it was done, to use his own emphatic words, 'spent *two apprenticeships and a fortune in building 29 unsuccessful carriages to succeed in the 30th.*'

The writer was particularly taken by the picturesque setting of Anderson's workshop:

> In approaching Buttevant Castle one is struck with its beautiful and romantic situation: you reach its hospitable entrance through an avenue of evergreens, and, perhaps, forget, in the beauty of the scenery before you (at least, so it was with us), that you have come to see a piece of mechanism manufactured there, entirely by Irish mechanics, in which the first engineers had hitherto failed. We had forgotten, but were awakened to the object of our visit by a gate opening as we passed the back of the castle, which discovered to our view

> the workshops and the *Lion* carriage. We were indeed astonished - from a scene of sylvan beauty we stepped at once into a 'mechanic's shop', and 'midst the din of anvils and the bellows blast' we found both the machine itself and its inventor. We do not profess to be an engineer, but the simplicity of the mechanism is such that a child may understand it and see its capability; and we confess, had we but known the fact, we should have doubted that such exquisite workmanship could be executed here. We are not boastful, but we can with truth aver, we never saw anything equal to it from the best factories in England.

Enthusiastically, the writer could predict how the steam engine was going to do the work presently done by horses and was looking forward to naming the day 'that we can breakfast in Cork and dine in Dublin.' He ended up proclaiming that 'if ever man deserved well of his country it is Sir James Anderson, and most gladly do we look upon the harvest ripening to him, after his weary season of toil and labour.'[27]

Yet, only a year later, the *The Engineers and Mechanics Encyclopedia* noted that Anderson, here referred to as 'Baronet of Buttevant Castle', while still working, had to admit that by now he had spent some £30,000 on the project. A trial run at Howth had been completed successfully, and it was proposed to expand further. Moreover, it had been decided that the company:

> should in the first instance, in conjunction with the railway trains from London, run from Birmingham to Holyhead, the passengers to be thence conveyed to Dublin by steamer: from Dublin to Galway the steam drags were to be employed and thence to New York per vessel touching at Halifax; thus making Ireland the stepping-stone between England, Nova Scotia, and the United States of America. It will be seen that Sir Jas. Anderson purposed great things with his steam carriages, but judging from the paucity of the literature dealing with his public trials, we fear that little practical running was accomplished.

The report then concluded that:

> want of success, however, does not appear to have caused him to relax his energies, for in addition to the carriages we have referred to, many more schemes were proposed and patented, the latest bearing the date of 1858, showing that Sir

James Anderson, Bart, devoted no less than thirty-one years of his life to the furtherance of steam locomotion on common roads.[28]

Surprisingly, there is little indication that the Andersons took an active interest in other parts of the town of Buttevant. Notwithstanding the fact that they had expended much on the restoration of the castle and the building of the mill, they are not known to have supported the building programmes of churches or educational facilities, nor to have become involved in the other activities of the town. This may well have been due to the financial difficulties faced by both father and, later, his son. Sadly, Buttevant was to prove the final straw in the demise of the Andersons. John Anderson, who had already been in debt when he purchased the estate, saw all his business undertakings crumble before his eyes. Eventually, as already stated, he had to declare bankruptcy and ended his life in London. His son James Caleb, although greatly innovative and famous for his inventions, equally overstretched himself in his endeavours.

By 1837, at the latest, James Caleb's situation seems to have been quite desperate. A letter written from France to the Chancellor of Exchequer by James Caleb's wife, Lady Anderson, pleaded for a pension which, she felt, she was entitled to because of the services rendered by her father-in-law to the government. Also, much of her own riches had been invested in his ill-fated undertakings, and she now found herself in the invidious position of having to rely on the kindness of friends in order to feed herself and her nine helpless and destitute children. Indeed, her husband's embarrassments, she declared, 'are so great that he cannot venture to stir out. Therefore 'tho' a kinder husband or a fonder father does not exist, it is impossible for him to assist his large family.'[29] There is no record as to whether her pleas were successful, but in 1831 the Buttevant estate was sold to Viscount Doneraile, who, it appears, allowed the Anderson family to continue living there until the mid 1840s.

The Doneraile Papers, now deposited in the National Library of Ireland, contain the leases taken over by the St Legers from the Andersons. These underline the latters' involvement in the houses and hotels clustered around the barracks, and list their ownership of a sizeable amount of land belonging to Buttevant manor. Much of the archive, however, bears testimony to the bitter exchanges in the course of the take-over by Hayes, the 3rd Viscount Doneraile. Correspondence from the 1820-30s provides lists of tenants to be evicted from the Buttevant estate, including James Anderson himself, who went on to describe bailiff Cornelius Garvan as a 'savage tyrant.' Viscount Doneraile was, by all accounts, an unpopular landlord at Buttevant and it is no wonder that Rev J.L. Cotter felt compelled to write that 'the people of Buttevant are greatly displeased with Lord Doneraile for feeling no interest for Buttevant and all declare that he will have <u>no vote</u> from this town and neighbourhood at the next election.' In many ways, the papers present the picture of a troubled place, an example of which may be a comment in the folder of 1847 concerning the local womens' habit of 'fore-startling and re-grading of potatoes.'[30] Significantly, the intervention of the clergy in a number of matters received much attention, in particular the complaints from this quarter about ongoing prostitution, a reality probably to be expected in a garrison town.

When Captain Grove White was finishing his account of Buttevant in 1905, he could nevertheless report that great progress had been made in the previous century. The initial expansion during the early part of the eighteen-hundreds had increased the number of houses to some 204 and the garrison had contributed greatly to the prosperity of the town, heralding the arrival of hotels, shops and banks. Little could Grove White have known what lay ahead for the town. World War I would see the large-scale deployment of the town's troops to foreign battle-fields, and the burning of the barracks by the Republican Army on 12 August 1922 effectively represented the end of the garrison town. This led to yet another decline in the fortunes of Buttevant, which had, perhaps, been relying too heavily on the presence of the army, and on the prosperity which ensued from the milling and other industries, initiated by the Andersons. While the mill was used for various businesses until recently, the barracks and their associated buildings and activities have all but disappeared. With the Andersons' castle, mill and work-shops now lying deserted, we are left in the somewhat fortunate position that, due to lack of further development, many of the town's buildings, both of medieval times and of the nineteenth-century, are still standing. In addition to Anderson's castle complex, Buttevant has three religious buildings that bear witness to the nineteenth-century boom in the town.

RELIGIOUS REVIVAL

St John's (Church of Ireland)
Part of the manorial estate was the parish church, which is situated on a slightly elevated site south-west of the castle (Plate 11).[31] The present church dedicated to St John may be the successor to previous ones, the 'ancient remains' of which were clearly visible in 1837 when Lewis described the present church as 'a handsome structure in the later English style, with a square embattled tower surmounted by a finely proportioned spire.' Lewis stated that the new church was 'near the site of an ancient church, of which there are still some remains, and on the site of another of more recent date.'[32] According to Smith, these churches were dedicated to St Brigid and the Virgin Mary respectively and were situated within the same church yard.[33] The Pipe Roll of Cloyne had already referred to 'the parish church' and to 'the church of St Brigid', although these may well have been one and the same.[34] In 1615, the church at Buttevant was described as

'repaired', while the chancel was ruined ('ecclesia reparata, cancella ruinata'), and in 1661 the establishment was without a curate.[35] In 1694, the church of 'de Bothon als Templebroody [Templebreedy] *als* Buttevant' had lapsed into ruin. This was probably the manorial church and, rather than rebuild it, it may have been decided to erect a new structure for the members of the Established Church, the consecration of which appears to have taken place *ca* 1698, when Viscountess Lanesborough, wife of Denny Muschamp, donated a communion cup to the church. In 1774, although the Protestant population of 'Bothon' was only 30, a permanent curacy had been re-established and the church was in repair, while the church dedicated to St Brigid had been abandoned.

Rather than referring to St Brigid of Kildare, this church, which gave name to Templebreedy, may have been dedicated to the sister of St Colmán, the patron saint of the diocese of Cloyne.[36] The bishop of Cloyne was also in possession of a manor in nearby Kilmaclenine, which is called after Colmán under the guise of Mac Léinín. The existence of an early Christian site, possibly the one that gave Buttevant its ancient name of Ceall na Mullach, could be supported by the presence of a number of holy wells, one across the river from Buttevant castle and one in nearby Mount Brigid, Churchtown. On the other hand, the 'temple' element of Templebreedy would suggest Anglo-Norman patronage, arguably associated with the Barrys. These probably adopted this dedication for their manorial church, which was also to serve as parish church. A number of Gothic worked stones housed in the present church are thought to have come from an earlier structure on the site, possibly the manorial church (see Plate 12). Such is their resemblance to the sculpture of the Franciscan abbey that these stones could also have originated there, or at least have come from the same work-shop. However, the *spolia* found in the abbey, which had not become part of Brash's attempt at restoration, would perhaps have been housed in the adjacent Catholic church.

It would appear that the church dedicated to St Mary, as mentioned by Smith, was the precursor of the present Church of Ireland church of St John's, which was dedicated *ca* 1698. However, writing in 1750, Smith introduces a note of confusion by mentioning a further church, a 'modern' structure, as well as two ruined churches. This may indicate that the 'new' Protestant church, tentatively dated to 1698, had already fallen into disrepair some fifty years later. If this was the case, then this church would then have been replaced by St John's in 1826. In that event, the steeple made famous by the steeple-chase which is supposed to have taken place in 1752 between the church at Buttevant and that of St Mary's in Doneraile would have been on the church newly built around 1698. Whether this church was already dedicated to St John is uncertain. Though the apostle was a popular dedicatee in the Established Church, the title could well have been taken from an earlier ecclesiastical structure, a nunnery, dedicated to St John the Baptist, of which some remains still exist in what is now the Mill Lane. The dedication to St Mary, on the other hand, was re-used for the Roman Catholic church, which began to be built a few years after that of St John's, while local devotion to St Brigid appears to have lost its previous status.

The Pain architects

We are on firmer ground with the history of the present St John's, which was built in 1826 by the well-known Gothic revival architects George Richard (1793-1838) and James Pain (1779-1877). The brothers had been pupils of the famous English architect, John Nash, who placed them in charge of work he had been commissioned to do at Lough Cutra Castle, Co Galway, in 1815. James went on to carry out work mainly in the County Limerick area, while George Richard established himself in Cork. In addition, until George Richard's death in 1838, the brothers carried out many works together, amongst which were several fine court houses, gaols, bridges and churches for both denominations. James was appointed architect to the Board of First Fruits for the province of Munster in 1823,[37] and Buttevant church must have been among his early projects, as it was dedicated only three years after he had received his commission.

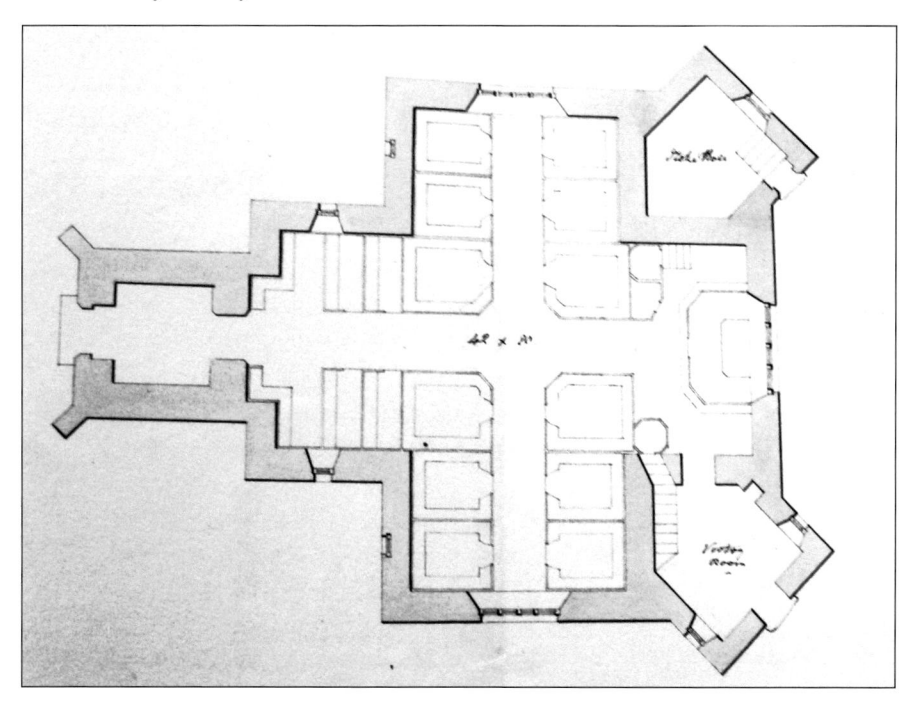

Fig. 2: Ground plan of St John's Church, Buttevant. Architectural drawings by James Pain of churches in the dioceses of Cashel & Emly, Cloyne, Cork & Ross, Killaloe & Kilenora, Limerick & Ardfert, Waterford & Lismore, Ms 138, no 12, 1: copyright Representative Church Body Library.

Most of the First Fruits churches display a plain rectangular 'Gothic box' architecture, with a square tower at the western side, where the main doorway was also located. Although some continued to be built along these lines when James, often assisted by his brother, was appointed, the Pains also branched out into different designs. One of the most unusual of these is shown by St John's, which follows the lay-out of an equal-armed Greek cross, accommodating the altar in the East end, the entrance in the West, and pews in both South and North arms (Fig. 2). Diagonally added to the back of the church are a 'Vestry Room' and a 'Stoke Room', the latter incorporating an under-ground heating chamber. Although the architects used this design for a few more churches, not many of these have survived, and St John's therefore provides an invaluable example of a very remarkable design. Described as 'aloof and independent, it is secure in its own style, solidly grounded, compact and stocky, it looks an immovable and timeless structure planted in tradition.' [38]

The cost of £1,476 18s was to be met through contributions from parishioners and a loan from the Board of First Fruits, which had to be repaid in yearly instalments of a quite substantial amount of nearly £60. The need for a more spacious church may have been felt when Bregoge, Kilbroney and Cahirduggan were joined to the Buttevant union in 1820, which previously had consisted of only some twenty Protestant families.[39] By 1830, the population had grown to two hundred or so parishioners, while the garrison church could accommodate another 450 people. The number of parishioners was apparently increased when a *cause célèbre* took place in Doneraile, as recorded by Grove White:

> In Buttevant Church there is a gallery, which was built about the forties of the 19th century. Owing to some serious misunderstandings between the Rev. H. Somerville, Rector of Doneraile, and some of his parishioners, it was decided by Viscount Doneraile, the Rev. F. W. Crofts, of Clogheen, and James Grove White, Esq., of Kilburn (Kilbyrne), who were also parishioners of Buttevant, though being in the Parish of Cahirduggan, to build, at their own expense, a gallery in Buttevant Church, with three pews and a private staircase. This was duly carried out. The first pew at the head of the staircase was occupied by Lord Doneraile, the next one became the Kilbyrne pew, and the end one that of the Rev. F. W. Crofts.[40]

Only two brass plates survive, those denoting the Kilbyrne and Springfort Hall pews respectively; the third pew now has no plate.[41]

St John's was, by all accounts, a most up-to-date building. It was centrally heated from an under-ground boiler room which heated hot water and one may wonder whether Sir Anderson's engineering abilities were responsible for this. Later, at the beginning of the twentieth century, the building could be lit electrically from a generating station placed 'near the Barrack Gate.' Now, as a result of Anderson's rerouting of the road leading to Cork, both the church and the ruins of earlier ones — all of which may have lain outside the outer city walls — are enclosed by a wall which contains some remnants of earlier buildings.[42]

The Roman Catholic church of St Mary's
There are no indications that relations between the Church of Ireland clergy and those of the Roman Catholic church in Buttevant were not amiable. Nevertheless, Fr. Cornelius Buckley of St Mary's soon after responded to the building of St John's by erecting a house of worship which would match that of his Protestant neighbours. Moreover, his church was to be located on the main street and not hidden away like St John's amongst a grove of trees, however romantic this location may have appeared to commentators. Furthermore, there was now to be a clear separation of the castle complex from the town, where the new church tied in with a cluster of previous and still-standing religious buildings, including a thatched mass-house, possibly a nunnery and, most importantly of all, the Franciscan friary. Although not quite half-way between the two then existing Buttevant hubs — the castle/church complex and the barracks — Fr Buckley established an ecclesiastical centre to which were also to belong schools and, later, a convent. Above all, he took account of the presence and architectural style of the friary, even incorporating what may have been part of the conventual buildings into the church. Two *spolia* from the friary, now part of the fabric of the church walls, underlined the continuity between the two religious establishments.

The building history of St Mary's is covered in a separate chapter of this book. However, it should be noted that Fr. Buckley's undertaking played a pivotal role in recreating Buttevant, partly in the image of its medieval past. By all accounts, as will be seen again below, the priest was very supportive of Windele and Brash in their efforts to preserve the fabric of the friary. And since he was so obviously aware of the friary, one wonders whether he had any say in the choice of architectural style for St Mary's. It has been claimed that 'the universal employment of Gothic by the Church of Ireland was a deliberate choice, for it denoted historical continuity with pre-Reformation Christianity'.[43] If so, Buttevant's Roman Catholic church was built in the same idiom. Indeed, it may have been Buckley's concern with the continuity of the tradition expressed by the friary that he did not favour a differing style from St John's. Thus, he didn't opt for a building in the classical style, which would arguably have underlined a stronger connection to Rome and a resurgence of power emanating from there. In the event, both Gothic revival churches differ greatly and Fr.

Buckley's stress on Catholic values was adequately addressed in the interior, particularly in the choice of subjects for the stained-glass windows.

The convent

The Catholic church of St Mary's, the anchor-point of the cluster of ecclesiastical buildings facing the main street of Buttevant, was complemented in 1879 by the erection of a convent, also dedicated to St Mary and run by the Sisters of Mercy. Attractively set within landscaped grounds adjoining Mill Lane, the convent mirrors in a small way the castle/church complex nearby (Plate 13). Following the work of the Pain brothers on St John's, and of Charles Cottrell on St Mary's, George Coppinger Ashlin (1837-1921), another Gothic-inspired architect, who had by then already distinguished himself by his designs for Catholic churches, monasteries and convents, was chosen for the convent.[44] Born in Cork, Ashlin had been apprenticed to Edward Welby Pugin in Birmingham and London, and was later taken into partnership and eventually put in charge of Pugin's Dublin office and of his Irish commissions. From 1875 onwards, Ashlin was involved in the building of St Colman's Cathedral at Queenstown/Cobh, probably his most famous commission. His extensive Cork portfolio, which included the church of SS. Peter and Paul, may have been due to the connections of his mother, who belonged to the old Cork family of Coppinger.

The Buttevant building, built at a cost of £3,000, was to accommodate 16 nuns and 100 pupils and received much local support. Lord Doneraile gave the lease for the site for £10 per annum and also provided a subscription on the condition that the school should be incorporated into the convent building. In this way, he was not seen to be providing for a religious institution. Further funds were raised by Mary Anne Walsh of Rathclare, Buttevant, a sister of Mrs Tracey who also provided money for the Chancel window in St Mary's in memory of her parents, brothers and sisters. Support was also received in 1879 from Mother Joseph Croke, superioress of the Convent of Mercy at Charleville and sister of Archbishop Croke of Cashel, both natives of nearby Kilbrin. With its pointed gables and massive chimneys, it displays Tudor-style windows and Gothic details which are mostly concentrated around the door-ways. Much thought and effort also went into the design of the convent grounds, which, unusually, also comprised a summer-house incorporating stained glass windows.

As is the case with Buttevant's other notable buildings, the nineteenth-century convent consciously echoed the town's past history. Thus, the sisters appear to have rededicated the section of the grounds containing their grave-yard into a memorial park, designed to hark back to previous times. Inserted into the wall bordering Mill Lane, is a tablet which reads:

> On the adjoining site stood the old thatched chapel of Buttevant and beneath are deposited the remains of the Rev.

James Roche, P.P. 1779-1807 which were laid at the gospel side of the altar without headstone or inscription. Hereon are likewise commemorated the names of the Rev. John O'Kane, O.S.F., martyred at Limerick, 1622; Rev. Boetius MacEgan, Guardian 1642, martyred Bishop of Ross at Carrigdrohid 1650; Rev. Redmond Barry, 1704; Rev. Francis Donegan, P.P. 1758-1779; Rev. Father Kingston, 1774; their resting places are unknown. Pray for their souls and the souls of the priests and people who worshiped in this lowly temple during the dark penal days. R.I.P. In their memory Fr. C.B. has erected and J.E. Davis has inscribed this tablet May 23rd. In the year of Our Lord, 1898.

While this inscription recalls Penal times and the thatched mass house that stood there, the site may previously have been the location of a nunnery, of which traces may still be seen in the wall facing the entrance to the castle. The nunnery, of which little is known, appears to have been dedicated to St 'Owen', or John the Baptist, and it may have been used as a parish church when the building in the castle demesne was taken over by the Established Church. The continuity of location between nunnery and convent was possibly deliberate. Although documentary evidence is scarce, there must have been local awareness of the nunnery, as the double headed window and some *spolia* drawn by Benjamin Woodward in the 1830s, are described as 'Scraps from the Nunnery of St John's'.

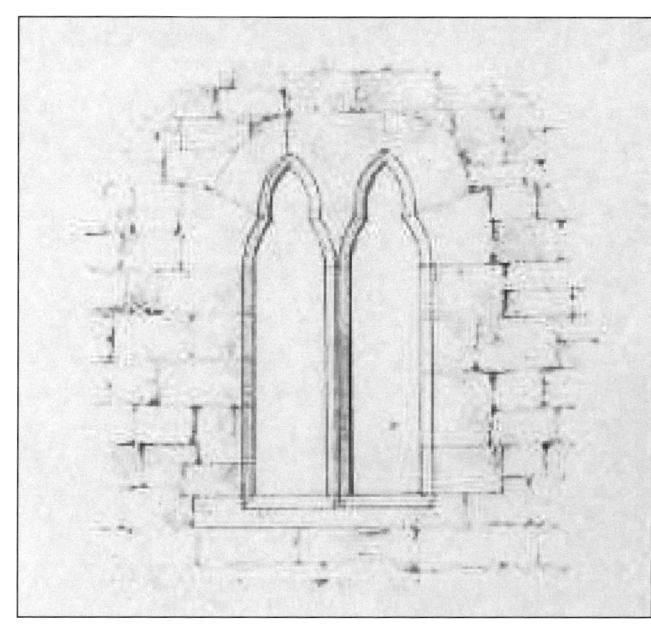

Fig. 3: 'Scraps from the Nunnery of St John's, Drawings by Benjamin Woodward, Ms 3 B 59, copyright Royal Irish Academy.

Brash, too, mentioned a 'small trefoil-headed two light window' and the same author described some *spolia* on this wall, noting that 'moulded caps are worked on the stone' (Fig. 3).[45] These are, no doubt, the three 'scraps' drawn by Woodward, which are now in a shrine dedicated to St Joseph, situated next to the memorial tablet (Plate 15).

PRESERVING THE PAST

'A sort of medieval museum for the curious': Antiquarian interest in the remains of the Franciscan abbey at Buttevant:
By the nineteenth century, Buttevant's erstwhile pride and beauty, the Franciscan friary, had fallen into serious disrepair. In the words of J.R. O'Flanagan, 'the ruins of the abbey...present the remnants of a once-glorious pile. Portions of the nave, chancel and steeple-tower yet plead haughtily for greatness vanished.'[46] Samuel Lewis had previously noted in his *Topographical Dictionary of Ireland* (1837):

> The ruins of the abbey are finely situated on the steep bank of the river Awbeg, and consist chiefly of the walls of the nave, chancel, and some portions of the domestic buildings; the upper part of the central tower, supported on arches of light and graceful elevation, fell down in 1814; the tomb of the founder, David de Barry, is supposed to be in the centre of the chancel, but is marked only by some broken stones which appear to have formed an enclosure.[47]

Robert O'Callaghan Newenham, in a comment accompanying his drawing of the friary bemoaned the fact that the tower, which had stood 'on light and graceful arches', had by now fallen and covered the interior with a heap of rubbish. He put forward the view that the 'remarkable pile of sculls and bones close to the western entrance, regularly built up and intertwined with ivy', represented the mortal remains of the soldiers who fell at the Battle of Knocknanuss (1647), when a large army of Irish Confederate soldiers was defeated. This explanation was, however, put to rest by Richard R. Brash who stated that these were the remains of burials from Ballybeg abbey which had been brought to the Franciscan friary for reburial when the lands surrounding the abbey were taken over by a farmer. Although Windele also recorded that Fr. Buckley (1798-1875) had removed these for reburial in the crypt, their presence there no doubt contributed to the eerie charm the abbey held for the romantic nineteenth-century antiquarians.

Fig. 4: View of Buttevant friary from Smith's History of Cork, c. 1750

Indeed, despite (or perhaps because of) its 'complete state of decay and neglect', the friary attracted the interest of painters, antiquarians and architects alike. Contemporary romantic sentiment may indeed have contributed much to this appeal, but there is no doubt that the rich architectural and sculptural details of the friary buildings also attracted the more knowledgeable antiquarians, which most certainly included Benjamin Woodward (1816-1861). A junior partner in the well-known architectural firm of Deane & Woodward — famous for its design of Queens College Cork (now University College Cork), the Museum at Trinity College, Dublin and the Oxford University Museum of Natural History — Woodward was taken into the Cork practice in 1851, most probably on the strength of an earlier exhibition of the drawings he made at Holycross Abbey, Co Tipperary. Many details of his later architectural work, including those displayed at University College Cork, have been credited to his deep interest in Irish Gothic architecture, which is also evident in his sketches of Buttevant friary. Though Woodward's drawings were never published, and can now only be viewed in the library of the Royal Irish Academy, this was not the case with the drawings made by Richard R. Brash, a noted Cork antiquarian and architect, who became interested in the friary on a number of levels. Apart from publishing an account of the antiquities of Buttevant, accompanied by expert sketches, Brash was also able to muster support for restoration work in order to halt any further decline.

Richard R. Brash (1817-1876)
In the *Transactions of the Kilkenny Archaeological Society* in 1852/3, Brash commented on the 'melancholy fact that most of our national monuments are falling to ruin, and in a few years little will remain to us of the past, unless this and similar societies stimulate and excite national feeling for their preservation.'[48] Two years prior to this he had already written in *The Builder* about the 'neglect of architectural antiquities in Ireland',[49] and Buttevant was, apparently, the place which spurred him into action. He not only published a detailed description of the friary, he also set about making safe some of the dangerous breaches then noticeable in the walls of the church. In a somewhat

dramatic way, he explained how:

> A large portion of the north wall of the nave had fallen, there was a fearful breach in the north wall of the chancel, which hourly threatened a fall, and which in all likelihood would have broken through the arching of the crypt, destroying that interesting feature, and have left the east gable in a very precarious condition; the walls were full of breaches, and the tombs and windows in a state of dilapidation, added to which the rubbish of the fallen tower and walls encumbered the nave and chancel to the height of several feet, and the whole place was open to every sort of desecration.

Fig 5: North Wall, Buttevant Abbey.

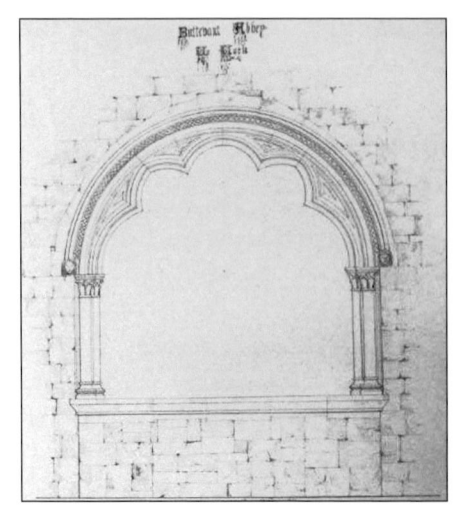

Fig. 6: Drawings by Benjamin Woodward, Ms 3 B 59, copyright Royal Irish Academy.

During the ensuing restoration process, Brash collected the many fragments strewn around the premises, particularly those of the cloisters, and incorporated them in what he called 'a sort of medieval museum for the curious' (Fig 5). Although opinions may be divided about the visual effect of this action, which displays the sculpted stones bereft of their proper context, he made at least sure that they were secured and thus preserved for future generations. Indeed, he may have come too late because, when commenting on the altar-tomb situated on the North side of the nave with labels 'terminated by carved heads, beautifully executed', he reported that one of them had been 'abstracted by an officer of the Buttevant garrison'. As Woodward's drawing shows, both carved heads had still been in position when he was in Buttevant a few years earlier (Fig. 6).

In 1852, Brash published 'The local antiquities of Buttevant' in the *Transactions of the Kilkenny Archaeological Society* and this was followed in 1853 by 'An account of some antiquities in the neighbourhood of Buttevant, in the County of Cork'. In the second article, which is mainly concerned with Ballybeg abbey, he was able to dismiss previous suggestions that the columbarium was the stump of a Round tower and to provide a detailed study of the history and architecture of the abbey. However, in his report on the *tumuli* of the neighbourhood, which he thought to be 'either memorial or sepulchral in character', he looked for *comparanda* not only in Ancient Greece but even in Siberia. Interesting, however, is his description of the 'once noble tumulus or barrow' at Kilmaclennan [Kilmaclenine], which had been opened some fifteen years earlier by the parish priest of Buttevant, the Rev. James Connery, who 'informed the people that he first heard of it in Paris.' Brash's informant was unsure as to what had been found, 'but the gold-seekers came afterwards, and excavated and ransacked the whole mound, and the farmers are now carting away the materials of which it is composed.' While Brash and his fellow antiquarians were not averse to some impromptu excavating themselves, he obviously saw himself in a more professional light than Fr. James Connery (†1835), who was an accomplished Irish scholar and used the manuscripts by his older kinsman Seán Ó Conaire († 1773), P.P. of the diocese of Cloyne and a member of the Society of Antiquarians. Although there are various manuscripts of the Ó Conaire family still extant, it is not known which was the 'Irish manuscript collection', which apparently also included transcriptions of the grave-stones of the friary, and which was mentioned by Brash and Windele, albeit in a not too flattering way.[50]

However, in his first paper, acting as an architect rather than an antiquarian, Brash provided valuable comments on, and drawings of, the friary. Regretting that notices were scarce in view of the historical and antiquarian importance of Buttevant, he nonetheless hoped that his comments would stimulate further research, and he would no doubt have been taken aback had he known that a publication of the kind he envisaged would not become available until more than a century-and-a-half later!

While writing appreciatively about the special attractions of the Buttevant friary, Brash had the knowledge that enabled him to place its architecture in the context of other Franciscan houses. Moreover, when deciphering the inscriptions on some of the grave-stones, he was able to correct readings and interpretations of such earlier writers as Charles Smith (1715-1762) and Sylvester O'Halloran (1728-1807), with the help of observations made by his fellow antiquarian, John Windele, who was then about to convert his interest in Buttevant into action.

The restoration of Buttevant Friary
John Windele (1801-1865) of Blair's Hill was the most active antiquarian of his time in Cork.[51] While his day job involved work in the Sheriff's office, most of his spare time was spent on antiquarian pursuits. He was a member of the Cork Cuvierian Society, the Cork Art Union, the Cork Archaeological Society, the South Munster Antiquarian Society, and the Kilkenny Archaeological Society. His special interest was in Ogham stones, and many of the stones in the University College Cork Collection were originally discovered, and often simply taken by him. His note-books and correspondence, now in the Royal Irish Academy, record his many tours around Munster, often in the company of his fellow-enthusiasts. On one occasion, while setting out with two companions, he described how they only had two horses between them, with each riding for 15 minutes and then walking for another 30. On arrival, he declared that this could be considered 'a good and saving method' of travelling. There are no such comments about his trips to Buttevant, although once, when travelling there from Ardpatrick, Co Limerick, he was moved to proclaim: 'Beamish & Crawford, my blessing on you: timely was the relief afforded at the cross-way house!'

Windele's documents, which are all the more valuable because of our ignorance of the present whereabouts of Brash's correspondence and manuscripts, describe the efforts made by Cork antiquarians to save the Buttevant friary from further deterioration. Windele, in the words of Brash, 'immediately set to work with his usual zeal and energy.' A printed leaflet, issued by him in Cork on 22 October 1850, expressed the anxiety which must have been felt by many concerned individuals at a time when monuments had not yet been taken under state control:

> Dear Sir,
> I beg to solicit your subscription, however small the amount, towards the Repair of one of the Walls of BUTTEVANT ABBEY. Its fall, now declared imminent by an Architect who inspected it with me, will, unless at once prevented, be accompanied by the destruction of the greater part of that Venerable Structure. A sum of £4 or £5 on the whole will suffice to effect its preservation.

Anxious letters to fellow antiquarians, Richard Sainthill, treasurer of the Buttevant Abbey Preservation Society, and to Crofton Croker were dispatched in haste. Stressing that he intended to raise £10, but aware of the fact that this was 'a great deal considering the low state of public taste among us', he feared that much more was needed. He went on to ask Croker whether he had 'found any Archaeological Samaritans with hearts compassionate enough to afford a fine old crumbling tottering Irish relic a mite of sympathy?'[52]

A volume of Windele's, entitled *Topography of Cork, Kerry, Clare and Limirick* (sic!), from the years 1818 through to the 1840s, also contains material which does not seem to have been written by him. Amongst the material not in his hand are a number of pages on Buttevant friary to which he added notes and corrections. In one case, he observed that the 'huge heap of sculls and bones carefully piled', some of which may have come from the adjacent cemetery and which blocked up the entrance to the friary, had been removed in 1833 by the Parish priest to the vault underneath the church. His own descriptions are accompanied by sketches and much effort was devoted by him to the deciphering of tombstone inscriptions. Although Windele's drawings are somewhat amateurish, he also included copies of Brash's more expert sketches, which duly appeared in the *Transactions of the Kilkenny Archaeological Society*.

Brash's efforts towards the restoration of the friary did not go unrewarded; some five years later, he was appointed as architect for the second building phase of St Mary's Catholic church. In documents relating to the selection process, Brash was described as an ally and fellow antiquarian of Fathers Matthew Horgan and Richard Smiddy, both of whom were, no doubt, friends of their colleague, the Buttevant Parish Priest, Fr. Buckley, who provided the materials for the restoration.[53] The antiquarian enthusiasm of Buttevant Parish priests appears to have persisted, as his nephew, Fr. Cornelius Buckley (1845-1922), was instrumental in the restoration of Lombard's Castle in 1886/7, as a plaque there confirms:

> Cead Mile Failte
> Lombard's Castle was reduced and restored by the Rev. Cornelius
> Buckley, C.C., 1886-7. God Save Ireland

The architecture of Lombard's Castle, more 'a substantial mansion of some wealthy burger than a purely defensive structure', according to Brash, received great praise from Windele. Although by then reduced to being the home of some labouring families, both Brash and Windele recorded the story that it had been built by a Galway man who found a treasure on the site.

Nineteenth-century romanticism

Local lore was, as we have also seen in Windele's account of Kilmaclenine, very much at the heart of contemporary antiquarianism and treasure seeking. Ninteenth-century romanticism brought about an interest in the past, whether this be marked by a revival of Gothic architecture, or by the importance given to local customs and traditions which were now, often for the first time, collected. It is no wonder, therefore, that Buttevant should also have had its share of legends, many of which were collected by Thomas Crofton Croker, particularly in his work *Researches in the south of Ireland*, published in London in 1824.[54] Some of Croker's material may have come to him through his friendship with fellow Corkonian Windele. Be this as it may, most of Buttevants ancient remains, the friary, the castle and the Augustinian abbey at Ballybeg, find mention in his work. Croker repeated Smith's theory, later to be discredited by Brash and Windele, that the heap of skulls in the friary were the remains of fallen soldiers at the battle of Knocknanuss:

> Close to the entrance of the abbey is a large square pile of skulls and bones, the relics of those who perished at the battle of Knockninoss, five miles distant from hence. It was fought on the 13th of November, 1647, between the English or parliamentary forces under the command of Lord Inchiquin, who was complimented by a pecuniary vote for his conduct on that occasion, and the Irish under Lord Taaffe; the latter were completely routed, and four thousand (half their number) left dead on the field.

An equally gruesome tale was reported of the castle:

> A legend relates that this castle was the chief residence of the Clan of Donegan, who rejected every offer of the English to surrender it, and repulsed every attempt made to take it; but it was ultimately surprised and captured by David de Barry, who gained it through the treachery of a soldier of the garrison. De Barry, having made himself master of the place, put its sleeping inmates to the sword, and rewarded the perfidy of the betrayer by striking off his head also. There was a small addition to this story related to me as possessing equal claims to belief;—the dissevered and ghastly head of the betrayer, as it went bounding down the stairs of one of the towers, yelled forth, in a sepulchral and terrible tone, the word—treachery!—treachery!—treachery!
> About the year 1812, in planting part of the castle grounds the

> labourers discovered, a little way below the surface, a human skeleton, with the appearance of a wig on the skull, which mouldered when exposed to the air; and apparently concealed in the caul were several shillings and sixpences of Elizabeth's: three or four of these coins are now in the possession of my friend, Mr. Samuel Richardson of Cork, and I recollect as many more being offered to me to purchase. There was no case or coffin round the body, nor was it buried in what is considered consecrated ground.

Croker recounted a further tale, which would have been tantalising for any antiquarian or treasure hunter, and which also had been told to him a decade or so earlier:

> Adjoining Ballybeg Abbey is a large field, called the Pigeon Field; in digging which some years since, a vault was discovered 'lined with images.' The person from whom I received the information added, that these images 'being handy to the road,' were broken up and thrown thereon to repair it. In 1815, the landlady of the inn, at Buttevant, gave me an account of a curious discovery made at Ballybeg Abbey, about five-and-twenty years back, by a blacksmith named Supple, who was induced, from a dream, to dig amongst the ruins in search of money, a superstition so prevalent with the lower orders of Irish, as to cause them, like the Arabs, to excavate near almost every ancient building, in expectation of finding concealed treasure. Supple, after some laborious days spent in disturbing the bones of the old Fathers, came to a stone coffin, containing a skeleton adorned with a cross and chains of gold, and a thin plate of the same precious metal stamped with a representation of the crucifixion. These relics were carried by the finder to Cork, and disposed of to a goldsmith, by whom they were consigned to the crucible; and the stone coffin converted to a pig-trough at the cabin of a farmer near the abbey. The accuracy of this narrative has been corroborated by a son of Supple's, whom I met accidentally, and entered into conversation with on the spot.

Almost all comments on Buttevant in the course of the eighteenth and early nineteenth century reveal a melancholy picture of past grandeur and present dereliction. The richness of its architectural remains served both as an attraction and a poignant reminder of what had once been and was now in the process of being lost. However, Buttevant, as I hope to have shown, had a second flowering in the nineteenth century. Once the Barry era came to an end in 1793, the new castle owners, the *parvenu* Anderson family, took the opportunity to style themselves in the manner of their medieval predecessors, or as they imagined it to have been. At the same time, however, they introduced new industry into what had been a rural community. Before they were forced to abandon Buttevant, the Andersons provided for the establishment of extensive army barracks, which brought prosperity to the town, and they also promoted the milling industry which continued after their departure. Although the Barry estate reverted back to the gentry in 1831, when it was bought by the St Legers from the by then bankrupt Andersons, the St Legers were never as interested in Buttevant as they were in their own *caput* at Doneraile. However, a dispute, which arose between the Doneraile parishioners and their rector, led to their patronage of St John's church at Buttevant. The successor of a number of earlier churches, St John's was now given added importance.

Not long after, the Roman Catholic Parish church of St Mary's was commissioned, and its funding through subscription over the next decade or so illustrates the prosperity which by then had arrived in the town. Although interrupted by the Famine years, this affluence ensured the success of fundraising towards a church building which was to represent a newly found Catholic confidence. Successive parish priests with an interest in history and architecture ensured that accomplished architects were employed with a view to designing a building which conformed to an image of continuity from the Middle Ages. Prominently located on the main thoroughfare through the town, St Mary's was followed by the equally prominent and adjacent Convent of Mercy, whereas the castle and church of St John's were confined to their hidden, if romantic, positions. Moreover, although for many centuries a 'fine old crumbling tottering Irish relic', the Franciscan friary now lay at the heart of both antiquarian and local sentiment. No wonder Thomas Crofton Croker could declare:

> The naked walls of this abbey are looked upon by the peasantry with the highest reverence, and thither many still resort to perform rites of solitary devotion. A small gravestone, marked with the cross, is placed on the shattered altar; and at the time of our entrance, an old man was kneeling before it, counting his rosary with an intense piety; having repeated there a certain number of prayers, he went from grave to grave, and from one recess to another, observing the same ceremony, and during the time of our stay, two or three devotees performed similar pious rounds.[55]

In sum, as the town gradually regained some of its earlier importance, it was its medieval inheritance that inspired many of the nineteenth-century buildings that still grace Buttevant to this day.

1. I would like to thank Eamonn Cotter, Albert Daly, Mary Lombard, Cal Hyland, Catriona Mulcahy, James O'Brien and Carol Quinn for providing me with important information. I also thank the librarians at the Royal Irish Academy for allowing me access to the Woodward drawings and the Windele correspondence and note books.
2. Lord Killanin and Michael V. Duignan, *Shell Guide to Ireland* (London, 1962), p 116
3. The two old friars which had formerly lived in the abbey, had previously 'begged about the Country': 'Report on the State of Popery in Ireland, 1731: Dioceses of Cashel and Emly', in *Archivium Hibernicum* 2 (1913), pp 108-156, at 122, 127.
4. Thomas Crofton Croker (ed), *The tour of the French traveller M. de La Boullaye Le Gouz in Ireland, A.D. 1644, edited with notes, and illustrative extracts, contributed by James Roche, Francis Mahony, Thomas Wright, and the editor* (London, 1837). Available online at CELT. [A translation of portions of 'Les voyages et observations du sieur de la Boullaye Le Gouz ...', Paris, 1653].
5. James Grove White, *Historical and Topographical Notes etc. on Buttevant, Castletownroche, Doneraile, Mallow and places in their vicinity* (Cork, 1906-1915), p 336.
6. Pigot & Co.'s *Directory* 1824: http://www.failteromhat.com/pigot/0025.pdf.
7. Charles Bernard Gibson, *The history of the county and city of Cork* vol. 2 (Cork, 1861), p 474.
8. For archival references, see http://www.landedestates.ie/
9. Jacques Louis de Bougrenet Chevalier de La Tocnaye, *A Frenchman's Walk through Ireland 1796–7 (Promenade d'un François dans l'Irlande), translated by John Stevenson* (first published Cork 1798; repr. Belfast, 1917; Dublin, 1984), p 73.
10. The following information is mostly based on Niall Brunicardi, *John Anderson Entrepreneur* (Fermoy, 1987)
11. Brunicardi 1987, 28.
12. Dictionary of Irish Biography 1 (Cambridge, 2009), pp 103-5.
13. Brunicardi 1987, p 80.
14. Brunicardi 1987, p 55.
15. Brunicardi 1987, p 107.
16. Brunicardi 1987, p 112.
17. Brunicardi 1987, pp 65-66; Grove White 1906-1915, p 4. The photographic album of the Scottish Captain Henry Brewster (1816-1905), while stationed at Cork, contains some of the otherwise rare depictions of the barracks and of the adjacent buildings in the year 1843. The album, is now in the Getty Museum, Malibu and the photographs can be viewed in: Photography: discovery and invention: papers delivered at a symposium celebrating the invention of photography, (J. Paul Getty Museum, 1990), p77. Also available on http://books.google.ie/books?id=XGHe5QQkmvkC&dq=david+brewster+photography+album+ireland&source=gbs_navlinks_s.
18. Second report of the Irish railway commission (1837-8), as quoted in J. Prunty, 'Military Barracks and Mapping in the Nineteenth Century: Sources and Issues for Irish Urban History', in H.B. Clarke, J. Prunty and M. Hennessy (eds), *Surveying Ireland's Past: Multidisciplinary Essays in Honour of Anngret Simms* (Dublin, 2004), pp 477-534, at 501.
19. Brunicardi 1987, p 75.

20. Prunty, 'Military Barracks and Mapping', p 478.
21. Paul McCotter and Kenneth Nicholls (eds), *The Pipe Roll of Cloyne (Rotulus Pipae Clonensis)* (Cloyne, 1996), p 29.
22. www.buildingsofireland.com
23. Lewis, *A Topographical Dictionary of Ireland* 2 vols (London, 1837), i, p 235: http://www.libraryireland.com/topog/B/Buttevant-Orrery-And-Kilmore-Cork.php.
24. Robert O'Callaghan Newenham, *Picturesque views of the antiquities of Ireland : Drawn on stone by J. D. Harding.* 2 vols (London, 1830), i, pp 4-5.
25. Thompson Cooper, 'James Caleb Anderson', in Lesley Stephens (ed), *Dictionary of National Biography*, 63 vols (London, 1885-1900), i, p. 382.
26. Thomas Kelly (ed), *The Engineers and Mechanics Encyclopedia by Luke Herbert* 2 vols, (London, 1839), p. 548.
27. The Farmers Magazine 1 (London, 1838), pp 210-215.
28. William Fletcher, *The History and Development of Steam Locomotion on Common Roads* (1891), pp 82, 143, 145: http://archive.org/details/historyanddevel00fletgoog.
29. Brunicardi 1987, pp 138-141.
30. The Doneraile papers have been catalogued by the National Library of Ireland: http://www.nli.ie/pdfs/mss%20lists/doneraile.pdf
31. Albert Daly, *A Corner of Buttevant* (Buttevant, 1997).
32. Lewis, *Topographical Dictionary*, p 236.
33. Charles Smith, *The ancient and present state of the county and city of Cork* 2 vols (Cork, 1815), i, p 293.
34. MacCotter and Nicholls 1996, pp 28, 50.
35. William Maziere Brady, *Clerical and Parochial Records of Cork, Cloyne and Ross* (1863-1864), pp 57, 59.
36. Pádraig Ó Riain, *A Dictionary of Irish Saints* (Dublin, 2011), p 58.
37. David Lee, 'James and George Pain - Gothic Architects', in David Lee & Christine Gonzalez (eds.), *Georgian Limerick 1714-1845* (Limerick Civic Trust, 2000).
38. David Lee & Debbie Jacobs, *James Pain, architect* (Limerick Civic Trust, Limerick 2005), pp 157-160. Drawings of St John's are included in James Pain's survey plans of the churches in the ecclesiastical province of Cashel, now in the Representative Church Body Library, Dublin (MS. 138). I would like to thank Dr Raymond Refaussé for allowing access to the material.
39. Lewis, *Topographical Dictionary*, p 70; http://www.libraryireland.com/topog/B/Buttevant-Orrery-And-Kilmore-Cork.php
40. Grove White, *Historical and Topographical Notes on Buttevant, Castletownroche, Doneraile and Mallow*, p 345. Grove White, whose family was involved in the dispute, had further gossip to add. He told how the family of Robert Crone, which had secured the townland of Byblox from Roger Langley, whose family had occupied it for nearly 100 years, and who made the drastic decision to give it up in order to disinherit his eldest son, were the cause for further discord amongst Doneraile parishioners and a subsequent increase in attendance at St John's. According to Grove White, Robert Crone's son, Major John Crone, 'made Byblox famous for extravagant parties and hunt balls. Unfortunately, he went one step too far in 1844, when he hosted a grand dinner party with music and dancing at Byblox on the night of the burial of his near relative, Mrs. Mary Hill, of Graigue. This evoked the fury of the local rector, Henry Somerville, who began a campaign against the wasteful habits of the local gentry from his pulpit. He also clashed with Major Crone over

the bequest to the poor of Doneraile by his grandfather, when the Major was unable to supply the rector with a satisfactory account of how the money had been distributed. What ensued was an unpleasant court case and permanently strained relations between the rector and his landed flock. This culminated in Lord Doneraile and other gentlemen of the area abandoning the church in Doneraile in protest.' The Doneraile papers, now kept in the National Library of Ireland, include papers relating to the case of Hayes, 3rd Viscount versus Rev. Henry Somerville concerning Rev. Lovell Robinson's 'intrusion on the duties of Somerville by baptizing the infant child of the Hon. Mr St Leger'. (2 folders 1844-70)

41. Mr Albert Daly, a representative of the Friends of St John's of Buttevant and previously a church warden, is of the opinion that this was the pew of the Crofts of Velvetstown, while he still recalls 'Lady Doneraile' sitting downstairs in the main church. I would like to thank Mr Daly for sharing his wide knowledge on the church and graveyard with me.
42. Albert Daly, *A Corner of Buttevant*, pp 17, 21.
43. David Lee & Debbie Jacobs, *James Pain, architect*, pp 147-148.
44. The following information mainly relies on the Biographical Index of the Irish Architectural Archives: www.iaa.ie.
45. R. R. Brash, 'The local antiquities of Buttevant, Co. Cork', *JRSAI* 1 (1852), pp 83-96, at 96.
46. J.R. O'Flanagan, *The River Blackwater in Munster* (London 1844; repr. Tower Books, Cork, 1975), p 146.
47. Samuel Lewis *Topographical Dictionary of Ireland*, p 236.
48. Brash, 1852, p 96.
49. The Builder 8 (1850), p 569.
50. On Donnchadh, Séamas and Seán Ó Conaire, see: Breandán Ó Conchúir, *Scríobhaithe Chorcaí 1700- 1850* (Dublin, 1982), pp 50-53.
51. On Windele and other Cork antiquarians, see Joan Rockley, *Antiquarians and Archaeology in Nineteenth-century Cork* (BAR British Series 454, Oxford, 2008).
52. Windele's appeal is also recorded in the minutes of the Cork Cuivierian Society, vol I (1850), p 181.
53. James O'Brien, *St. Mary's Church, Buttevant, Co. Cork 1828-1886. Notes on its Building History* (Rome, 2011), p 37.
54. Thomas Crofton Croker, *Researches in the south of Ireland illustrative of the scenery, architectural remains, and the manners and superstitions of the peasantry, with an appendix containing a private narrative of the rebellion of 1798* (introduction by Kevin Danaher, Shannon, 1969), p 113-118; also available on: http://www.ucc.ie/celt/online
55. Thomas Crofton Croker, *Researches in the south of Ireland*, p 115.

CHAPTER 10

ST MARY'S CHURCH, BUTTEVANT, CO. CORK 1828–1886:
Notes on its building history

~ JAMES O'BRIEN ~

The history of the building of St Mary's Church, Buttevant affords not only a precise identification of those immediately involved with the provision of a new parish church in the nineteenth century but also allows some insight into the world view of those people and of the profound religious values which motivated them and resulted in a religious *tropaion* bequeathed to their descendants.

Much of the building history of St Mary's can be reconstructed because of the survival of extensive material from its building archive. This is due to the diligence of Fr. Cornelius Buckley (1845-1922) who maintained systematic transcripts of many of the records relating to its construction.[1] Copied primarily from the account books of the parish of Buttevant, his records also included material transcribed from the books maintained by the building committees, which were active between 1829 and 1864, and from the registers maintained by specific members of those committees. Fr. Buckley's notes were probably drawn up prior to July 1886, shortly before the death of the then parish priest, Canon Timothy Buckley (1808-86). They refer to events as early as 1828 and terminate with several miscellaneous items dating to 1899. The material of immediate interest here dates from the period 1828 to 1864. These two dates mark the point of departure and the point of completion for the building of the new parish church in Buttevant. However, Fr. Buckley also records the installation of specific fixtures and fittings after 1864 – mainly during the 1880s – which are included in this account for the sake of completeness.

The transcriptions made by Fr. Buckley are invaluable as a contemporary source for the construction of Buttevant parish church. Through them, it is possible to identify all of the major phases of the church's building history. They detail those responsible for the planning and design of the new building. Most importantly, from a local history perspective, they identify those who contributed the funds necessary for the realization of those plans. Without this set of records, there would be little immediate archival evidence to identify the architects for the church, especially Richard Brash who carried out extensive works during the second building campaign of 1853-1864. Neither would it be possible to identify those who very zealously supported the building programme with their generous subscriptions.

Fig. 1. Fr. Cornelius Buckley (1845-1922), extreme left, attending a general council meeting of the GAA in 1888.

A supplementary archival source for the building history of St Mary's, Buttevant, is the *Visitation Register* of Bishop Michael Collins, Coadjutor (1827-1830) and subsequently Bishop of Cloyne and Ross (1830-1831). He made two canonical visitations of the parish, one on 12 June 1828, and the other on 24 June 1830. Not only does he note the spiritual and temporal conditions of the parish in his *Register*, he also comments succinctly on a particular problem encountered by the parish in its efforts to provide a new church more suitable for divine worship. The roots of this problem were to be found in the medieval enfeoffment of the Barry family, their disposal of the manor of Buttevant in 1793, its acquisition by the Scottish entrepreneur John Anderson, and the end of the Napoleonic wars with the ensuing general financial crisis and catastrophic consequences for speculators such as Anderson.

The picture of the building of St Mary's provided by both of these archival sources must, of necessity, be viewed against the background of the contemporary social history of the parish. To that end, the archive of the Doneraile estate, in the National Library of Ireland and in the Cork City and County Archive, contains much interesting material, especially with regard to the administrative overhaul of the Buttevant estate that took place subsequent to its acquisition by Lord Doneraile in 1831. Also of importance is the correspondence of the Buttevant Famine Relief Committe with the government's Famine Relief Commission which is conserved in the National Archives of Ireland.

The extensive manuscript collection of the Cork antiquarian John Windele, some of it dating from the 1830s, which is conserved in the library of the Royal

Irish Academy, is also an interesting resource for the local history of Buttevant and contains several important items which, unfortunately, do not appear to have been much used in local studies.

The foregoing primary material can be supplemented by extracts from contemporary newspapers, especially the *Southern Reporter*, contemporary printed sources such as the *Catholic Registry*, Samuel Lewis's *Topographical Dictionary of Ireland (*1837) as well as travel guides and commercial directories. A useful source of local information is James Grove White's *Historical and Topographical Notes etc. on Buttevant, Castletownroche, Doneraile, Mallow and places in their vicinity* which provides an invaluable record of many of the townlands of the parish and extensive genealogical material which was most useful in identifying several of the persons mentioned in Fr. Buckley's building lists.

With regard to the Gothic revival movement of the early nineteenth century in Ireland, of which St Mary's is a very distinct product, attention has to be drawn to several important scholarly works which began to appear from the end of the eighteenth century and which quickly became standard reference works for architects working in the Gothic idiom. Most influential in this literature are Joseph Halfpenny's *Gothic Ornaments in the Cathedral Church of York* (1795-1800); James Murphy's *Plans, Elevations, Sections and Views of the Church of Batalha, in the Provence of Estremadura in Portugal, with the History and Description by Fr. Luis De Sousa* (1795); John Milner's *Treatise on the Ecclesiastical Architecture of England* (1811); John Britten's *Cathedral Antiquities of England* published in fourteen volumes (1814-1835); and Thomas Rickman's *An Attempt to Discriminate the Styles of Architecture in England, from the Conquest to the Reformation* (1817). Also of importance is the corpus of ecclesiastical law enacted in the united dioceses of Cloyne and Ross from the mid eighteenth to the mid nineteenth century. The fount for this material is the *Monita et Statuta* issued by Bishop John O'Brien in 1755. These were subsequently updated in Bishop Coppinger's *Monita Pastoralia et Statuta Ecclesiastica pro unitis Dioecesibus Cloynensis et Rossensis* of 1821, and again updated by Bishop David Walsh's *Statuta Dioecesana* of 1847. The *Decreta Synodi Plenariae Episcoporum Hiberniae apud Thurles Habitae Anno MDCCCL* also enacted several statutes that would ultimately have effects on the building of churches in Ireland.

COMPLICATIONS

The diocese of Cloyne and Ross experienced a concerted programme of church building from the late eighteenth century which continued unabated to the eve of the famine. Within this period, practically all of the penal chapels mentioned in the *Report in the State of Popery* of 1731 had been replaced by more dignified places of worship. This campaign of providing churches to every parish in the diocese was especially promoted by Bishop Michael Collins. He had built the ambitious pro-Cathedral of St Patrick in Skibbereen in 1826 and was directly responsible for the building of a new central parish church in Ballyhea as well as in several other parishes in the dioceses where he insisted parish priests build proper churches. The registers of his pastoral visitations for 1828 and 1830 leave no doubt that he brought considerable pressure to bear on the parochial authorities in Buttevant to advance their plans to build a more suitable church for the parish.

By 1832, the general church building campaign had borne fruit with new churches in several of the surrounding parishes – (Charleville [1812], Doneraile [1827], and Ballyhea [1831] – following explicit instructions from Bishop Collins). In Buttevant, however, nothing happened and the penal chapel continued in use. On 12 June 1828, Bishop Collins visited the parish and found that 'the chapel [was] almost a ruin'. By 1829, it would appear that some efforts had been made to build a new church: a site seems to have been identified for it and a building committee had been formed. However, these efforts had been hampered by 'the unsettled state of the property which forms the town and a principal portion of the parish...it being under these circumstances difficult to procure a certain term of the site'.

The precarious situation of the Manor estate of Buttevant had arisen because of the bankruptcy of the Scottish entrepreneur John Anderson (1747–1820). By 1793, he had acquired the manor from Henry, eight earl of Barrymore, and had made considerable improvements to it. With the collapse of his banking enterprises at the end of the Napoleonic wars, and the dramatic failure of an investment in Welsh coal mining, much of his estate was lost or had passed to his creditors. When John Anderson went bankrupt, the Buttevant estate came under the receivership of Hayes, third viscount Doneraile who made initiatives to buy its freehold in July 1830[2] and eventually acquired it in 1831.[3]

The impossibility of obtaining a secure tenure on a site for the new church also halted all progress at diocesan level. While church building was primarily in the hands of the local parish priest who determined the kind of church he wanted and awarded the contract as he saw fit, he did not, however, enjoy complete discretion in matters of church building. Certain conditions and standards laid down by diocesan statute had to be met with before building a church. These were enforced by the diocesan Bishop. This was especially true with regard to the site chosen for the church and the terms of the lease on which the parish priest might have been able to acquire ground to build. In his *Monita Pastoralia et Statuta Dioecesana* of 1821, Bishop William Coppinger (1791-1831) explicitly required that no church building was to be undertaken in the dioceses of Cloyne and Ross unless and until the diocesan bishop's permission had been sought and obtained. Moreover, he required that no lease of a site for a church was to be accepted until such time as he had been consulted as to its terms and had approved them.[4]

The diocesan bishop's concern is partly explained by the need to ensure that the site for a church was appropriate and conformed to the general criteria laid down in works such as San Carlo Borromeo's *Instructiones Fabricae et Supellectilis Ecclesiasticae* (1577) and partly by a concern that a site could be held on terms that would allow it to be consecrated in which case something close to freehold would be necessary as a church held on a tenuous lease could not strictly be consecrated, i.e. perpetually and formally made over to God for the purpose of public worship.

For consecration, it was also necessary that the church be debt free – which was something that may have taken a considerable period of time to accomplish in some cases.[5] In Buttevant, however, construction proceeded on the basis of available credit and the initial expenditure appears to have been cleared sufficiently quickly to allow for the consecration of the building on the 9 October 1836. The Catholic Registry of 1838 records that up to that year of all the churches that had been built in the dioceses of Cloyne and Ross, St Mary's, Buttevant, was the only one to have been consecrated.[6]

Fig. 2 Fr. Cornelius Buckley (1798-1875) founder of St Mary's Church, Buttevant.

When he returned to visitate the parish of Buttevant on 24 June 1830, Bishop Collins had no progress to report on the efforts to replace the penal chapel. He noted that 'the chapel [is] an old thatched fabric altogether unfit for this parish or any other...[and] the multitude in attendance at the chapel [was] immense'. In addition to the legal difficulties surrounding the Buttevant estate, failure to make any advance on the situation of 1828 may also have been due to the declining health of the parish priest, Fr. James Connery (1807–1835), a noted antiquarian, Gaelic scholar and early member of the Royal Irish Academy. In his 1828 visitation, Bishop Collins noted that 'the state of this parish is such as may be expected when the p.p. is incapable of administering it and the actual administrators are unable'.

From 1817, a series of coadjutors had been appointed to Fr. Connery to administer the parish, the last of whom was Fr. Cornelius Buckley of Jordanstown who was nominated administrator on 23 September 1823. Following the 1830 visitation, Fr. Buckley appears to have assumed greater responsibility in running the parish and in progressing the building of the new parish church. It is interesting to note that in the transcriptions of the building accounts, this Fr. Cornelius Buckley is specifically referred to as the *founder* of St Mary's Church although he did not become parish priest of Buttevant until 1835 by which time most of the initial building phase had been completed.

THE FIRST BUILDING COMMITTEE 1829-1847

By 1831, the complications surrounding the building of a new church in Buttevant had begun to be resolved. The prime instigator of the work, Bishop Michael Collins, had succeeded as Bishop of Cloyne and Ross in 1830; Lord Doneraile acquired the property of the manor of Buttevant between 1830 and 1831; and Fr. Cornelius Buckley began to assume greater responsibility for the government of the parish with the increasing incapacity of the parish priest, Fr. Connery.

Lord Doneraile, shortly after purchasing Buttevant, presented a site for the construction of the new church and presbytery. It consisted of the ruins of the Franciscan friary with its attiguous graveyard to the north of the friary, in what had been its cloister, as well as the ruins of the Desmond tower and the vacant lots on the main street between two existing terraces. He made an additional contribution of £30 to the building fund. The church wardens in Buttevant also contributed some £20 for the enclosure of the existing graveyard.

The site for the new Catholic church was a prominent one on the main street of the town and, when built, St Mary's would become the principal architectural element on the street prospect. The siting of the church directly on the main street reflected the benefits of the act for Catholic emancipation of 1829 which removed the restrictions prohibiting Catholics from building churches or chapels immediately on the king's highway[7] In the case of Buttevant, the penal chapel was typically hidden away from public view in Mill Lane.[8] The new church, in contrast, is a clear example of the departure from this architecture of repression, as Richardson calls it, which saw Catholic churches built out of public view in alley ways or in side streets. It was a very clear statement of the self-confidence, optimism and prosperity of Catholics in the immediate post-emancipation era.

By 1831, plans for the building of the church, in accordance with diocesan regulations, must have already been approved by Bishop Collins and a foundation stone was laid in that year. The new church was estimated to cost something in the region of £3,000. This sum would represent a very ambitious building project for the parish. It would, however, turn out to be somewhat optimistic and eventually secured little more than the erection of the walls and the roofing of the building. The completion, decoration and fitting of the new church were postponed to later periods. As matters transpired, the final estimate for the building of the church exceeded £7,000.[9]

A building committee was formed on 31 May 1829 – six weeks subsequent to the passage of the Act for Catholic Emancipation.[10] It consisted of: Solomon Mulqueen, John Hutch, Thomas Blake, William Linehan, Michael Rogers, James Connors, Thomas Linehan, Snr., Michael Madden, Thomas Hayes, William Walsh, Edmond Fitzgibbon, Cornelius Corbett, John Upton Supple, and E. M. Darce, who acted as secretary. Its principal task was to raise the funds necessary for the new church. Three subscriptions were taken in 1831 (see Appendix 1). The first recorded list raised £282-15-0. The second represents the proceeds of an applotment levied on the farmers of the parish. It consisted of one shilling per pound paid in rent. Raised in two moieties in the Spring and Autumn of 1831, it brought in £411-10-0. The third list of subscriptions raised in 1831 consisted of an applotment on the farmers of the Lisgriffin part of the parish. It was stipulated that this levy was to be considered a loan to the parish of Buttevant to be repaid when the church in Lisgriffin was re-built.[11] The levy raised £21-15-0.

A further popular means of raising cash for church building in the nineteenth century was the celebrity sermon. Here, a well known preacher was hired by the parish priest to come and preach a sermon in the parish to which the public were admitted by ticket. One such sermon was preached at Buttevant in December 1842 and raised £41-8-0, with Fr. Theobald Mathew contributing £5.[12] A further means of collecting subscriptions for the Buttevant building fund was to charge entry for the consecration ceremony which took place on 9 October 1836. An advertisement placed in the *Southern Reporter* on 27 September 1836 offered tickets at five shillings each or £1 for a family ticket to admit five persons. The tickets were available from the local clergy and from outlets in Mallow and in the city of Cork.

The records of the building committee were audited five times between 1829 and 1853. The examination of the books carried out on 15 March 1839 showed that £2,811-7-5 had been collected since 1828. This amount included a loan from the Board of Works for £600 which had been repaid by 1839. Of the £2,811-7-5 collected in this period, some £1,495-19-9 $^1/_2$ had been subscribed in chapel gate collections.

The audit conducted on 16 May 1841 showed that £401-0-4 had been collected, mostly through the gate collections, occasional gifts and from the sale of graves.

The third audit conducted on the books of the building committee was effected on 26 March 1843. It revealed that some £457-13-8 had been collected in gate collections and occasional items.

On Christmas day 1847 a further audit was conducted and showed that some £344-8-10 had been collected towards the building account. As with previous audits, most of the subscriptions came from the gate collection. The sale of material from the old chapel to William Linehan had raised a further £5.

While a gallery collection continued from 1847 to 1853, and was audited as having raised £179-0-7 $^1/_2$ for that period, the gate collection was abandoned at Christmas 1847 due to the severity of the famine. Thus for the period from 1829 to 1853 a sum of £4,221-14-6 $^1/_2$ had been collected for the building of the new church.

The success of the building committee's efforts to finance the new church can be gauged by the fact that it was possible formally to consecrate the building in 1836 which would indicate that the works carried out were substantially debt free. On 27 September 1836 *The Southern Reporter*, amid concerns about a revolution in Portugal, the advantages of mangel wurzel sugar, teeth replacement, and advertisements announcing the arrival in Cork of consignments of Lisbon grapes, French brandy and Malaga rum, carried a notice concerning the consecration of Buttevant Church which was scheduled to take place on Sunday, 9 October 1836. The insert read:

This impressive ceremony will be performed by the Rt. Rev. Dr. Murphy, Bishop of Cork (sic) assisted by the other Prelates of the Province. The consecration sermon by the distinguished and Very Rev. Dr. Kirwin of Galway. A Grand selection of sacred music by distinguished performers. Admission by ticket, the proceeds of which will be applied to liquidate the Debts due of the Church. The Grand Pontifical High Mass will commence at 12 noon. Single ticket 5/-; Family ticket (admits 5) £1. To be had in Cork at Seymours Music ware-house; Gallagher's, Mallow; and from the Roman Catholic clergy of the surrounding towns and parishes. Buttevant, 27 September 1836.

The notice was repeated in the issues of 1 and 8 October 1836 in what was clearly a publicity drive to attract as many as possible to the consecration – the first to have been carried out since before the reformation.

FAMINE

The Buttevant church building lists are also notable for the interruption made by the famine and the consequent cessation of all building activities from 1847 until 1853. This area of North Cork would not generally be associated with the extreme destitution experienced in other parts of Ireland during the famine.[13] Nevertheless, the area did suffer considerable distress from 1846 and a full blown social crisis was in train by late 1847. The extent of the problem can be appreciated through a reading of the correspondence of the Buttevant Famine Relief Committee with the government's Famine Relief Commission (1845-1847).[14] By February 1847, the local poorhouse, which had been built to accommodate 800 persons, had 1,790 inmates, many of whom had already pawned all their possessions.[15] Jemima Deane Freeman of Castlecor House had, independently of the Relief Committee, collected £155 for two soup kitchens and appealed for a grant to the Famine Commission to match that amount.[16] In nearby Charleville, Daniel Clanchy, secretary of the local relief committee had to cater for 5,000 persons whose support had now fallen on 'the exertions of the shopkeepers and other industrious classes of this town'. In May of 1846, Christopher Crofts, secretary of the Buttevant famine relief committee requested a grant from Henry Laboucher, the treasurer of the Famine Relief Commission, as the level of destitution in the area was beyond the ability of his committee to handle. Drs. Cotter and Sheehan of the Buttevant Fever Hospital requested the Commission in May 1846 to provide funds for an extension to the hospital. By November of that year, they reported that some 288 persons had been admitted since the beginning of the year and they requested money for soup boilers. They enclosed a list of subscribers and hoped that the Commission would match the amount. That did not always happen, especially where the Commission decided that locally subscribed funds were sufficient to cover expenditure. In Killbolane, William Barry requested the Commission to make money available for 'the decent burial of paupers'.[17]

Clearly, with such a range of urgent charitable demands, building subscription lists could neither be maintained nor be given any priority. They were, accordingly, suspended until better times – and that is what happened to the Buttevant church building subscription list from December 1847 until it was resumed in November 1853 in preparation for the second phase of works which was eventually executed by Richard Brash in 1855.

THE SECOND BUILDING COMMITTEE 1853-1864

A second building committee was formed in 1853 to complete the church. Jeremiah O'Connor, a shopkeeper in the town, acted as secretary to this committee and kept the books.

While a gate collection 'was resumed on 1 November 1853 for the further completion of the church which works had been suspended by the distress of the famine years', a second applotment of the parish was also levied. As with the applotment of 1831, the amount to be paid was reckoned at the rate of 1 shilling per pound of rent. The 1853 applotment list was drawn up by James O'Sullivan of Boherascrub and realised a total of £338-11-9 (see Appendix 2). This sum represented a decrease of £72-18-3 on the applotment of 1831. While the 1831 cess appears to have been confined to the farmers of the parish, that of 1853 also included shopkeepers in the town of Buttevant. It probably also reflects a lower rate of rents being paid in the economic depression of the immediate aftermath of the famine as well as the problem of the shortage of money in the immediate post-famine years, a factor not without consequences in the land sales forced by numerous bankruptcies. The point is well illustrated in the failure of the Encumbered Estates Court sale of Castle Cor where the auction of various parcels of property had to be abandoned due to lack of bidders.[18]

Further funds were raised by means of a public sermon preached by Dr. Cahill on 22 January 1856. The event raised £85-15-4. This was augmented by a gift of £100 from Michael Rogers, a native of Buttevant, then living in the United States. Further donations were received from James Ryan, also in the United States, Miss Peel, Henry Munster, Rev. Laurence Mahony, James Morrogh esq.,[19] Mrs Harold Barry, Rev. C. McCarthy, Alderman Rynolds of Dublin, the men at Grange quarry; Sergent Berin of the 51st Regiment, as well as a sum of restitution money. The total amount generated in January 1856 came to £218-15-4.

At this time, a window fund to cover the cost of glazing the main windows of the church was established among the ladies of the parish (see Appendix 3). In February 1856, they contributed £38-16-0 to the building committee.

In June 1855, Richard Brash of Cork contracted to execute works for the internal completion of St Mary's. His tender was £650-0-0. However, other additions were made to the contract (including two side altars, 12 gothic seats, removing the bell from the new tower to the old one) which brought the final cost of the contract to £753-3-5 'which was paid in full (with something off) in April 1858'.

Brash's contract involved two major items: the building of the sacristy and the completion of the church interior by laying out the chancel, installing the ceiling and providing tracery and glass for three of its main windows.

The final works carried out by the second building committee was the enclosure of the church grounds by the erection of gating and pallisading in front of the church in 1863/64. While the buildings lists are tacit on the subject, it may not be altogether unreasonable to suggest that Richard Brash was also the architect retained for this work. 'The stone was got at Copstown quarry. It was cut by Regan of Doneraile. A man named Murphy supplied the railings and W. H. Lysaght is credited with the erection of the massive gates'.[20] The works in front of the church cost £224-10-3. With the enclosure of the church grounds, the building campaign, begun in 1853, effectively came to a close. In 1864, the gate collection, which had been taken from 1829, was given up and it was determined that all future building expenses would be taken from the gallery collection.

THE ARCHITECTS

The building accounts of St Mary's, Buttevant, identify Charles Cottrell of Hanover Street, Cork, as the architect for the church.[21] Cottrell remains something of an enigma to Cork architectural history and is particularly resistant to historical probing.[22] The earliest references to him date from 1816 and 1817 when he exhibited a number of architectural works, including a design for a steeple for Christ Church, at the Cork Society for Promoting the Fine Arts. He is subsequently listed as a builder or architect in several sources and his name is associated with Wandesford Bridge, Hanover Street, in Cork.[23] While John Windele (1801-1865) numbers him, with Deane, Hill, and Pain, among those chiefly responsible for the regeneration of architecture in the city of Cork in the first half of the nineteenth century, nonetheless, only one edifice can securely be attributed to him, namely St Francis's in Grattan Street, Cork City, which was demolished in the 1940s to make way for the present structure (Fig. 3).[24] A note in the Buttevant building accounts records that he supplied the description of the new church to Samuel Lewis which was published in the 1837 edition of Lewis' *Topographical Dictionary of Ireland.* The description reads:

> 'It is a very handsome structure of hewn limestone, in the later English style, consisting of a nave and transept, between which, on each side, rises a square embattled tower crowned with richly crocketed pinnacles; the walls are strengthened with buttresses at the angles and between the windows of the nave, terminating in crocketed pinnacles above an embattled parapet carried round the building; and the gables of the transept are surmounted by Maltese crosses, beneath which, on each side, is a cinquefoiled niche resting on a projecting corbel. The nave is lighted by a range of three windows of two lights ornamented in cinquefoil, with a quatre-foiled circle in the crown of the arch; and the transept is lighted at each end by a noble window of five lights, 26 feet high, and elaborately enriched with tracery: the tower on the east side was a detached watch-tower belonging to the abbey, erected by one of the Earls of Desmond for the protection of the brethren in times of violence, and incorporated with the present building'.[25]

Fig. 3 St Francis's Church, Grattan St, Cork, before demolition c. 1950.

This description, however, would appear to derive from Cottrell's plans rather than from the church as it was built since it differs in several points of detail from the actual building, e.g. only the west gable was surmounted by a Maltese cross (the east gable having a simple metal cross and the south gable having a small Latin cross), the absence of a cinquefoiled niche on the east gable, the parapet is carried around the west and south elevations only, the eventual tracery installed in the transept windows has six lights rather than five and was not executed until the 1850s.

Further discrepancies between the description published by Lewis and the church as built may be noted in its reference to the church as belonging to "the later English style" without reference to any earlier period of English Gothic. While Lewis's description is true of elements such as the depressed and hooded arches of the doors on the south and west elevations, the monumental windows of the transept, and the stages of the west tower, it is pointedly at odds with the transept doors on the east side, or the blank windows on the south elevation of the east transept, with mouldings copied from the nearby friary which clearly belong to the early period (1250). Perhaps too much surprise should not be expressed on this point as Lewis's description of Sts Michael and John's in Dublin, was subjected to similar criticism by Richardson. Here again, Lewis focused on the door mouldings of the façade to determine the period after which the church was built and omitted to mention anything of the periods to which the windows belong.[26] Lewis mentions the incorporation of the Desmond tower into the new building at Buttevant, but it would be hard to describe it as an example of the perpendicular style.

Perhaps these discrepancies can be explained by an editing of the material supplied to Lewis. By virtue of his use of terms such as 'later English style' it is obvious that Cottrell was aware of the chronological categories for identifying the historical evolution of English Gothic proposed by John Milner in his *Treatise on the Ecclesiastical Architecture of England, during the Middle Ages* (1811) and of Thomas Richman's refinement of the theory in his *An attempt to Discriminate the Styles of Architecture in England from the Conquest to the Reformation* published in 1817. As Cottrell must have known, and as was typical of Georgian architects working in the Gothic idiom, St Mary's does not afford us a pure or consistent example of the perpendicular style. Indeed Francis Johnston had employed a similar approach in building the Chapel Royal at Dublin Castle. Rather, like the English cathedrals, Cottrell's architectural essay incorporates an accumulation of stylistic phases which, in this case, embraces perpendicular, middle, and early English Gothic. Beneath the apparent disharmony between its east and west elevations, the church plots 'the orderly and poetic march of time, [with] each successive building campaign contributing elements in its distinctive stylistic voice'.[27] In this historical progression, the incorporation of the Desmond tower afforded the architect an opportunity historically to re-connect with the Gothic of the fourteenth century thereby asserting not only an architectural continuity but also a religious continuity with the historical elements of the site on which the new church was built.

Fig. 4 John Windele's drawing of Buttevant Friary dated 4 October 1833.

The earliest extant image of St Mary's, Buttevant, is a sepia drawing done by John Windele and dated 4 October 1833 and conserved in the Windele manuscripts in the library of the Royal Irish Academy (Fig. 4). It documents the progress that had been made since the building works began in 1831. The drawing shows the ruins of the abbey from a vantage point already used by Anthony Charnley for his engraving of the ruin published in Smith's History of Cork in 1752. What is of interest in Windele's drawing is his representation of the Desmond tower before its incorporation into the new structure. It is clear that the original crenellation has been embedded in a mass of some ten feet of masonry which was subsequently superimposed on the tower to take it above the height of the east transept of the new church. The drawing also shows the east transept gable which appears to have been recently built but which remains incomplete with elements of the internal scaffolding of the building visible above the walls. From the drawing, it may be inferred that Cottrell followed the traditional method of church building which began works with the chancel area, moved to the transepts and ended with the building of the nave.

Integrating the Desmond tower, a genuine element of medieval architecture, into his new church posed particular challenges for Cottrell.[28] On the east side of the new church, he does not use finely cut ashlar blocks but a more coarse rubble so that the east gable, transept and east wall of the nave would better resemble the building techniques used in the medieval Desmond tower. On the south and west elevations, however, he uses finely cut blocks laid in regular horizontal courses. While this latter method reflects the building techniques of Tudor Gothic, it was criticized by A.W.N. Pugin in his *True Principles of Pointed or Christian Architecture* (1841). Pugin, in his efforts to achieve a genuine medieval surface texture, pointed out that small and irregular stones produced a richer effect while large blocks laid in strong horizontal courses tended to compete with the vertical thrust of Gothic architecture.[29] Although built before the publication of Pugin's *True Principles*, St Mary's, Buttevant, illustrates both of Pugin's observations on surface texture.

It is also interesting to note that in a few instances in the buttresses, Cottrell used elements decorated with tracery copied from the nearby friary to augment the architectural and religious continuity between his new church and its medieval precursor.

Cottrell's commission for St Mary's at Buttevant exhibits a very assured exercise in an historiated English Gothic idiom. It is clearly the work of an accomplished architect who had mastered the principles of the Gothic revival as they were known and understood before the arrival of A.W.N. Pugin. St Mary's reflects the interests of the revival movement of the 1820s and 1830s which were firmly fixed on English models of the period between 1380 and 1450 and draws inspiration for its elements from many of the great English prototypes e.g. York Minster, Winchester Cathedral, Edington Priory, King's College, Cambridge,

Westminster Hall, and St George's Chapel, Windsor. However, Cottrell displays considerable originality in his massing of the church in Buttevant, particularly by placing the tower at the angle of the nave and transept rather than on the west front, as was the case with medieval English parish churches, or at the crossing which was customary in medieval monastic or collegial churches. While the original plans for the church do not appear to have survived, it is clear that Cottrell's original intention was substantially adhered to in the second building phase of the 1850s, carried out under the direction of the Cork architect Richard Brash.

In contrast with the elusive Charles Cottrell, Richard Brash (1817-76) is a well known architect and antiquarian with a substantial and highly accomplished oeuvre scattered throughout the county of Cork.[30] He was the son of a Cork builder and received his initial training in his father's workshops. In 1852, he exhibited three architectural designs at the National Exhibition of the Arts, Manufactures & Products at Cork. Among his earliest works are the Convent of Mercy in Mallow (1850), a flax mill in Bandon (1851) and a presbytery in Mallow (1851-1852). Brash unsuccessfully competed for the building of Sts Peter and Paul's in Cork (1859) but did win the contract for the substantial re-building of St Peter's, Dungourney (1869). Through the pages of the Irish Builder he expressed his reservation on Burgess' plans for the building of St Finn Barre's in Cork and on Street's re-construction of St Bridget's Cathedral in Kildare.

It is, however, as an antiquarian that Brash is best remembered. His posthumously published *The ogam inscribed monuments of the Gaedhil in the British Isles* (1879) remains a standard reference on the subject of ogham inscriptions. But his antiquarian interests also involved systematic study of ancient ecclesiastical buildings and especially of Round Towers. In 1875, he published a dissertation entitled *The Ecclesiastical Antiquities of Ireland to the Close of the Twelfth Century* having already published *Notes on the Ecclesiastical History of Ireland* (1872-1874).

Brash was an active member of the Kilkenny Historical and Archaeological Society, and a fellow of the Scottish Society of Antiquaries and of the Cambrian Archaeological Association, contributing regularly to their learned journals on subjects of antiquarian interest. For many years he was a member of the Cork Cuvierian & Archaeological Society, becoming its president in 1870.[31]

Richard Brash's first encounter with Buttevant appears to have been in about 1850 when, together with John Windele and Fr. Cornelius Buckley, he was a driving force in a restoration campaign to save the ruins of the Franciscan friary from total collapse. Indeed, the present aspect of the friary is the result of that restoration, an account of which Brash gave to the Kilkenny Historical and Archaeological Society in 1852.[32]

Sometime prior to June 1855 tenders were invited for the completion of St Mary's, Buttevant. The building lists for the period indicate that several tenders were received but the parish priest 'evidently decided to give the preference to Mr. Brash who was an architect, archeologist and local historian of repute, friend to the Windeles and Father Matt Horgan and Fr. Smiddy'. Clearly, Fr. Buckley must also have shared the archeological and antiquarian interests of the Windeles and of Fr. Horgan and Fr. Smiddy.[33] Brash's letter of tender of 10 June 1855 reads as follows:

Fig. 5 Richard Brash (1817-1876)

'I propose to execute the alterations and plastering at the Catholic Church of Buttevant according to the plans and specifications furnished by me for that purpose. That is one set of plans and a specification for the plastering.

And another plan and specification furnished for building the chancel and sacristy. In addition to which I propose to make and erect three sets of red pine frames in the window opes built up and to fill same with metal sashes glazed with C[oloured] glass.

Also to provide chiseled limestone window sills for the above three windows.

Also to flag with limestone flagging that portion of the nave where the platform is.

Also to fix a platform across the chancel 6 feet wide as pointed out to me by Mr. Buckley with 10 inch step and to cut fix and regulate all the railings.

The above work I engage to execute finding all labour and materials except sand and lime for the sum of Six Hundred and Eighty Pounds.'

Clearly, Richard Brash was retained to carry out two principal works and supplied a set of plans and specifications for both: to build the sacristy and to complete the interior of the church. In the former case he erected the present west sacristy, a mono-cameral unit with a large pointed window in the west gable and two other (domestic) windows in the north elevation. Presumably, the new sacristy was also furnished at this time, the principal items being in pine. In the latter case, the completion of the church interior was more complicated in that it involved opening three of the main windows of the building and providing them with tracery and simple coloured glazing.

The other significant item which Brash installed was the ribbed ceiling in the Tudor style, having provided a set of plans and specifications for what he calls 'plastering'. As an inspiration for the ceiling in Buttevant, Brash could turn to medieval prototypes such as that over the chancel and sanctuary of Edington priory in Wiltshire.

In addition, Brash laid out the present sanctuary according to the directions given to him by the then parish priest, Canon Cornelius Buckley. A platform raising the sanctuary above the nave floor was installed, and a subsequent platform for the high altar was put in place – although the definitive high altar would not be built until 1876 – and the sanctuary was railed off from the nave.

As built by Brash, the sanctuary has two doors as required by the rubric for the Solemn High Mass. These allow for the sacred ministers to come to the altar from the left and to leave it by the right. In the churches at Fermoy and Kanturk (built approximately at the same time as the completion of the sanctuary in Buttevant) the sacristy doors are more conventionally located at either side of the altar on the rear wall of the chancel. In Buttevant, this was impossible due to the constraints of the site. Instead, the problem was solved by having two sacristies, one on west side, the other (earlier) on the east side allowing the sacred ministers to come from the western sacristy and return to the eastern sacristy, with doors set in the west and east walls of the sanctuary. Both sacristy doors are in the pointed style and elaborately decorated in blind tracery.

The 1855 contract eventually included the installation of two side altars in the sanctuary, one at either side of the platform of the high altar.

As works progressed, other items were added to the contract including the supply of two side altars, twelve Gothic seats, and the removal of the bell from the new to the old tower. These further adjustments brought the final contract to £753-3-5 which was paid, 'with something off' in April 1858.

Fig. 6 St. Mary's Church, Buttevant before 1900.

FIXTURES AND FITTINGS

In 1884, Fr. Buckley recounts that 'a movement was set on foot to seat the church and carry out the internal furnishings of it and to erect a gallery at the southern end. Plans were got from Mr. Newstead, Fermoy, and the contract was given to the Galweys of Charleville. Subscriptions for this were collected by Canon [Timothy] Buckley and Fr. O'Connor' (see Appendix 4). He also records that the amount of money subscribed for these works, £301-1-6, fell short of the sum required to pay the contractor. In these circumstances, a sum of £250 was borrowed from the National Bank and a second charge was placed on the gate collection to repay the loan. The ceremonies held in 1885 to mark the completion of these improvements were attended by Archbishop Croke of Cashel and by four other bishops.[34]

1. *The High Altar*

The erection of the high altar of St Mary's Church, Buttevant, was completed on 12 April 1876 when the Cork sculptor Samuel Daly was paid a fee of £200.[35] The altar was intended as a memorial to Canon Cornelius Buckley, the church's founder, who had died on 4 March 1875. Subscriptions for the work were collected by Dr. James P. Sheehan in February 1876 (see Appendix 5). In addition to the altar, a tablet was erected in the church to Canon Buckley. This too was executed by Samuel Daly at a cost of £48.[36]

The memorial high altar was raised on three steps in the centre of the chancel and was free standing. The mensa was backed by an elaborate reredos of three bays on either side of a pinnacle which contained a crucifix under its canopy and the tabernacle at its base. The altar was flanked by two credence tables. In 1974, the high altar was inexplicably demolished. All that survives of it are the mensa, which acts as the current altar, and the columnar bases of its credence tables which have been deployed to act as plinths for the statues of the Sacred Heart and of the Holy Family following the removal of the votive altars which once supported them.

2. *The Memorial Altar for Canon Timothy Buckley*

The altar of the Easter sepulchre in the east transept was erected as a memorial altar to Canon Timothy Buckley, who had succeeded Canon Cornelius Buckley as parish priest and who died in 1886. The altar cost £50 and was executed by J. F. Davis, College Road, Cork. A further £30 was expended on the erection of a memorial cross, also done by J. F. Davis, which was erected in the church yard. The cost of the memorial altar exceeded estimates because a foundation had to be built in the church crypt to support it. These extra expenses were met by Fr. Timothy's successor, another Fr. Cornelius Buckley, and from the proceeds of the auction of Fr. Timothy's effects. Fr. John Kelleher and Fr. Cornelius Buckley acted as treasurers for the collection to defray the expense of the altar and cross. The collection amounted to £73-5-6. (see Appendix 6).

3. *The Altar Rail*
The Altar rail for the sanctuary was the gift of Mrs. Tracey, Rathclare. It cost £80 and replaced the rail that had been installed by Richard Brash in 1856. In the 1974 interventions, the rail was partially demolished and its gates removed. These were subsequently used as a frontispiece for an ambo in Lisgriffin church.

4. *The Pulpit*
The provision of a pulpit in 1884 necessitated another round of questing. On this occasion, it seems that the brunt of the operation was concentrated on the Cork merchants. (see Appendix 7) The usual contributors obliged: Murphy's Brewer, £10, Cork Distilleries, £5, the Mallow Brewery, £3, Philip Punch £1, William Egan, silversmith, £1; no fewer than three butter merchants (John O'Connor, Matthew Scanlan, John Daly) contributed £1 each; Lambkin Brothers, tobacco manufacturers, £1, Alderman Madden £1, Louis Egan, dentist. In addition, Archbishop Croke of Cashel contributed £5, the parish priest and curate, £5 each, Dr. Hutch[37] gave £1, Mr Waters, Shandon Street, 10 shillings, and £30 was raised from lectures given in Cork, Queenstown, Mallow, Fermoy, Charleville and Tipperary. A subscription of £10 was received from the United States. In all, £120 was collected for the pulpit which was duly erected in the church. The pulpit, as built, was of white Carrara marble standing on a base of red marble with green colonnettes. The pulpit was octagonal and had seven carved panels all in a late English Gothic idiom.

Unfortunately, and incomprehensibly, the pulpit was demolished in 1974. Five of its panels, two of them with an inscription, were inset into the present marble dado under the chancel window. A sixth panel was used as a frontispiece for a fixed ambo incongruously placed in the sanctuary. The seventh panel was used in a base for the tabernacle in St Mary's Church, Lisgriffin, while the red marble base of the pulpit now acts as a credence table in the same church.

5. *The Chancel window*
One of the most prominent features of the church is the chancel window (Fig. 7), supplied in 1886 by Franz Borgias Mayer (1848–1926) of the *Mayer'sche Hofkunstanstalt* in Munich.[38] The form of the window would appear to have been inspired by the great east window of York Minster dating from 1405 (Fig. 9). It is an excellent example of Mayer's attention to detail in providing a perfectly worked out architectural frame for the glass which has strong colours, naturalistic and exactly delineated figures, and a balanced composition within the window opening. The window displays excellence in design and execution and is the result of very sophisticated team work involving master painters, academic designers and highly skilled assistants.[39]

From the building lists for the church, it is clear that the prime mover in the installation of this window was Fr. Cornelius Buckley. He recounts that the window had been opened by Richard Brash in the works carried out in 1855 and, at that time, it had been glazed with simple coloured glass similar to the glass still extant in the south window of the church. Designs for the present window had been drawn up in the early 1880s but lack of a patron to finance the work delayed its installation. Fr. Buckley recounts that he had spoken of the window to Mrs. Tracey of Rathclare but, at first, she was unable to promise anything towards the new window. However, it transpired that, after her death, she left a provision in her will of £200, which was the estimate given by Mayer's for the new window. She intended that it would be a memorial to herself and to her family.[40]

The order for the window was placed in 1886 following a determination by Bishop McCarthy of Cloyne that the bequest left by Mrs. Tracey was to be applied to the purpose of erecting a new chancel window. The window, which was recorded as order no. 867 by Mayer (Fig. 8), was despatched from Munich to Buttevant on 26 November 1886.

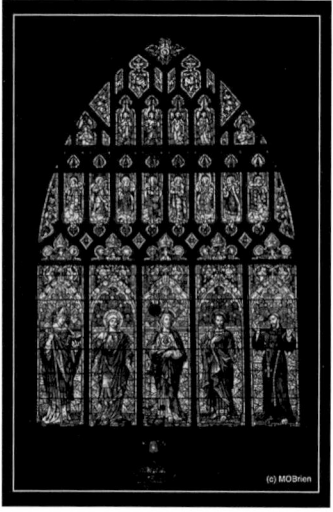

Fig. 7 The Chancel window installed by Franz Borgias Mayer of Munich in 1886.

Fig. 8 Extract from the ledger of the Mayer'sche Hofkunstanstalt, Munich, recording the despatch of the Buttevant window. (Third entry from top pg 221)

The five lights above the dedicatory inscription depict the Sacred Heart, flanked by the Blessed Virgin, patroness of the church, and by St Joseph. The outer figures represent St Colman, patron of the diocese of Cloyne, and St Francis whose appearance here once again asserts the religious continuity with the Franciscan tradition of the parish. The upper registers of the tracery are filled with representations of two celestial choirs of angels playing a variety of musical instruments.

This iconographic design appears to have been a standard one used by Mayer's changing the figures in accordance with the needs of particular churches. Shortly before the erection of the Buttevant window, Mayer erected a similarly designed chancel window in St Patrick's church at Fermoy with St Patrick as patron of the church, St Colman, patron of the diocese and St Bernard in reference to the medieval Cistercian abbey on which the town is built.

6. *The Transept Windows*

The transept windows, especially the west transept window, are the most conspicuous external elements of the building. The models for these are clearly English dating from around 1300. Two obvious prototypes are to be found at York Minster. Here the great east window provides the formal outline for the Buttevant window. The transept windows at York also provide further stylistic prototypes for those at Buttevant (Figs. 9 and 10).

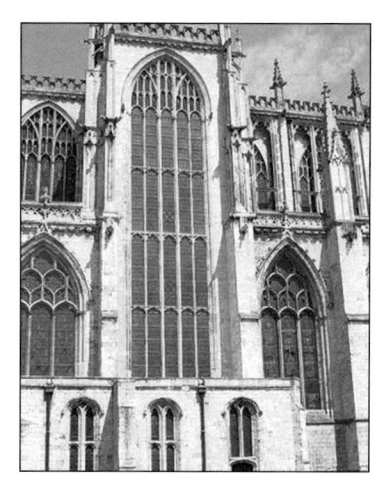

Fig. 9. (left) York Minster, east window. Fig. 10. (right) York Minster, transept window.

York as representative of the epitome of the 'chaste' period of English Gothic, pitched mid-way between the brute 'Norman' period and the decadent 16th century, had been popularized by John Milner in his *Treatise on the*

Ecclesiastical Architecture of England during the Middle Ages published in 1811. It is, therefore, perhaps not surprising that Charles Cottrell should have looked to York Minster when planning St Mary's, Buttevant.

According to Brash's contract of 1855, he was obliged to open three windows, supply cills for them, as well as red pine tracery frames to be filled with metal sashes of coloured glass. From the building lists, it is certain that one of these windows was the chancel window which remained in place until substituted by the Mayer window in 1886. It can probably be taken that another of these windows was the west transept window and the third was the probably the south window which continues to retain its original non-figurative coloured glass. However, the contract makes no mention of the east transept window and the building lists are also silent on that subject. This may mean that the east window was left blocked up until its present glazing was installed in 1906 when a copy of the west tracery was made for it. Otherwise, it may have been included in Brash's contract which, as the building lists mention, was substantially exceeded by the inclusion of further works.

The tracery for the transept windows was supplied by Richard Brash in his contract of 1855. The prototypes for the tracery are again English Gothic with the west window of Winchester Cathedral (Fig. 11) providing a very likely source of inspiration for the Buttevant transept windows. It is also worth nothing that the north window of Westminster Hall in the Palace of Westminster was rebuilt shortly before the Buttevant window and in a similar style. The tracery is an excellent example of the so called "carving-knife" effect so much criticised by John Ruskin.

Fig. 11 Winchester Cathedral, west window.

The plain coloured glass installed by Brash in the west transept window was replaced in 1906 when both transept windows were re-glazed with figure glass representing pendants of the ascension (east side) and of the assumption (west side) representing the specific title under which the church was dedicated.

7. South Window

The south window appears to be one of the windows installed by Richard Brash in his contract of 1855 and appears to be the only window installed by him to retain its original simple coloured glazing. Again, the window is inspired by English prototypes, the arrangement of a large "half window" over the main doors of churches being a hallmark characteristic of English Gothic.

An example of this arrangement, well known to the nineteenth-century Gothic revival and which survived the ravages of the reformation, is the priory church of St Mary, St Catherine and All Saints at Edington in Wiltshire built between 1350 and 1360 (Fig. 12). The west facade affords an example of the kind of medieval precedent which was followed for the main (south) entrance facade at Buttevant.

Fig. 12 Edington Priory, Wiltshire 1350-1360.

Figure 13 gives an impression of what the internal south prospect of St Mary's, Buttevant, would have looked like had the present choir gallery not been built.

Fig. 13 Edington Priory, Wiltshire, internal west prospect.

8. *The Sanctuary Lamp*

The Sanctuary Lamp was also erected during the works carried out in 1884 at a cost of £16. The subscription list reads as follows:

Mrs. Buckley, Jordanstown, Mrs. Ada O'Brien, Springville, Mrs. Roche, Castleisland, Miss Bethel, Thurles, Miss Bridget Sullivan, Miss Lizzie Morris, Miss Dunlea, Churchtown, Miss Maggie Culhane, Miss Mary Herbert, Mrs. Buckley, Jordanstown in memory of James Buckley; additional general subscriptions of £6.

9. *The Stations of the Cross*

Mayer's of Munich also supplied a set of Stations of the Cross at the cost of 10 guineas each which included a painted label indicating the donors of each of the stations.

Most of the stations were sponsored by individuals in the parish: the parish priest took one while his two nephews took another two and his niece took a third. One each was taken by Mrs. Tracey, Denis and Norah Nunan, Mr. and Mrs. Nagle, Mrs. O'Connell, Miss Blake in memory of Fr. Blake who had died in America, Mrs. Thomas O'Sullivan, The League of the Cross, the Reverend Cornelius and Norah Buckley in memory of Hanorah Buckley, and Mother Joseph Croke for Mrs. Tracey. The remaining station was erected by general subscription.

The Stations of the Cross were canonically erected by Dr. John McCarthy, Bishop of Cloyne, on the first Sunday of Lent (1 March) 1885.

10. *The Choir Gallery*
According to the building lists, 'in 1884 a movement was set on foot to seat the church and carry out the internal furnishing of it and to erect a gallery at the southern end. Plans were got from Mr. Newstead, Fermoy, and the contract was given to Galweys, Charleville'. The pine benches in the church were executed under this contract.

ARCHITECTURAL STYLE

The architectural style of St Mary's Church, Buttevant, is neo-Gothic. It is inspired by English prototypes and architectural features built in the period extending from about 1330 to 1480. It also incorporates some details derived from the adjacent Franciscan Friary dating from a slightly earlier period.

While St Mary's is a parish church, it does not exhibit the general ground plan of typical English parish churches of the fourteenth century which usually consisted of an externally defined chancel, a nave with side aisles, sometimes with transepts, and a west tower. Rather, the monocameral ground plan with transepts of Buttevant parish church reflects more the general form of English collegiate chapels, such as that at King's College, Cambridge, or perhaps Westminster Hall which, because of its legislative function, was probably the best known medieval Gothic structure in the British Isles.

The massing of St Mary's, which clearly draws on English models, is again a-typical of those same models, in that, for example, the tower which is archetypically characteristic of English medieval parish churches is not to be found in the west (or main entrance) façade but at the juncture of the nave and transept – which is also a-typical of English collegiate or monastic churches where the tower was usually placed at the crossing of the nave and transept. The tower itself appears to reflect something of the towers of York Minster or of Magdelen College, Oxford (1458).

In order to identify the architectural context to which St Mary's belongs, it is necessary to situate it within the general history of the Gothic Revival in Ireland, and in North Cork, during the first third of the nineteenth century. As will be seen, it shares many of the features of this particular strand of the revival movement and clearly drew on the prototypes inspiring many of the churches built during the period. While the revival movement was championed at this early period by the Anglican Church for various reasons, Buttevant parish church represents an early essay in the neo-Gothic style for a significant Catholic church and an almost conscious departure from the typically Palladian style more generally employed in the building of Catholic churches up to then.[41]

As a style for church building, the Gothic revival began in earnest in Ireland with the construction of the Chapel Royal at Dublin Castle (Fig. 14). Designed by Francis Johnston, architect for the Board of Works, construction had begun in 1807 and was completed in 1814 at the phenomenal cost of £42,000.[42] With this important and paradigmatic essay in Gothic church building, Johnston was hailed by contemporary commentators as the principal native architect responsible for the revival of Gothic architecture in Ireland.[43] The Chapel Royal set a precedent 'for intractable materials, heavy massing, aggressive profiles, repetitive detailing, [and] Irish iconography which were echoed for decades in [Ireland]'.[44]

Fig. 14 Francis Johnston (1760-1829), Chapel Royal, Dublin Castle built 1807-1814

The exterior side elevations of the chapel reflect an admixture of elements drawn from the various phases of English Gothic architecture. Tall windows, with hood moulds, from the middle English period are assigned to the galleries of the interior. Below them smaller windows with depressed openings are assigned to the lower stages of the chapel. On the north side, where the ground inclines, an undercroft is supplied with square-headed windows. The transoms and mullions of the tracery in the principal windows, however, are perpendicular. The north entrance is through a Tudor Gothic style door with depressed archway. Inspiration for the exterior of the Chapel Royal was drawn from Westminster Hall, York Minster and Christ Church Cathedral, Dublin.

The neo-Gothic made an early appearance in North Cork with John

Anderson's remodeling of Buttevant Castle (c. 1810) and with the Pain brothers' building of Mitchelstown Castle (1823). Through the Board of First Fruits, George Pain began promoting the style in Anglican church building with the construction of St James's, Mallow (1824), St Mary's, Castletownroche (1825), and St John's, Buttevant, (1826). By 1827, the Pain brothers were active in the rebuilding of the North Cathedral in Cork where they supplied the elaborate polychrome Tudor ceiling. They also supplied a similar interior and ceiling to St Patrick's Church, Fermoy, at around the same time.

Remarkably, Douglas Scott Richardson makes no reference to St Mary's, Buttevant, in his survey of early or Georgian Gothic in his *Gothic Revival Architecture in Ireland*, although he treats extensively of the work of George and James Richard Pain and of their work in North Cork. The omission of St Mary's from this survey is difficult to explain. Both in its conception and execution, the building exhibits many of the period concerns of architects working in the Gothic revival idiom, regardless of denominational adherence. While the Pain brothers executed their building projects to a very high standard, it has to be noted that their use of Greek Cross plans is anomalous in terms of the architecture of Western Christianity during the Gothic period and appears to derive directly from the classical revival of the renaissance. The Pain brothers certainly drew on the available vocabulary of English Gothic prototypes. However, their massing and consistent use of those elements do not display the more accomplished approach of Charles Cottrell at St Mary's, Buttevant, where no hint is to be found of any admixture of forms deriving from the classicism so excoriated by Pugin in his *True Principles of Christian Architecture*.

CONCLUSION

From the foregoing, it is clear that the building of St Mary's church, Buttevant, extended over a period of almost sixty years. The present parish church was not built as a unit during a single building campaign as tends to be case in more recent times. Rather, what emerges is that the building, which was massively expensive in terms of the population and means of the parish, was built in two main phases: the initial one extending from 1828 to 1847, and the subsequent one from 1853 to 1864. Even then, the internal fitting of the church would not be completed for another two decades: the high altar in 1875, the pulpit in 1884, the choir gallery in 1884 and the chancel window in 1886.

While the Famine was a very significant factor in delaying the building process, it is also clear that the prohibitive costs of the works which the parish engaged in required a long term strategy in order to raise the necessary funds. From the building records, it is noteworthy that the greater part of the resources needed for the realization of St Mary's was raised within the parish itself with supplementary resources mainly coming from the commercial hub that was then Cork City. Apart from one or two, albeit substantial gifts, practically no resources derived from the great centres of the nineteenth century Irish diaspora such as the United States and Great Britain.

The protraction of the building process over such a long period of time is also, in part, due to a conservative approach to financial administration which excluded borrowing from the banks or elsewhere to finance works. It is clear from the building lists that works did not commence until sufficient capital had been amassed and appear to have continued on a pay-as-you-go system. Apart from a grant from the Board of Works which was quickly repaid, the only mention of borrowing to fund works appears in the 1880s and then to supplement a short fall in the payment of contracts.

The building of the church reflects a high degree of social cohesion directed towards a common purpose which was achieved by a sense of commitment and generosity extending right across the parish. For the entire building process, practically everyone had, and availed of, the opportunity of contributing in some way to the building of the new church which resulted in quite a remarkable place of worship which was, and remains, a clear statement of the new found social assertiveness and self-confidence of early nineteenth century Catholics.

As an architectural essay, and in terms of expenditure, St Mary's certainly accomplished any objective that its builders may have had of rivalling the efforts of the Board of First Fruits in its provision of churches to areas of low protestant population density. This becomes obvious when the building is compared with the Pain brothers' essays in Gothic revivalism at St James's, Mallow, built in 1824 for £3,700, St Mary's, Castletownroche, built in 1825 for £1,250, and St John's, Buttevant, built in 1826 at a cost of £1,500.

It is also notable that the parish retained the services of two accomplished architects to design and build the church. Both clearly were aware of the contemporary trends in Gothic revival architecture and produced a competent essay in that idiom which is of local, regional and national significance.

ACKNOWLEDGEMENTS

The author wishes to acknowledge the kindness of those who granted permission for the reproduction of photographic material: to Michael J. O'Brien for his fine photograph of the chancel window; to Cork City Library for the photograph of St Francis's Church, Grattan Street; to Herr Wilfried Jaekel, archivist of the *Mayer'sche Hofkunstanstalt* in Munich, for the image of the dispatch register with the reference to the Buttevant chancel window; and to the Royal Irish Academy for permission to print an image of John Windele's drawing of Buttevant Friary. Efforts were made to contact the owners of images 9, 10, 11,

12 and 13. These have proved to be unsuccessful. The author, however, will be pleased to include an acknowledgement in any future edition should the owners so desire. The image of the Chapel Royal at Dublin Castle is by Jtdirl and is available in the public domain on Wikipedia.

APPENDIX 1 - The 1831 subscription lists

First list 1831:
Rev. Cornelius Buckley,[45] Lord Doneraile,[46] Messrs. Bemish and Crawford (Cork),[47] Samuel Perrott Esq., Dr. Curtin, Mallow; Church wardens Buttevant to enclose the abbey grave yard, Lord Egmont,[48] Lord Bandon,[49] Dr. Crotty,[50] Jeremiah Murphy Esq., Cork,[51] James Murphy and Co.,[52] William and Thomas Wise; Anthony O'Connor, Mallow; C.D.O. Jephson, Mallow,[53] Dr. John Glover Gregg, Buttevant,[54] Dr. Mac Fadsan,[55] Soldiers of the 51st Regiment,[56] Soldiers of the 22nd Regiment,[57] Soldiers of the 14th. Regiment,[58] Mr. William MacGarry, Buttevant; Mr. Richard Beare, Cork,[59] Thomas Lyons and Co., Cork,[60] Keeffe O'Keeffe esq. Cork, Mr. James Demson, Cork, William Harrington esq., Mr. Denis Lenehan, Cahirmee, Denis Murphy, Charleville, Rev. Lawrence Mahony, PP,[61] Jeremiah O'Mullane, Templemore, Mr. Joseph Morrogh, Cork, Mr. Charles Higgins, Mallow, John Walsh esq., solicitor, Dublin, Soldiers of the 58th Regiment,[62] George O'Callaghan, Mallow, Mr. Devine, Buttevant, Capt. Saunders, Saunders Park, Charleville, Soldiers 76th Regiment,[63] quarter master Kenny, William Wagget, Recorder,[64] Mr. James O'Brien, Cork; Michael Sygne, Cork; Carden Terry, Cork,[65] Dr. Verling, RN,[66] John Daly, Cork,[67] Mrs Wilson, 65th Regiment,[68] Mr. James Punch, Cork,[69] Mr. James Cremin, Cork,[70] Daniel Leahy esq., Cork, William Murphy esq., Cork, Cornelius Moylan, Granard, Rev. John Power, Ballyhea,[71] Restitution money per J.W., Mr. John Joseph Galwey, Cork,[72] Mr. Richard Malone, Cork, Mr. P. Hurley, Youghal, Major Galwey, Cork,[73] Mr. Michael Hennessey, Cork, Dr. Kelly, Maynooth,[74] Denis Kelleher, Ballinhassig, John Cowhey, Annagh, Captain Kidd, 22nd Regiment, James Morgan, Limerick, James Dennehy, Mr. Guinee, Liscarroll, Restitution money, George Harding, Doneraile, Mr. Michael Guinee, Sergant Marshall, Lieutenant Fontaine, Mr. John Byrne, Charles Williams esq., Mr. O'Grady.

Second list 1831:
The contributors were: The Rev. Fr. Connery, P.P., Thomas Lenehan, Ballincurrig, William Rogers, Spittal, John Hutch, Bregogue, Jeremiah O'Mallane, John Sullivan, Boherascrub, Denis Cronin, Boherascrub, John Supple, Grange, Thomas Blake, Knockbarry, William Lenehan, Knockbarry, Daniel Herlihy, Bregogue, John Connell, Tullig, James Nagle, Bregogue, Richard Hutch, Bregogue, John Deloughery and Brothers, Denis Coughlan, Kilclousa, Robert Heafy, Currymount, John Cowhey, Bregogue, John Clifford, Knockbarry, Michael Clifford, Knockbarry, Michael Connors, Farrangibbon, Edmond Cowhey, Snr, Bregogue, Edmond Cowhey jnr, Bregogue, Denis Connell, Bregogue, William O'Donnell, Bregogue, Maurice Stack, Bregogue,

John Walsh, Ballyvorisheen, William Connors, Ballinguile, Cornelius Coughlan, Ballinguile, Thomas Hallinan, Ballinguile, Matt Coughlan, Ballinguile, Daniel O'Brien, Ballinguile, Simon McAuliffe, Ballinguile, David Crotty Snr, Jeremiah O'Keeffe, Ballincurrig, Michael Madden, Morgan Madden, Owen Madden, William Madden, Daniel Crotty, Edmond Burke, Eliza Coughlan, Edmond Connors, John Connell, Jordanstown, John Sullivan, Denis Linehan, Velvetstown, Denis Sheehan, Miles Regan, Knockanare, John Regan, Michael Byrnes, Cornelius Garvan, William Elliott, Timy Cronin, Boherascrub, Owen Sullivan, Boherascrub, John Coleman, Boherascrub, Jeremiah Connell, Boherascrub, Thomas Sullivan, Boherascrub, Mrs. Geare, Boherascrub, Michael Browne, Boherascrub, John Hayes, Boherascrub, James Corbett, Grange, Murt Connors, Grange, John Madden, Grange, Timothy Stack, Grange, David Leahy, Grange, John Connors, Grange, Mrs. Sullivan, Grange, William Roche, Grange, Robert Healy, Grange, Denis Connors, Grange, Thomas Connell, Spittal, John Coughlan, Spittal, Cornelius Garvan, Spittal, Denis Sweeney, Morgan Sweeney, Widow Connors, Daniel Conway, John Bourke, Thomas Long, Thomas Beechnior, John Beagley, Joseph Coughlan, George Clancy, Michael Ryan, Thomas Williams, Widow Roche, Robert Pigott, Christopher Brien, Richard Brien, Horgan, Knockbarry, Pat. Mullane, James Mullane, Cornelius Collins, Pat Glover, Currymount, James Lenihan, Tenniscart, Daniel Connell, do, James Walsh, do, Timothy Horrigan, do, Pat Walsh, John Connors, James Ahern, Maurice Connell, Greggs, John MacKesy, Tom MacKesy, Tom Bourke, James Roche, John Fitzgerald, Grange, Widow Barrett, Grange, Widow Roche, Grange, Edmond Carley, Boherascrub, Edmond Connors, Boherascrub, William O'Brien, Boherascrub, Thomas O'Brien, Boherascrub, Jeremiah Leahy, Boherascrub, Garrett Roche, Boherascrub, John Roche, Boherascrub, John Daly, Boherascrub,Thomas O'Brien, Boherascrub, Fitzpatricks, John Carley, Watergate, David Fitzpatrick, Watergate, James Connors, Watergate, Roches, Kearney, Maurice Reilly, Copstown, John Cronin, John Long, David Guinee, Thomas Cowhey, John Hayes, Boherascrub, Daniel Connors, Boherascrub, Maurice Barrett, Boherascrub, Michael Sheehan, Ballybeg, Thomas Coughlan, Ballybeg, Cornelius Lenihan, Ballybeg, Michael Linehan, Ballybeg, John Cremin, Ballybeg, William Coughlan, Ballybeg, John Connors, Velvetstown, Michael Coleman, Velvetstown, David Coleman, George Ellard, Thomas Connell.

Third list 1831 – Lisgriffin parish:
The subscribers were: James Garvey, Drinagh; Thomas Barry, Templemary; Edmond Walsh, Garrane; Patrick Flynn, Ardaprior; James Regan, Ardaprior; Thomas Sheehan, Clonturk; Patrick Dundon, Ardskeagh; Jeremiah Connell, Ardskeagh; Thomas Walsh, Drinagh; Patrick Regan, Curriglass;William Guinee, Greymiles; James Fitzpatrick, Greymiles; William Donough, Greymiles; David

Regan, Drinagh; Daniel Warren, Ardskeagh; John Sullivan, Boherascrub; Thomas Browne, Boherascrub; William Regan, Curriglass; Denis Sheehan, Poulnaree.

APPENDIX 2 – the 1853 applotment

Those who contributed to the 1853 applotment were: Alexander McCarthy, MP, Currymount,[75] Thomas Lenihan, Balincurrig, James Buckley, Jordanstown, Danile Flynn, Boananagh, Richard Hutch, Tullig, John Hutch, Bregogue, Dr. James P. Sheehan, Jeremiah O'Connor, Buttevant, Cornelius O'Connor, Ballybeg West, Denis Coughlan, do, George Green, Grange, James McGrath, Cregane, Mary Sullivan, Buttevant, Daniel Herlihey, Bregogue, James Nagle, Bregogue, Timy Lenihan, Knockbarry, Thomas Hallinan, Ballinguile, Maurice Cronin, Boherascrub, John Sullivan, Boherascrub, William Lenihan, Grange, Edmond Fleming, Daniel O'Brien, Ballinguile, William Greene, Grange, James Sullivan, Grange, Simon McAuliffe, Ellen Hayes, Buttevant, James Woods, Buttevant, Morgan Madden, William Daly, Buttevant, Michael Sheahan, Buttevant, Cornelius Coughlan, Buttevant, Thomas Costelloe, William Blake, Lackaroe, Cornelius Buckley, Templeconnell, James Nagle, Knockanare, Jeremiah Sullivan, Boherascrub, Edmond Burke, Ballinatrilla, John Walsh, Ballyvorisheen, Thomas Hallinan, Ballyvorisheen, Maurice Carley, Grange, James Lenihan, Tenniscart, Robert O'Connell, Buttevant, Timy Coughlan, Buttevant, Mrs. Pigott, Buttevant, Mrs. Rogers, Buttevant, Miss Barry, Buttevant, Robert Barry, Buttevant, Patrick Barrett, Buttevant, James Hayes, Buttevant, Jeremiah O'Donnell, Miss O'Connor, Buttevant, Mrs. Walsh, Buttevant, John Roche, Buttevant, Miss. O'Connell, Buttevant, Mrs. Buckley, Buttevant, John Coughlan, Buttevant, Maurice Hennessey, Buttevant, Thomas Walsh, Buttevant, William Roche, John Sheehan, Ballybeg, Jeremiah O'Brien, Ballybeg, Edmond O'Connor, Ballybeg, William Lenihan, Ballybeg, Michael Lenihan, Ballybeg, William Lenihan, Ballybeg East, Michael Morrissey, Ballybeg East, John Cowhey, Ballybeg, Widow Carley, Ballybeg, Cornelius Callaghan, Ballybeg, John O'Connell, Ballybeg, Michael O'Keffe, Ballybeg, Edmond Carley, Ballybeg, Maurice Carley, Ballybeg, James Regan, Teniscart, Peter Sullivan, Teniscart, Patrick Walsh, Teniscart, Patrick Dunworth, Teniscart, Michael Madden, Ballinatrilla, John Guinee, Ballyvorisheen, William Connell, Boherascrub, Mary Coleman, Boherascrub, Morgan Byrnes, Boherascrub, Matthew Blake, Boherascrub, William O'Donnell, John Cowhey, Bregogue, Maurice Stack, Bregogue, Timy Mackesy, Mary Connell, Bregogue, Thomas Coughlan, Rathclare, Myles Regan, Cornelius Garvan, Tomas Regan, Knockanare, John Blake, Knockbarry, Patrick O'Connor, Ballinguile, Patrick O'Brien, Ballinguile, Patrick Connors, Knockrundaly, William Coughlan, Spittal, Thomas Regan, Spittal, Michael Ellard, Spittal, Luke Ellard, Spittal, Thomas Connell, Spittal, William Blake, Lagfrancis, Thomas Coughlan, Lagfrancis, Thomas Blake, Lagfrancis, Owen Madden, Kilbroney, Matt Simcox, William O'Donnell, Cregane, Cornelius Collins, Maurice Burke, Grange, Thomas Leahy, Grange, James Stack, Grange, John Madden, Grange, William Madden, Grange, Patrick Supple, Grange, Ellen Weldon, Grange.

APPENDIX 3 – the window fund

Those who contributed to the window fund were: Mrs. M.A. Walsh, Miss Leonard, Miss Coughlan, Kilclusa, Mrs. O'Connor, Mrs. O'Sullivan, Mrs. Coughlan, Mrs. Robert O'Connell, Mrs. Lenihan, Grange, Mrs. O'Connell, Ardskeagh, Mrs. Nagle, Bregogue, Mrs. Richard Hutch, Mrs. Buckley, Jordanstown, Miss. Barry, Buttevant, Mrs. John Cowhey, Mrs. Sheehan (Dr's mother), Mrs. Costelloe, Mrs Greene, Grange, Mrs. Ryan, Mrs. John Hutch, Mrs. Morgan Madden, Mrs. Burke, Mrs. D. Flynn, Mrs. Timy Coughlan, Mrs. M. Cronin, Mrs. Carley, Mrs. J. Sullivan, Mrs. Connor Buckley, Mrs. Weldon, Mrs. P. O'Connor, Mrs. P. O'Brien, Ballinguile, Mrs. Sheehan, Mrs. Dunne, Mrs. Pigot, Mrs. Guinea, Mrs. Dundon, Mrs. Tresey, Mrs- Owen Madden, Mrs. J. Linehan, Mrs. Herlihey, Mrs J. Blake, Mrs. Connell, Mrs. C. O'Connor, Mrs. Corbett, Mrs. Daniel O'Brien, Mrs. Fleming, Mrs. W. Greene, Mrs. Rogers, Bregogue, Mrs. Myles Regan, Mrs. Sheehan, Ballybeg, Mrs. P. Roach, Mrs. M. Blake, Mrs. Cunningham, Miss Sheahan, Mrs. Coughlan, Mrs. Burke, Mrs. Collins, Mrs. Egan, Mrs. O'Donnell, Mrs. Coleman, Mrs. Dillon, Mrs. William Connell, Mrs. Macksey, Mrs. Hennessey, Mrs. Leahy, Mrs. Regan, Mrs. J. Sullivan, Grange, Mrs. Coughlan, Mrs. Michael Madden, Mrs. Morgan Burns, Mrs. P. Sullivan, Mrs. Linehan, Teniscart, Mrs. John Madden, Mrs. Walshe, Mrs. Sheehan, Mrs. Lenihan, Boherascrub, Mrs. Regan, Teniscart, Miss Dwane, Mrs. Regan.

APPENDIX 4 - Subscription list for internal furnishings, 1884

The following was the initial subscription list which amounted to £301-1-6:
1. Canon Buckley, P.P., £5
2. Rev. C.S. O'Connor, C.C., £3
3. William Guinee, £10
4. Mrs. Buckley, Jordanstown, £5
5. Mathew Nagle, £5
6. Daniel O'Keeffe, £5
7. Miss Lynch, Balincurrig, £5
8. Miss O'Brien, £5
9. Mrs. Hallinan, £5
10. Thomas Garvey, £5
11. Denis Nunan, £5
12. Doctor Corbett, £3
13. Thomas Foley, £3
14. Denis Cronin, £3
15. Timy Coughlan, £3
16. Daniel Byrne, £3
17. Mrs O'Connell, £3
18. Miss Walsh, £3
19. John Coleman, Snr., £3
20. Miss Ellie Corbett, £3
21. Mr. Ellard, £3
22. William Coughlan, £3
23. Mrs. Nagle, £3
24. James Culhane, £3
25. Daniel Flynn, £3
26. Pat Frawley, £3
27. Denis Connell, £3
28. Arthur O'Leary, £3
29. Tim Sheahan, £3
30. Jeremiah Connell, £3
31. Daniel O'Brien, £3
32. William Lenehan, Grange, £3
33. James Mullins, £3
34. Daniel Coughlan, Kilclousha, £3
35. John Harold Barry, £3
36. P. Walsh, Kilmallock, £3
37. Michael Hayes, £2
38. James Condon, £2
39. T. Sullivan, £2

40. William Coughlan, £2
41. William Daly, £2
42. William Connell, 32
43. Thomas Russell, £2
44. Timy Stack, £2
45. David Herlihy, £2
46. Matthew Burke, £2
47. Daniel Madden, £2
48. Mrs. Madden, £2
49. Garrett Fleming, £2
50. Eugene Sullivan, £2
51. William Coleman, Boherascrub, £2
52. Con Nunan, £2
53. J. W. Coleman, £2
54. Miss Blake, £2
55. Denis Dundon, £2
56. William Greene, £2
57. Mrs. Lynch, Bregogue, £2
58. William Hallinan, £2
59. James Cronin, Boherascrub, £2
60. Miss Carley, £2
61. Frank Blake, £2
62. Maurice Hickey, £2
63. Matthew Blake, £3
64. Patrick O'Connor, £1
65. Tom Barry, £1
66. Mr. Ryan, £1
67. Denis Fitzpatrick, £1
68. Myles Regan, £1
69. Thomas Walsh, £1
70. Patrick Sims, £1
71. Thomas Beechnior, £1
72. Mrs. Cowhey, 31
73. John Roche, £1
74. Miss Quinn, £1
75. Bridget Costelloe, £1
76. Timy Lenahane, £1
77. John Mackesy, £1
78. Mrs. McDonald, £1
79. James Barry, £1
80. Martin Gorey, £1
81. John Connell, £1

82. Timy Cronin, Ardaprior, £1
83. David O'Leary, £1
84. Mrs. Warren, £1
85. Maurice Foley, £1
86. Edward Hutch, £1
87. Mrs. Morris, £1
88. Cleary and Company, Cork, £1
89. J. Madden, Grange, £1
90. William Tobin, £1
91. Timy Egan, £1
92. James Lenihan, Ballybeg £1
93. John Barry, £1
94. Con Lucy, £1
95. Charles Corbett, £1
96. Michael Hannon, £1
97. Richard Hutch, £1
98. Mrs. Cleary, £1
99. Nat. Simcox, £1
100. James Greene, Ballygrace, £1
101. Dan Murphy, Egmont, £1
102. George Carley, £1
103. Patrick Corke, Twopothouse, £1
104. Patrick Walsh, Station, £1
105. Rev. J. Buckley, Mourne Abbey, £1
106. Rev. P.J. Doyle, Castlemagner, £1
107. Thomas Lynch, 17/6
108. Michael Motherway, 10/
109. Maurice Walsh, 10/
110. William Lenihan, Smith 10/
111. James Coughlan, £1
112. Mary Keeffe, £1
113. Con Barry, 10/
114. Roger O'Donnell, 10/
115. Mrs. Houlihan, 10/
116. Thomas Henry Ryan, 10/
117. Mrs. Kenealey, 10/
118. Robert McCarthy, 10/
119. Michael Saunders, 10/
120. Mrs. Callaghan, 10/
121. Patrick Barrett, £1
122. Peter Sullivan, £1
123. Mrs. Lenahan, 10/

124. Thomas Harris, 10/
125. Micahel Sheehan, 10/
126. John Cronin, 10/
127. Mrs. Garvan, 10/
128. Constabulary, 12/6
129. Thomas Leahy, 10/
130. James Stack, 10/
131. John Ryan, Lisgriffin, 10/
132. Michael Rogers, 10/
133. Miss Lee, 7/6
134. Mrs. Conway, 5/
135. Mrs. McDermot, 5/
136. Michael Sims, 5/
137. Robert O'Brien, 5/
138. Nannie Regan, 5/
139. John Barry, 5/
140. John Sheedy, 5/
141. Mrs. Roche, 5/
142. Mrs. Monahan, 5/
143. Patt Nolan, 5/
144. Phil Fahy, 5/
145. John Curtin, 5/
146. Mrs. Saunders, 5/
147. James Dempsey, 10/
148. Mrs. Harrington, 5/
149. Paddy Collins, 5/
150. Con Kelleher, 5/
151. Francis Flannry, 5/
152. Denis Barrett, 5/
153. William Coughlan, 5/
154. Lizzie Callaghan, 5/
155. Smaller sums £6-14-0
156. Messers Murphy, Cork, £25
157. Distilleries, Cork, £5
158. Beamish and Crawford, £10
159. Harley and Co., £2

APPENDIX 5 - subscription list for the high altar, February 1876:

1. Anonymous, £100
2. Dr. Sheehan, £20
3. Rev. T. Canon Buckley, £10
4. Rev. C. Buckley, £10
5. A.M. Darce, Fermoy, £10
6. Thomas Waters, Cork, £10
7. The Most Rev. Dr. McCarthy, £5
8. John Purcell, J.P., £5
9. John H. Barry, Ballyvonare, £5
10. James Murphy, Dublin, £5
11. Michael O'Grady, Limerick, £5
12. Dr. Reardon, Doneraile, £5
13. Captain Stewart, Springfort Hall, £5[76]
14. James Buckley, Jordanstown, £5
15. Mrs. Tracey and Patrick Walsh, £5
16. James McCarthy, Currymount, £5
17. Tim Hennessey, Cregane, £3
18. Michael O'Connor, Newtown, £3
19. Charles Stewart, London, £2
20. Archdeacon O'Regan, £2
21. The Very. Rev. Dr. Dilworth, £2
22. Jeremiah O'Grady, Patrickswell, £2
23. The Rev. E. Neville, £2
24. The Rev. J. Barry, Glauntahane, £2
25. Miss O'Geran, Killura, £2
26. Mr. McGarry, Castleview, £2
27. Mr. Nagle, Liskelly, £2
28. Mr. Daniel Flinn, Boana, £2
29. The Rev. John Ryan, Ballyhea, £1
30. The Rev. C. Cahill, Charleville, £1
31. Dr. Walsh, Buttevant, £1
32. Dr. Corbett, Buttevant, £1
33. James Murphy, London, £1
34. Abraham Sutton and Son, Cork £1

APPENDIX 6 - list of subscribers for the memorial altar for Canon Buckley:

1. Mother Joseph Croke, £5
2. Most Rev. Dr. McCarthy, £2
3. Rev. C. Buckley, £3
4. Rev. J. Kelleher, £2
5. Fr. Ashlin, £2
6. Archdeacon Cullinan, £1
7. Very Rev. Canon Walsh, £1
8. Fr. Blake, St Colman's, £1
9. Rev. M. Walsh, £1
10. Rev. T.C. Buckley, £1
11. Rev. R. Aherne, £1
12. Rev. Thomas Rice, P.P., £1
13. Colonel Davidson, £1
14. Mr. C. Buckley, Mallow, £1
15. Mrs. Buckley, Mallow, £1
16. Mrs Buckley, Jordanstown, £1
17. Mr. Oliver, Mills, £1
18. Dr. Corbett, £1
19. Mr. Arthur O'Leary, £1
20. Thomas Foley, £1
21. J. Lenahan, £1
22. Thomas Ryan, £1
23. P. Frawley, £1
24. W. Daly, £1
25. Mrs. Kinkead, £1
26. Mr. Denis Nunan, £1
27. Fr. Lee, Kilfinane,
28. Mrs. Cunningham, £1
29. Mrs. Lynch, Ballincurrig
30. Cork Distilleries, £3
31. Mr. J. H. Barry, £2
32. Miss.Walsh, £1
33. Mr. Roche, Sol., Castleisland, £1
34. Mr. Taylor, £1
35. Mr. Thomas Sullivan, £1
36. Mr. Thomas O'Brien, £1
37. Mr. Denis Cronin, £1
38. Mr. William Greene, £1
39. Mr. Ball, Charleville, £1

40. Mr. Kearns, Charleville, £1
41. Fr. Doyle, PP, £1
42. Captain Stewart, £1
43. Fr. Ellard, Shanklin, £1
44. Patrick Galwey, £1
45. Patrick O'Leary, Cork, 10/
46. Miss. Costelloe, 10/
47. Miss. Dundon, 10/
48. Jeremiah O'Connell, 10/
49. John Coleman snr, 10/
50. Mrs. Ellard, 10/
51. Mr. James Culhane, 10/
52. Mrs. Blake, 10/
53. John Coleman, 10/
54. Edward Dunlea, Churchtown, 10/
55. Mrs. Cronin, 10/
56. Mrs. Motherway, 10/
57. Thomas Walsh, 10/
58. John Mackesy, 10/
59. Mrs. Cowhey, 10/
60. Maurice Roche, 10/
61. Daniel McCarthy, Mallow, 10/
62. Mrs. O'Connell, 10/
63. William Coleman, 10/
64. Mrs. Garvey, 10/
65. James Dempsey, 10/
66. Constabulary 10/6
67. Mr. Bullen, Mallow, £1
68. Mr. Dan Regan, 10/
69. Daniel O'Brien, Ballinguile, 10/
70. James Coughlan, 7/6
71. Mrs. McDonald, 7/6
72. Mrs. Mulcahy, 7/6
73. Mrs. Julia McAuliffe, 5/
74. Mrs. J. Regan, 5/
75. William Linehan, 5/
76. Mr. Hutton, 5/
77. J. Connell, Ballybeg, 5/
78. James Cahill, 5/
79. Denis Ring, 5/
80. Mrs. Houlihan, 5/
81. Miss Kate Conroy, 5/

82. Thomas Coughlan, 2/6
83. John Dogherty, 2/6
84. Mr. John Regan, 2/6
85. Miss. Lee, 2/6
86. Miss. Fitzpatrick, 2/6
87. Philip Moloney (sculptor, Ballyclough), 2/6

APPENDIX 7 - subscription list for the pulpit, collected in 1884:

1. Lady's Well Brewery, £10
2. Francis Sullivan, Philadelphia, £10
3. Archbishop Croke, £5
4. Cork Distilleries, £5
5. Brewery Mallow, £3
6. Canon Buckley, £3
7. Very Rev. Dr. Browne, Maynooth, £2
8. Samuel Daly, Cork £2
9. William Egan and Sons, Cork, £1
10. Louis Egan, dentist, £1
11. Philip Punch, Cork, £1
12. Thomas Burke, Kanturk, £1
13. E. A. Beytagh, Solicitor, £1
14. Edward O'Connor, Mallow, £1
15. Stephen Perry, Cork, £1
16. Cornelius Buckley, Mallow, £1
17. Denis Flynn, Cork, £1
18. John Leader, Cork, £1
19. Charles Sugrue, Cork, £1
20. John O'Connor, Butter Merchant, £1
21. Mathew Scanlan, Butter Merchant, £1
22. John Daly, Butter Merchant, £1
23. Patrick Riordan, £1
24. Lambkin Brothers, £1
25. Alderman Madden, £1
26. George Reynolds, £1
27. Michael Barry, Belgrave Place, £1
28. Francis Lyons and Co, £5
29. Dominic Daly, £1
30. James O'Connor, £1
31. B. J. Alcock, £1
32. John Harte, Queen's Counsel, £1
33. Edmond Dunlae, Churchtown, £1
34. Mrs. Buckley, Jordanstown, £1
35. Miss Walsh, Ballyvorisheen, £1
36. Rev. Dr. Hutch, £1
37. Rev. Michael O'Connor, £1
38. Rev. James Barry, PP, £1
39. Rev. P.J. O'Callaghan, Adm. Fermoy, £1
40. Jeremiah Roche, Solicitor, £1

41. Joseph Cremin and two Companions in the USA, £3
42. Thomas Bresnan, 10/
43. Edmond Walsh, 10/
44. M. Jones, 10/
45. Alex McCarthy, 10/
46. William Lunham, Cork, 10/
47. Dominic Cronin, Cork, 10/
48. Mrs. Waters, Shandon St, 10/
49. Mrs. P.J. Sheehan, Mallow, 10/
50. Michael Ryan, Bruree, 10/
51. Mr. J. H. Barry, Ballyvonare, 10/
52. Declan Clancy and Michael Harding, 10/
53. Rev. Martin Hennessey, 10/
54. Proceeds of lectures in Cork, Queenstown, Charleville, Tipperary and Mallow, £30.

---

1. Fr. Cornelius Buckley (1845-1922) was born at Jordanstown, Buttevant. Ordained in 1869, he served in the parishes of Ballyclough, Kanturk and Buttevant. He was a cousin of Canon Timothy Buckley (1808-1886). An ardent promoter of Gaelic games, Cornelius Buckley was involved with the GAA from its inception. The Buttevant GAA pitch is named for him. A number of items from his papers survive. See Jim McCarthy, 'Priests of Buttevant and Churchtown' in *Mallow Field Club Journal*, no. 8 [1990], pp. 132-136.
2. Cork City and County Archives, U188 [Doneraile papers], Box 1/ f.10/7, letter 15 July 1830.
3. John Robert Robinson, *The Last Earls of Barrymore* 1769-1824 (London, 1894), p. 248. Robinson also mentions that Barrymore made a life reservation of £3,000 for himself and a further life reservation for his countess of £1,000 on the estate. Such charges made it difficult to assess the annual value of the estate with the former continuing until the earl's death in Paris on 18 December 1823 and the latter until the death of the Countess of Barrymore on 6 May 1832. Indeed, what appears to have been the final settlement paid to the Countess of Barrymore was discharged on 27 March 1835 (See Cork City and County Archives, U188 [Doneraile papers], Box 2/f.13/24, receipt of 27 March 1835). See also Richard Brash, 'Local Antiquities of Buttevant' in *The Transactions of the Kilkenny Archaeological Society*, vol. 2 (1852-3), p. 87; Susan O'Loghlen and Ciara McDonnell, Collection List no.62: The Doneraile Papers (National Library of Ireland, 1998-2002), p. 9.
4. 'Quandocumque sacellum aedificandum est caveat parochus ne hoc opus aggrediatur antequam Ordinarii consensum postulaverit obtinueritque, non solum quoad situm sed etiam quoad terminum aliasque locationis conditiones' [William Coppinger, *Monita pastoralia et statuta ecclesiastica pro unitis dioecesibus Cloynensi et Rossensi*', (Cork, 1821)].
5. Fr. Murray, parish priest of Castlehaven, acquired a lease for the site of St Barrahane's from Lt. Col. Townsend in 1840 and built the church by 1841. However, it was not consecrated until 30 September 1883. Cf. James Coombes, 'Catholic Churches of the Nineteenth Century:

Some Newspaper Sources' in *The Journal of the Cork Historical and Archaeological Society*, vol. LXXX [1975], no. 213, p. 7.

6. Catholic Registry (1838), London 1838, p. 380: 'The chapels in this diocese, as in most other places of Ireland, have been very much improved. The only one as yet consecrated is that at Buttevant; the ceremony was performed on the second Sunday of October 1836. The building stands pre-eminent amongst the many beautiful churches that have lately been erected in this country. It is built near the old abbey of the Franciscan order, one of the best preserved in the South of Ireland. The style of architecture is Gothic, the design beautiful and chaste, executed in cut stone'.
7. Prior to Catholic emancipation in 1829, it was not uncommon to evade the law by acquiring two sites, one in front of the other. The site on the king's highway was left vacant and the church was built on the site behind it. Local examples of this practice can be seen at St Mary's in Mallow (1818) and the Nativity of the Blessed Virgin in Doneraile (1827).
8. The present convent graveyard is located within the ruin of the penal chapel which, itself, incorporated a medieval building.
9. As a comparative example of the contemporary value of money, James Grove White relates that Springford Hall and demesne were purchased in 1854 through the Encumbered Estates Court for £4,500 and re-sold about 1858 for £7,000. See also Mary Cecelia Lyons, *Illustrated Incumbered Estates: Ireland 1850-1905*, Whitegate Co. Clare 1993, p. 37.
10. The tenth George IV cap. 7, the Roman Catholic Relief Act being an Act for the Relief of His Majesty's Roman Catholic Subjects, was approved by parliament on 24 March 1829 and received royal assent on 13 April 1829.
11. The penal chapel in Lisgriffin was eventually replaced in 1897 by the present church which was designed for Fr. Francis Murphy, C.C. by Samuel Francis Hynes (1854-1931), the contractor being Thomas A. Walsh of Charleville and Kilmallock. The new church was dedicated to the Immaculate Conception of Our Lady on 8th December 1897.
12. Fr. Theobald Mathew (1790-1856), Capuchin friar attached to Holy Trinity friary in Cork city, and apostle of temperance. He began the building of Holy Trinity church in 1832 to designs drawn up by George Pain in 1825. The effectiveness of his temperance crusade was felt in Cork by 1835 when the breweries and distilleries experienced as much as a 25 per cent decline in their sales.
13. For a study of the effects of the famine in the Poor Law Union of Skibbereen see Patrick Hickey, 'Famine, mortality and emigration: a profile of six parishes in the Poor Law Union of Skibbereen, 1846-1847', in P. Ó'Flanagan and C. Buttimer, (eds), *Cork: History and Society* (Dublin 1993), pp. 873-918.
14. National Archives of Ireland, Archive of the Famine Relief Commission 1845-1847.
15. Famine Relief Commission, letter of Jemima Deane Freeman, Castlecor, 1 February 1847.
16. Charlotte Flora Jemima Allen, daughter of John Lee Allen of Erroll Park, Perth, Scotland, and of the Lady Henrietta Duncan, married Edward Deane Freeman of Castle Cor on 28 October 1841. James Grove White notes: 'The famine, non-payment of rents in those bad years, coupled with lavish hospitality to the poor in those bad times, and the greatest hospitality to everyone coming their way, at all times, were the causes of the downfall of the Deane-Freemans, and Castle Cor and their vast estates in seven counties were sold in that merciless Court, "The Encumbered Estate Court"'.
17. Famine Relief Commission, letters
18. An account of the auction in The Newspaper, 22 February 1851, p. 63 read: "The principal estates of Edward Deane Freeman, of Castle Cor, which are distributed in the counties of

Cork, Tipperary, Limerick and Kerry, found no purchasers, except at ruinous terms. The first lot, comprising of the mansion house and demesne of Castle Cor, valued at £550 a year, only obtained a bidding of £21,500, not 11 years purchase. The sale was consequently adjourned. The next lot met the same fate, the highest bidding for a clear £230 per annum rental only reaching £2,000, about nine years purchase. Twenty-six lots of impropriated tithes, producing the aggregate of £930 a year, sold for £12,600 or about 13 years purchase. Three lots in the county of Kerry, of a separate estate, giving a rental of £280 a year, sold for £4,800 or about 17 years purchase". See also Mary Cecelia Lyons, *Illustrated Incumbered Estates: Ireland 1850-1905* (Whitegate, Co. Clare, 1993), p. 46.

19. A brother in law of Alexander McCarthy, MP, having married Helena McCarthy, daughter of Alexander McCarthy. He died in 1868. (Grove White, vol. 1, p. 295, sub Curry-mount)
20. W H Lysaght of Hazelwood operated very substantial steel and iron mills in Newport and Coventry. The company is credited with the invention of corrugated iron.
21. See also Richard Brash, 'The Local Antiquities of Buttevant', *Transactions of the Kilkenny Archaeological Society*, 2 (1852-3), 95.
22. There is some evidence to suggest that Charles Cottrell, the architect, is the son of Edward Francis Cottrell, architect, Hanover Street, who appears to have married a Miss Colthurst, daughter of Wallace Colthurst, in 1793. Charles Cottrell married Mary Meade in 1828 and appears to have had left only one surviving daughter, Eliza, who married Thomas Henry Jermyn. This information was kindly supplied by Mr. Andrew Jermyn of Kinsale, a great-great grandson of Charles Cottrell.
23. Pigot & Co.'s *City of Dublin and Hibernian Provincial Directory* (1824) link him with Wandesford Bridge; the Cork Constitution, (9 June 1831), the Cork County and City Post Office Directory for 1842-3, Slater's *National Commercial Directory of Ireland* (1846) and Laing's *Cork Mercantile Directory* for 1863 all list him as an architect.
24. John Windele (1801-1865) was an antiquary who lived at Blair's Hill, Cork. He was a member of the Cork Cuvierian Society, the Cork Art Union, the Cork Archaeological Society, the South Munster Antiquarian Society, and the Kilkenny Archaeological Society. After his death, the Royal Irish Academy purchased Windele's manuscripts. There were 150 items in all, including 24 volumes of notes on Irish history and antiquities, many with pen and ink sketches of particular antiquities, 11 volumes on antiquities in County Cork and a further 6 on Munster and the south of Ireland. Other specialised volumes in the collection relate to architecture, druids, and ogham inscriptions. The collection includes 33 volumes of Windele's correspondence, covering the years 1820 to 1863. He had a wide circle of contacts among people interested in Irish antiquities, and this is reflected in his correspondence. In his *Notices of the City of Cork and its Vicinity*, (Cork 1839), p.45 and p. 65, Windele notes that St Francis's church had been rebuilt in 1830 at a cost of £4,500. Charles Cottrell, together with Fr. Matthew Horgan, also drew plans for a school in Cobh to be built on the Midleton estate which appears never to have been executed *(Kilbrin Revisited*, published in Conjunction with the Ballygraddy-Curraghs National Schools Re-Union 1993, (Cork 1993), p. 151).
25. Samuel Lewis, *A Topographical Dictionary of Ireland* (London 1837), p. 236
26. Douglas Scott Richardson, *Gothic Revival Architecture in Ireland* (London 1983), vol. 1, p. 212.
27. Michael J. Lewis, *The Gothic Revival* (London 2002), p. 48; see also Chris Brooks, *The Gothic Revival* (London 1999), pp. 135-137.
28. Anna-Maria Hajba, *An Introduction to the Architectural heritage of North Cork* (Dublin 2009), p. 84, notes that it remains the only example of a nineteenth century church in North

Cork incorporating a medieval ruin.

29. A good example of Pugin's employment of this principle can be seen in the Convent of Mercy, Birr, Co. Offaly where the stone work closely resembles that on the east elevation of Buttevant.

30. Brash dedicated his *The Ecclesiastical Architecture of Ireland* to his wife Jane Jackson 'the congenial companion of many a pleasant pilgrimage', whom he married on 14 September 1847. He died at his house, College View, Sunday's Well, Cork, on 18 January 1876 and was buried in St Finbarr's cemetery, Cork. He was survived by his wife and daughters and a brother in the USA. His library was sold in April 1876. His widow made herself responsible for the posthumous publication of her husband's writings on ogham monuments. The data base of the Irish Architectural Archive lists some twenty-seven projects designed by Brash.

31. The Cork Cuvierian Society originated as a committee of the Royal Cork Institution in October 1835. Its meetings were held on the first wednesday of the autumn and winter months in the Institution's library. The Society was named after the noted French naturalist and zoologist Georges Cuvier (1769-1832) who was a notable early 19th century proponent of catastrophism. In its early years, the Society concentrated on the natural sciences but by 1850 it had evolved into an archaeological society. Fr Matt Horgan of Blarney, John Windele, Abraham Abell, Thomas Crofton Croker and Richard Sainthill were all members. The minutes (1835-1878) and transactions (1853-1875) of the Society, as recorded by Richard Caulfield, are deposited in the Manuscripts Collection of the Boole Library at University College Cork (MS 227).

32. The minute books of the Society, conserved at University College, Cork record that John Windele gave a report on the restoration in November 1851.

33. Fr. Matt Horgan (1775-1849) was parish priest of Blarney (1816-49), and an architect who built churches at Waterloo, Whitechurch and Cobh as well as two round towers at Waterloo and Whitechurch which are regarded as the earliest specimens of neo Romanesque in Ireland. He was also a member of the Cuvierian Society in Cork and something of an expert on ogham inscriptions. He was immortalized in Daniel Maclise's famous picture Snap Apple Night painted in 1833 and depicting the events of Fr. Horgan's hoolie in Blarney held on Halloween 1832. See Patrick Long's entry on Matthew Horgan in James McGuire and James Quinn, Dictionary of Irish Biography, (Cambridge 2009). Fr. Richard Smiddy (1811-78), archaeologist and antiquarian, was born on 20 July 1811 at Ballymakea, Killeagh, and educated at the Irish College, Paris (1832-38). Ordained in 1838, he served in the parishes of Killeagh (1838), Donoughmore (1838), Glantane (1838-40), Youghal (1840-51), Charleville (1851-53), and Mallow (1853-57). He became parish priest of Aghada in 1857. He published extensively on theological subjects and on archaeology. His earliest book, The Holy Bible and the manner in which it is used by Catholics, was published in 1850. He was responsible for the revision of the Irish language catechism for use in the diocese of Cloyne which was published as *An tagasc Chriostaidhe, de réir ceist is freagra*. His best known work, *Essays on Druids, Ancient Churches, and the Round Towers of Ireland*, was published in 1871, reprinted in abbreviated form in 1976 and reprinted in 2010. He died on 11 June 1878 and was interred in Aghada graveyard. Cf. Rev. Robert Forde, 'Diary of Very Rev. Richard Canon Smiddy', in *Mallow Field Club Journal*, 7 (1989), 70-84.

34. The *Building News and Engineering Journal*, 47 (1885), 644.

35. Sculptor and marble cutter, of 11 Cook Street, Cork, listed as such in the Cork Mecantile Directory for 1863. Daly is also credited as sculptor for the High Altar in Sts Peter and Paul's in Cork which was designed by G.C. Ashlin and erected in 1875.

36. The inscription reads: 'Very Rev. Cornelius Canon Buckley, P.P., of Buttevant. For more than half a century he laboured for the spiritual and temporal welfare of his flock, by whose generous aid he was enabled to build this church. To perpetuate his memory, the high altar has been erected by some devoted friends; died 4th March 1875 aged 77'.
37. Born at Tullig, Buttevant, in 1844 and educated in Rome, he was ordained for the diocese of Cloyne in 1866. As parish priest of Midleton he commissioned G.C. Ashlin to build a new parish church there in 1894. He died in 1918.
38. The company was founded by Joseph Gabriel Mayer in 1847 and quickly assumed a leading role in ecclesiastical artwork, especially after the Great Exhibition of 1851. Mayer eventually opened offices in London and in New York. The London office closed at the outbreak of the First Work War and its archive disappeared. A similar fate befell its New York office. The home studio of the company in Munich was bombed in 1942 with the loss of most of its archive. The company continues today under the direction of Gabriel Mayer and his son Michael Mayer. Since 2006, three despatch legers have emerged noting orders completed at the Munich workshops between September 1878 and July 1899. The author wishes to thank Herr Wilfried Jaekel, Mayer Company Archivist, for this information.
39. Gabriel Mayer, *Franz Mayer of Munich: Mayer'sche Hofkunstanstalt*, (Munich, 2011) (private printing), p. 14.
40. The dedicatory inscription, now occluded, reads 'For the glory of God and beauty of His temple, this window was erected by Mrs. Margaret Tracey, of Rathclare in memory of her parents John and Mary Walsh, and her brothers and sisters, John Joseph, Robert Francis, Patrick and Mary Walsh. St Mary's Church and Convent, Buttevant, are deeply indebted to the generosity of this worthy family. May their souls rest in peace. July, 1886....Timothy, Canon Buckley, P.P.'
41. Examples of contemporary Palladian churches would be old Charleville (1812), Mallow (1818), Skibbereen (1826), Doneraile (1827), Ballyhea (1831), Kinsale (1832). St Patrick's in Cork City was consecrated a week after St Mary's, Buttevant, in October 1836.
42. Francis Johnston (1760-1829), born in Armagh and trained in Thomas Cooley's practice, he moved to Dublin in 1793 and was appointed architect to the Board of Works in 1805. His works include Sackville (O'Connell) Street, Dublin, Nelson's Pillar, the General Post Office, and Charleville Forest Castle.
43. See Thomas Bell, *An essay on the Origin and Progress of Gothic Architecture, with reference to the Ancient History and present State of the Remains of such Architecture in Ireland, to which was awarded the Prize Proposed by the Royal Irish Academy, for the best Essay on that Subject* (Dublin 1829), p. 256.
44. Douglas Scott Richardson, *Gothic Revival Architecture in Ireland* (London 1983), vol. 1, pp. 62-63.
45. Administrator (1823-1835) and subsequently parish priest of Buttevant (1835-1875).
46. Hayes St Leger, third Viscount Doneraile [second creation] (1786-1854).
47. The brewery was founded by William Beamish and William Crawford in 1792. By 1805 it was the largest brewery in Ireland and the third largest in the British Isles with an output of 100,000 barrels per annum, up from 12,000 barrels per annum in 1792.
48. John Perceval, 4th Earl of Egmont (1767-1835).
49. James Bernard, 2nd Earl of Bandon (1785-1856). The Earl of Bandon acquired much of the Gregg interest in the parish, especially in the townland of Ardaprior.
50. Bartholomew Crotty, Bishop of Cloyne and Ross (1833-1846), born Clonakilty 1769; ordained Lisbon 1792, appointed Bishop of Cloyne and Ross 1833; died 4th October 1846.

51. Jeremiah Murphy (1779-1853) a co-founder of Midleton distilleries.
52. James Murphy (1769-1855) was a tanner and leather merchant who developed his father's business into one of the largest commercial enterprises in Cork City. Together with his brothers Nicholas (1785-1852), Daniel (1780-1856) and Jeremiah (1779-1853), he founded the Midleton distilleries in 1825.
53. Charles Denham Orlando Jephson Norreys (1799-1880) of Mallow castle. M.P. for Mallow 1826-1859. Best remembered as an amateur architect with a fascination for the Gothic revival. In 1828, he retained the Pain brothers to build the Spa House in Mallow in a replica Elizabethan style and, in 1858, the iconic Clock House in the town in the same style. In 1836, acting as his own architect, advised by Edward Blore, he carried out an extensive rebuilding of Mallow castle, again in the Tudor Gothic idiom, resulting in the present revival country house. He also commented on the rebuilding of the Houses of Parliament in a correspondence with Thomas Greene, M.P., chairman of the commons' committee for the rebuilding of the Houses of Parliament (Parliamentary Archive, Correspondence of Thomas Greene, M.P., GRE/1/47 of 15 June 1850). He died on 10 July 1880 at Queenstown.
54. Doctor of Medicine, and Surgeon of the 87th South Cork Light Infantry Militia, son of Barry Gregg and Eliza Glover of Castleview. Died unmarried 19 November, 1862, living at Castle Kevin, Doneraile. (J. Grove White, *Topographical Notes*..., vol. 1, p. 79, sub Ardaprior).
55. Doctor of Medicine, Buttevant, married Eliza Gregg, daughter of Barry Gregg and Eliza Glover of Castleview. (see Grove White vol. 1, p. 79)
56. The 2nd Yorkshire West Riding, or The King's Own Light Infantry Regiment.
57. The Cheshire Regiment.
58. The Buckinghamshire Regiment of Foot.
59. Richard Beare, Bruin Lodge, Lower Glanmire Road.
60. Thomas Lyons, painters of Abbey Street, Cork.
61. Parish priest of Milford. Died 5 November 1834 aged 105.
62. The Ruthlandshire Regiment of Foot.
63. The 76th Regiment of Foot had returned from border duties in Canada in 1827 and was despatched to the West Indies in 1834.
64. William Waggett (1771-1840) of Kitsborough, Cork, King's counsel, elected Recorder of Cork in 1808. He was a descendant of Richard Waggett and Ann Perceval who had settled at Spittal, Buttevant, ante 1680. [The Diaries of the First Earl of Egmont (1730-1733), London 1923, vol. 1, p. 166 and p. 398. Also Grove White, Topographical Notes, vol. 4, p. 214 sub Spittal].
65. This appears to have been a trade subscription made under the name of the deceased Carden Terry. Terry (1742-1824), a very notable Cork silversmith, was apprenticed in 1758, and registered his mark in 1784. He married Catherine Webb by whom he had two sons and seven daughters. His eldest daughter Jane Terry married John Williams in 1791 and entered into partnership with his father-in-law in 1795. Williams died in 1806 but the partnership was continued by his widow, Jane, until Terry's death. Jane died in 1845. Three of her sons married three sisters of the Crofts family of Buttevant. In addition, Carden Terry's sister, Sarah, had married Richard Crofts of Kilclusha House. Richard Crofts was murdered by the Whiteboys on 5 June 1823.
66. James [Roche] Verling (1787-1858), born Cobh, Co. Cork; studied medicine under Sir Arthur Clarke in Dublin and subsequently in Edinburgh, graduating in 1809; joined the Ordinance Medical Department and served in Spain during the peninsular war; transferred to the Royal Artillery Company in 1815 and journeyed to St Helena with Napoleon; succeeded Barry

O'Meara as Napoleon's physician but resigned the office in 1818 leaving St Helena in 1820; promoted to surgeon in 1827 and senior surgeon in 1843; he left the Ordinance in 1854 and died at Bellavista in Cobh in 1858. For a transcript of Dr. Verling's Journal while on St Helena (25 July 1818–23 April 1820) see J. David Markham, *Napoleon and Doctor Verling on St Helena* (Barnsley, 2005), pp. 26-118.

67. A notable butter merchant.
68. The 65th or the 2nd Yorkshire North Riding Regiment of Foot returned from service in India in 1821 and was moved to Canada in 1837.
69. Distiller and green distiller, North York Street.
70. A wines and spirit merchant at 6 Cook Street.
71. Parish priest of Ballyhea 1811-1849.
72. John Joseph Galwey of Lota, Cork.
73. A member of the family of Galwey of Lota, son of John Galway of Westcourt and Jane, daughter of William O'Brien of Ahacross. The Galway family was also connected to the Norcotts of Springfield by marriage.
74. Dr. Thomas Kelly entered Maynooth in 1814, was ordained and appointed dean in 1820, appointed Professor of Theology 1825, made Bishop of Dromore 1826, Coadjutor of Armagh 1828, and Archbishop of Armagh 1832. He died 1835.
75. Alexander McCarthy (1803-1868) a descendant of the McCarthys of Drishane, M.P. for the City and subsequently for the County of Cork in the O'Connellite Repeal interest; High Sherriff of Cork (1848); Barrister at Law; left Currymount to his brother James, who subsequently left it to his grand-nephew, James McCarthy Morrogh. The McCarthy monument on the Blackrock Road in Cork was erected to his memory by his brother Daniel.
76. Captain Spencer Stewart, J.P., eldest son of Colonel the Hon. James Henry Keith Stewart, C.B., son of the seventh Earl of Galloway, bought Springford Hall . He was born 24 June 1820; m. 1846, Frances Olivia, 3rd daughter of Miles McSwiney, Esq. Captain Stewart was in the 4th Foot and Rifle Brigade. He died at Springfort Hall 19 May 1893 without issue. An Englishman named Mr. Wyatt bought Springfort Hall in the Landed Estates Court in 1854 for £4,500, and sold it about 1858 to Captain Spencer Stewart for £7,000. Grove White, *Topographical Notes* etc., vol.1 p. 277.

Index

Anderson, James Caleb 5, 114, 117-22; John 16, 113-19; founder of Fermoy 115

Agmondsham, family lands 106; Mary, marriage to William Muschamp 106, 110

Aquitaine, Duke of 24; new towns in, 44

Aragon 24-5, 40

Ashlin, George, architect of Buttevant convent 128

Ballybeg 12, 32, 83, 118, 130, 133, 136-7; foundation date of 30-31; mill at 14

Ballyclough, troops at 16; Ballyclogh, fee of 36, parish 36

Barry 29-37; at Castlelyons 9, 16; at Liscarroll 37, 51, 55, 63; at Manorbier 10; David 2, 5, 30, 31, 36, 63; David, First Earl of Barrymore 104, 111-2; family motto 31; founders of Buttevant 3; Henry 146; John 13, 34, 36; Lady Elizabeth 104; monastic foundations of 71-4, 80, 83-89, 130; Nicholas of Annagh 34; Philip 30, 31; Philip of Kilbrin 35; Robert 36; William 30; William of Caherduggan 35; William fitzPhilip 2, 30;

Barrymore 30; David, Lord 104-5, 108, 111; estate 104-5, 115-6, 138, 144, 146, 187; Henry eight Earl of 146; Lady 104; muniments 36; Richard seventh Earl of 117

Bastides 3, 19, 21-27, 39, 42-46

Beresford, Maurice 22, 25, 27, 46

Borough, of Buttevant 2, 32-3

Boutavant , Bouttavant, Botavant, Botevant, Betavaunt 2, 26-8, 31-2

Boyle, Alice 104; Elizabeth 107; family vault 111; Michael, Bishop of Waterford and Archbishop of Dublin 104-5, 107; Richard Earl of Cork 104-6; Robert 105-6, 108, 111

Brash, Richard 8, 13, 124, 127, 130-1; and Buttevant friary 133-6; and St. Mary's 143, 151-2, 157-9, 161-2, 164-5; antiquarianism 157

Buckley, Fr. Cornelius (1798-1875) 127-8, 130, 135; Fr. Cornelius (1845-1922) 135, 143, 148, 157-60, 162; Canon Timothy 143, memorial altar for 160

Burgesses, of Buttevant 32, 33

Buttevant, borough 32-4; bridge 14; convent 120-21; ; French origins of 26-7, 31; Irish name of 29-31; and James Anderson 119-23; manor of 36-7, 108, 146; market house 2, 5, 6, 8, 13; market place 4-7, 35; military barracks 3, 115-17; mill 14, 30, 33; nunnery 13-14, 129; town foundation 2, 31-2; town layout 3-7, town walls 2, 7-8; grant of market 2, 31

Buttevant castle 2-3, 9-10, 30-31; restoration of 113, 117-19

Buttevant Franciscan friary 10-12, 29; foundation date of 32, 72; location of, 78-9; plots owned by 3; phases of construction of 83-9; preservation of 130-5

Carcassonne 24, 43-4, 48
Carmelites, at Castlelyons 9, 74
Castles, Ballintober 51-2, 59, 62, 66; Boutavant, Brittany 26; Bouttavant, Burgundy 26; Buttevant 9-10, 30-31, 113, 117-19; Chateau-Gaillard 26; Corfe 26; Dinefwr 10, 17; Dublin 52; Kilbolane 51; Kilcrea 74, 80; Limerick 52; Liscarroll 51-66; Lombard's 13, 33, 135; proliferation of in southwest France 24, Roscommon 52; Trim 52
Castle villages castelnaux 20, 22, 24-5, 27, 44-5
Catalonia 22, 40
Cottrell, Charles, architect of St. Mary's 128, 153-7, 164, 169, 189; Francis 189; Robert, inhabitant of Buttevant in 1260 34
Desmond tower 11, 153, 155; incorporation into St. Mary's 147-8; Windele's drawing of 148
Franciscan friaries, at Buttevant 7-10, 17, 29, 32, 34, 72; at Carrickbeg 72, 75, 79, 83-101; at Cashel 72, 75, 78-9; at Clonmel 72, 77-9; at Cork 71-73; at Kilcrea 72, 74-5, 77, 79-82; at Moor abbey, Galbally 73, 75, 77, 79-80; at Timoleague 72, 74-5, 79-80, 85; at Youghal 70-1, 74-5, 77, 79, 88; at Waterford 71-3, 75-80; in east Munster 67-82
Garonne 23, 41, 45
Gascony 15, 20, 24-5, 27, 39-40, 46
Grange, townlands of 103-12
Higounet, Charles 20, 22, 25, 27, 43, 47-8
Iberia 25-6, 40
Kilmaclenine 30; church of 31; manor of 124; town of 15, 32; tumulus at 133
Languedoc 24, 27, 43, 47
Lombards, castle 13, 135; family 34-5
Liscarroll, Battle of 111; castle 51-66; manor of 36-7; parish of 37;
Magners 36-7
Muschamp, Agmondsham, 106-8, 112; Anne 106-7; Denny 103-110, 112; family origins 106; family tree 110; Martha 107; Mary 106, 108-9; William 106
Muscridonegan, cantred of 30, 31, 35-7, 74
Market (market square, market place) 42, at Buttevant 4-7, 13, 35, 46; in bastides 20, 25-6, 46
Market towns, in France 24-5; 41-3; in Ireland 76, 83
Navarra 40
New Towns, and feudalism 22, 24; in southwestern France 19-27; origins of 21-5; phases of development 20-1, 39-44
Pain, architects of St. John's 125-6, 128, 140-1, 153, 169
Pipe Roll of Cloyne 5, 9, 14, 123
Provence 24, 43, 74
Pugin, architect 128, 156, 169, 190

Pyrenees 24, 39-40
Sauvetés 20, 22, 24, 39-40, 46
St. Brigid, 29-31, 123-5
St. Colmán 30, 31, 37, 124, 128, 163
St. John's Church of Ireland 123-7
St. Mary's Roman Catholic church 127, 143-71; architects for 153-59; architectural context of 167; architecture of 148, 154-6, 163-5, 167-9; beginnings 146-8; fundraising for 149-53, 160-1, 166, 173ff; sources for history of 143-5
Toulouse 20-21; Count of 24-5; new towns near 23
Vesey /de Vesci, Arthur 104; family origins in Ireland 105; family tree 110; John, Archbishop of Tuam 105-8; John Thomas 103; Thomas, first Viscount de Vesci 104, 107-8